GULLHANGER

For Julie and Em

GULLHANGER

Or How I Learned to Love
Brighton and Hove Albion

Mike Ward

MAINSTREAM
PUBLISHING

EDINBURGH AND LONDON

First published in Great Britain in 2002 by
MAINSTREAM PUBLISHING (EDINBURGH) LTD
7 Albany Street
Edinburgh EH1 3UG

ISBN 1 84018 645 3

A catalogue record for this book is available from the British Library

'When You're Young', by Paul Weller ©1979 reproduced with permission.

Typeset in Garamond and Courier New

Printed in Great Britain by
Mackays of Chatham Ltd

Acknowledgments

A lot of people have helped make this book happen, even if many of them can't possibly realise it. This is my thank-you bit:

FOR ALL-ROUND ENCOURAGEMENT: Alison Barrow, Jane Middleton, Andy 'Super Brighton Factman' Garth, Jo Morrow, Claire Morrow, Fergus Kelly, Nikki Murfitt, Tim Curran, Paul Cheston, Kathryn Spencer, Simon Spinks, Mel Whitehouse, Veronica Clark, Hugh Whittow, Richard Leifer, Dawn Neesom, Irvine Hunter, Brian Dunlea, Andy Griffin, Stephen and Denise Taylor, Dominik Diamond and his wee brother Michael, and, obviously, Mum and Dad.

FOR INSPIRATION: everyone at Brighton and Hove Albion, in particular Dick Knight, Martin Perry, Bob Booker, Paul Camillin and, needless to say, all the players. Also: Paul Samrah, Adrian Newnham, Tim Carder, Liz Costa, Sarah Watts, Matthew James, John Cowen and the rest of the FFA team, plus Micky Adams, Cyril Edwards, Ian Hart, Andrew Hawes, Paul Hayward, Bennett Dean, Paul Hazelwood, Simon Levenson, Terry Garoghan, Liz Fleet, Nicky Keig-Shevlin and, OK, Peter Taylor.

FOR THEIR BELIEF: Peter Hill, Phil Walker, Richard Stott, Katy Bravery and Bill Campbell.

FOR THE SOUNDTRACK TO A SEASON: Paul Weller, Billy Bragg, the Electric Soft Parade and Attila's ever-inspired matchday selections.

FOR THEIR LOVE AND INFINITE PATIENCE: Julie and Em.

And never forgetting Charlie Morrow.

'. . . but you find out life isn't like that . . .'
– 'When You're Young' – The Jam

The ticket-office woman flashed me a wary half-smile. A split second later, she was making this strange, low-level grunting sound which I'm not sure I know how to spell. Something like 'urrggggh', I suppose. Possibly with a couple of extra Gs.

Call me naïve, but it wasn't quite the reaction I'd expected. Had I dipped into my trouser pocket and whipped out a rasher of fluffy bacon, or flicked open my wallet to reveal a topless snapshot of Ann Widdecombe's slightly less attractive sister, then fair enough. But all I'd said was: 'I'd like a season ticket for block B, please.'

So why the unspellable grunt?

Well, I think we can rule out shock. Since Brighton and Hove Albion finished last season as Division Three champions – the club's first honour in 36 years, unless you count signing a sponsorship deal with Fatboy Slim's record label, or hiring Des Lynam to narrate their videos, or getting name-checked by Terry Wogan on *Auntie's Sporting Bloomers* – the poor soul must have processed God knows how many of these things.

So maybe it was the 'block B' bit. Perhaps, in my ignorance, I'd requested a seat in a section of the ground notorious for black magic and half-time ritual goat-sacrifices, or directly above a fracture in the Earth's crust.

Or maybe – and this seemed the most likely explanation – she'd simply got me sussed. Maybe she'd taken one look and thought, 'Here we go, another lousy bandwagon-jumper.'

In which case, she'd have been spot-on. That's exactly what I became this afternoon, shortly before 1 p.m., for the sum of £380, charged to my NatWest Visa card. Probably the most despised of all football-supporting types: the glory-seeker. The sort who ignores his local club through all the rough times – such as, in my case, a few years back when the Albion were 90 minutes away from plunging out of the League altogether. The sort who blanks them completely when their very existence is under threat, as I did for two years – or was it three? – when they were left to share a stadium 75 miles away, in Gillingham, following the demolition of their famous Goldstone Ground. The type who waits until the club is back in its home town and doing rather well again – and the goals are flying in, and the points are piling up, and an Albion car-sticker would no longer single you out as a sad case – before scuttling shamelessly, louse-like, out of the woodwork. The type who has only ever ambled along to a measly handful of the club's matches in the 15 years he's lived in the city – and these so long ago that he couldn't even begin to put a date on them, let alone recall the opposition. In short, a bit of a git.

Yep, I'm afraid that's me. And if it's that transparently obvious, then I may as well be wearing my own personalised T-shirt – 'Glory-Seeker: Please Knee In Goolies' – when I start turning up at the actual games.

So at least let me explain why I'm doing this – forking out all that money, disrupting my Saturday routine (plus a fair few evenings) well into next spring, risking being singled out as a slappable phoney. Because the point is, this isn't really about Brighton and Hove Albion. Not as such. It isn't even about football. Not specifically.

What it's really about is caring. Or, to be precise, finding out if I still know *how* to care. About anything.

I'm serious.

I don't mean caring in that low-key, gently-ticking-over kind of sense – about my family, my friends, my job, regularly changing my underwear etc. Obviously I care about them. Lots. Especially the underwear bit. But that's the routine, taken-for-granted type of caring. What I'm talking about here is something altogether different: a passionate, irrational caring which doesn't even begin to stand up to common-sense scrutiny. The sort which gets you worked up about stuff when you've no logical, grown-up excuse for doing so. The sort which, to the more sceptical outsider, might suggest you're a bit of a half-wit. The fun sort, which we allow to burn out – or, almost worse, fizzle – as middle age creeps up on us.

Ah, middle age. To be honest, I've never entirely understood what that means. How can you possibly know when you've hit the mid-point of your life unless you can say for certain when it's scheduled to end? But by the loose definition which most people seem happy to go by – too old to be young, too young to be old – I suppose I have to cut the crap and accept that I've reached it. Indeed, by some people's definition I probably hit it years ago. Sure, I'm still some way short of the stage where I'd consider investing in one of those funny baths with the door on the side; but I've also edged well clear of the age bracket where I could order a watermelon-flavoured Bacardi Breezer without suspecting that I looked like a tragic wanker.

I'm 41, for God's sake.

Forty-flipping-one. Blimey.

Believe me, turning 41 is a lot worse than turning 40. When you turn 40, you've been gearing up to it for months, possibly even planning a big party where you and your peers can compare bellies and bald patches, especially if you're male. People buy you profoundly amusing cards, hilariously hinting at imminent senility or death, or comedy mugs daubed with rib-tickling slogans such as 'Old Fart'. All of which helps you to cope. OK, you get quietly depressed about it, but if you're anything like me you've been so busy assuring everyone it's going to be 'just another day' that you've more or less ended up believing that.

Forty-one, on the other hand, is a bugger. Not just because it seems to arrive only about a fortnight after you've turned 40, but also because it's a clinical reminder that your ageing process hasn't suddenly ground to a halt. It's daft, but a part of me expected to be allowed a couple of years to get used to the idea of being 40 before having to face the next step. But it didn't turn out that way. Odd, that.

And, like I say, what scares me most at this age – other than the distended freak who confronts me whenever I catch my naked profile in our bedroom mirror – is that when it comes to this business of caring, I seem to have shut out all the mad, irrational parts.

In certain cases, of course, that's just as well. I'd have to be a deeply troubled soul, for example, if I still sat nervously gnawing my nails as the Sunday night Top 40 rundown reached its climax. Likewise, I'd be considered a tad pathetic if I continued to hold a grudge against whoever it was that failed me at Chemistry O Level in 1976. Although obviously I do hope they've suffered a horrible, lingering death.

The trouble is, whenever I do manage to get worked up about anything these days, it's almost invariably sad, moany-old-man stuff. I'm in serious danger of becoming Victor Meldrew before my time. Indeed, to illustrate this very point, I've been keeping a note of things which have riled me during the past week alone. I should warn you, it's pretty long and quite staggeringly petty. Still want to see it? Thought you might:

1. The bloke in the advert for Gillette Mach 3.
2. Economy binliners.
3. Service charge in restaurants. ('So let me get this straight: I'm paying you to cook me some food, right? And then I have to pay you extra if I actually want you to bring it to me?')
4. Anyone over 20 riding a skateboard.
5. People saying 'alternate' when they mean 'alternative'.
6. Highway Code Rule 198. I'm not sure if it's only happened here

in Brighton, but a reminder of this rule (well, I say 'reminder' – they could be making it up for all I know) has been pasted to the back of all the city's buses. What it says is: 'Ha-ha! I'm allowed to pull out right in front of you, Mr Anti-Social Car-Driving Fascist Scum, and there's stuff-all you can do about it. In fact, I think I'll do it right now! Wahey! Here I come! Up yours, matey!!' (Admittedly, I'm paraphrasing.)

7. The use of the word 'workshop' in any sense more pretentious than as a place where my car gets fixed.

8. The person at the till who makes a big drawn-out deal of examining my credit card signature.

9. Sellotape substitute: the bargain alternative which looks exactly like the real thing, until you try peeling some off, at which point it shreds itself into half a dozen useless gummy shards.

10. My daughter Emily's inability ever to switch anything off – lights, TV, stereo, bath taps – when she leaves a room.

11. Cyclists who ignore red lights.

12. Cyclists who ignore one-way systems.

13. Cyclists.

14. The bloke I encountered on Saturday afternoon when I popped into a 'major' electrical retailer and asked whether, in his role as a sales assistant, he could possibly talk me through the operation of a JVC micro system which I'd taken a fancy to. I'd actually have stood a more realistic chance of success if I'd asked this knobhead to translate Jamie Oliver's fish pie recipe into Serbo-Croat. 'Look, I hate to sound fussy, mate,' I told him. 'But I'm not very likely to buy this thing if you can't show me how it, y'know, *works*.' To be fair, though, he acknowledged my point. 'No, you're right,' he admitted, before walking off to serve some bloke wanting batteries.

15. The way 'our Graham', the announcer on Blind Date, always says 'Blind Daaayyyyyyyyyte'. And 'Cilla Blaaaaaaaaaaack'.

16. TV weather forecasters who talk to me as if I'm six.

17. Those fish-shaped stickers which religious people put on the back of their cars. 'God is great,' I assume they're saying. 'And, while I've got your attention, this is what a fish looks like.'

18. Grown men flying kites.

19. Lisa's eyebrows in *EastEnders*.

20. Fast-food joints where it's assumed I'll have chosen exactly what I want within four seconds of stepping into the store.

21. Sales people in fast-food joints who inquire if I'd like milk and

sugar with my coffee when I've just asked for it black.

22. Anyone who seriously believes that the political opinions of a total stranger walking past your house will be influenced to the tiniest degree by a poster you've stuck in your window.

23. People moaning that 'there's never anything on TV'.

24. People setting their office phones to go straight to voicemail on the very first ring, so that they can decide, at their leisure, whether or not you deserve a call back.

25. Wacky ties.

26. Wacky socks.

27. Wacky anything.

28. The word 'wacky'.

29. Clipboard-wielding blokes who turn up at my front door every fortnight and try to persuade me to switch gas/electricity suppliers. I particularly enjoy the bit where they brandish their price comparison chart, which confirms that their own service is by far the best value and that to have subscribed to one of their competitors singles me out as a feeble-minded fuck-wit.

30. People who say 'oriented' when they mean 'orientated'.

31. The bloke walking up North Street in front of me yesterday, who lit his last B&H and then let the screwed-up packet fall to the pavement. (I'd have had a word, but he looked as if he might use my face as an ashtray.)

32. The expression 'pro-active'.

33. The receptionist at our local health club last Friday, who refused to pass on my message that somebody had left their lights on in the car park, on the grounds that it wasn't 'company policy' to use the public address system except in emergencies. 'I think the person who's left their lights on might feel it's an emergency,' I'd suggested. 'But I'll tell you what: just to make sure it qualifies, I'll pop back outside and slash their tyres as well.'

34. Anyone who defends a decision as 'company policy' while failing to appreciate that all it really means is, "Cos we said so, so there.'

35. Second-hand shops with pretensions.

36. The avalanche of useless leaflets which tumbles out of my free newspaper.

37. People in bookshops who are standing in front of the very section I'm trying to get to. (There's a whole bloody A–Z to choose from, for God's sake. Fuck off and find a Jeffrey Archer.)

38. Check-out operators who start serving the next person before I've been able to pack all my shopping.

39. People urging me to 'enjoy' without adding another word to explain what it is I'm meant to be enjoying.

40. People who insist on thrusting their promotional flyers into my hand as I'm walking through town.

41. People who don't bother thrusting their promotional flyers into my hand because they're advertising a new nightclub and the last thing they want to attract is some speccy old lardarse.

42. The expression 24-7.

43. Killer dogs who are 'just being affectionate'.

44. Keith Chegwin's laugh.

45. *Big Issue* sellers who politely tell me to have a nice day when I've just made a special point of blanking them.

46. Ashley's voice in *Coronation Street*.

47. Setting off the security alarm when you leave a shop and having everyone gawp at you and assume you're a thief, even when it's the shop's fault because they forgot to remove the plastic tag at the till, but they still don't say sorry or offer you compensation or a free biscuit.

48. The personalised message on the front of buses, saying: 'Sorry, I'm not in service.' (I'd hazard a guess that you didn't really write that yourself, did you, Mr Bus? On the basis that you're a frigging bus.)

49. The assumption, by whoever's responsible for the above, that we're so profoundly simple as to find it endearing.

50. Guests who turn up for the weekend and announce they're on a wheat-free diet.

51. The expression 'What are you like?!'

52. Motorists who aren't me.

53. The fact that I let all this stuff annoy me.

So, like I say, quite a long list. And, remember, it only covers the last seven days. What we're talking about here is a permanent, on-going condition. Come to think of it, I hate the expression 'on-going' as well. Make that 54.

For all I know, these rants may well be textbook midlife-crisis material. And if they are, well, fine. So be it. Even if the diagnosis isn't quite that extreme, if they're just the inevitable result of my priorities and perspectives shifting as I get older, it leads me to pretty much the same conclusion – namely, that there's not a lot I can do about it.

But that doesn't mean I should let them become my only fixations. Even if I'm stuck with being this way – just as I'm wearily obliged to accept that for the rest of my time on Earth, my hair will be increasingly reluctant to sprout from those areas where I've previously taken its emergence for granted (the top of my head being quite a good example) and increasingly keen to pop out of places where it can only possibly be of comedic value (ears, nostrils, upper cheeks) – it shouldn't mean that this stuff is *all* I'm allowed to get worked up about. Should it? Just because I now devote so much time and energy to griping about the dreary, the petty and the niggly, it doesn't mean I can't counter-balance this by getting equally worked up about something fun, something uplifting, something indulgent, the way I used to. Of course it doesn't.

And that's where the football bit comes in.

Watching football is the only pursuit which has ever had the power to excite me in that euphoric, pulsating, lost-in-the-moment sense. In public, at least. Only at a football match have I ever been prepared to sit (or, ideally, stand) among a bunch of complete strangers and howl like a nut. The trouble is, I'm talking mostly in the past tense here. Quite a distant past at that.

Now and again, the game can still work its magic on me – but not with that consistent, aching intensity which I crave. In the last few years, watching football has largely meant slumping in front of Sky Sports – occasionally getting myself into a temporary tizzy if the match merits it, but usually ceasing to care much beyond the final whistle.

It was an incident during Euro 2000 which suggested that perhaps all is not yet lost, that my passion may be dormant rather than clinically dead. When Phil Neville lunged in like a lummox to give away that fatal last-minute penalty against Romania, thus ensuring that the England players would be back home in time to watch the highlights on their own TVs, so bitter was my frustration (God almighty, I thought, will it be this way forever until I die?) that I leapt up from the sofa and kicked the skirting board, temporarily forgetting that, if you intend to make this sort of histrionic gesture, it's usually best if you're wearing shoes at the time. By the following morning, three of the toes on my right foot had taken on a dramatic, intense purple hue; it would have been rather beautiful, had it not also felt as if a fridge-freezer had been dropped on them. When the hospital assured me nothing was broken, however, I wasn't sure whether to be relieved or disappointed. If I'd caused myself some genuine, high-profile damage, wouldn't it at least have demonstrated, albeit in a somewhat twattish fashion, that I still cared about something? I think it would. Instead, I had to make do with semi-convincing myself.

In a way, I feel as if I've become the opposite of Nick Hornby in his book *Fever Pitch*. Whereas Nick began to feel that football – or at least Arsenal – continued to matter way too much to him as he grew older, to me it doesn't matter nearly enough. I want to be round-the-clock obsessed, and I'm patently not.

But I do have one thing in common with Nick – namely, that, in theory at least, I'm an Arsenal fan. My uncle first took me to Highbury when I was ten, after which I'd head up there quite a lot – not fortnightly or anything daft like that, but several times a season – right up until the mid-'80s. But then marriage, relocation, fatherhood, the fact that each excursion started costing more than a decent filter-coffee-maker, all combined to put paid to that routine. That, plus the fact that, if I'm being honest, I stopped really caring that much.

I still continued to think of them as 'my' team. I still do, I suppose. I still went stupid with delight, hammering the floor with my fists, on that famous night back in 1989 when they snatched the title from Liverpool by winning 2–0 at Anfield. I still cry whenever I see that clip of Michael Thomas 'storming through the midfield', in the words of Brian Moore, to nab that decisive second goal in stoppage time. But I've only been back to see them once in more than 15 years, and only then because I joined a mate – a Bradford fan – in the away end one Tuesday night. I'd like to say I miss them, but if I really felt that way I'd have done something about it a long time ago.

Even so, how can I really justify this sudden switch of allegiance to Brighton and Hove Albion, other than through the fact that they're my local club? From the traditional football fans' perspective, I clearly can't. But given that, for me, this season isn't so much about football as it is about learning how to care again, the simple truth is that I think I stand a far better chance with the Albion.

Clubs such as Arsenal aren't just in another league; they occupy a world beyond reach. From my own strictly selfish point of view, they're simply too big, too rich, too powerful, too remote, to help me re-ignite that raw passion. They're just not up to the job. The Albion, on the other hand, are a far more exciting prospect. They're comparatively small, they're human, they seem to be prone to the occasional spectacular fuck-up – on face value, they're exactly what I'm looking for. Admittedly, I've always found their old-fashioned name – the 'Albion' part, I mean – a bit odd, not least because it's an anagram of 'albino'. But if I allowed myself to be put off by an archaic name with peculiar letter-juggling potential, I'd hardly have followed the Arsenal for so long.

I'd like to think, however, that this isn't *such* an easy option. After all, there are no cast-iron guarantees with glory-seeking. Bandwagons can break down, or veer off course, or lose a wheel or two, or maybe even plough into the central reservation (do stop me if I'm overdoing the analogies here). Division Two *could* mean more glory, sure – but equally there could be a desperate relegation battle in store, or a season of dour mid-table mediocrity. Look, I'm taking a gamble, OK?

And in a funny way, I'm not sure I'll mind if it fails, at least on the footballing front. If, four or five months from now, I find I'm sweating over a midweek injury crisis, or getting steamed up about a goal drought, or staring in horror at a Division Two table in which 'my' team have slumped to 19th, I don't think I'll feel I've made a horrible mistake.

If they've reduced me to a gibbering wreck by Christmas, that would have to be considered real progress.

Male Support – SATURDAY 28 JULY

Andy dipped his finger into the creamy topping of his Guinness, then began swirling it around in lazy circles, as if he hoped this might somehow produce one of those corny little shamrock patterns. I couldn't help wondering when he'd last washed his hands.

'So you're serious about this, then?' he remarked.

Oh, here we go.

'What, about supporting the Albion?' I replied. 'Yeah, of course. Why?'

'But you've never been to see them in your life.'

'I have, actually, smartarse. A couple of times, several years ago, at the Goldstone. But, no, you're basically right. I'm a glory-seeker. I admit it.'

I took a slurp and grinned, trying to make light of the whole thing, hoping Andy might at least appreciate the fun side to all this. I wasn't planning to take the conversation to the next level, to explain the more serious motive behind my decision ('Oh, and also, Andy, I'm on a semi-spiritual mission to rekindle my inner passion and to avoid being sucked into the emotional vacuum that is middle age') because I knew he'd just scoff. Trust me, Andy's like that. He doesn't even cry during *Surprise Surprise*.

As it was, I could already sense he was about to dismiss the whole idea. I knew that look of old. He was going to tell me I was wasting my time.

'If you ask me,' said Andy . . .

Wait for it.

' . . . you're wasting your money.'

I was close.

'Yes, well, I didn't, did I?' God, he could be such a negative, sour-faced sod.

'Didn't what?'

'Didn't ask you. I don't really care what you think, Andy. I'm doing this for me.'

I was beginning to sound like a neglected suburban housewife, finally asserting her independence by taking up naked salsa-dancing.

'So what happened to the Arsenal, then?' asked Andy. 'I thought you were a Gunners fan.'

'Well, I *am*,' I insisted. 'Sort of. It's just that, oh, I don't know . . .'

'What?'

'Well, the thing is, I can't really bring myself to care about them that much. I'm happy enough if they win, but it's not really that big a deal.'

'So?'

'So it should be, shouldn't it, when your team wins?'

'Why?'

'Because it just should.'

'Ah, right. That explains everything. Thanks for making it so clear.'

'Oh, come on, you must know what I mean.'

'Nope. Enlighten me.'

I was at a turning point here. Carry on this way and, against my better judgement, I'd have to own up to my real motive. This might be a mistake. In fact, there was very little 'might' about it.

Still, what the heck?

'Well, I'm 41, OK?'

'Uh-huh. So, about time you grew up, then.'

'Well, that's my point, you see. I *have* grown up. I've grown up so fucking much that nothing gets me excited anymore.'

'Really? I'm sure Julie would be flattered to hear that.'

'No, I don't mean in that sense. I mean in the sort of . . . the silly sense.'

'The *silly* sense? Oh, I understand entirely now.'

'You do?'

'Nope. Sounds like you're talking out of your bottom.'

God, why was I even wasting my breath?

'Look, remember when you'd still get really thrilled about how your team were doing, and winning the FA Cup really mattered, and so did,

I don't know, having the best haircut or the coolest shoes or whatever?'

'Jesus, yeah. Pathetic.'

'All right, so most of it was. But don't you feel hacked-off that middle-age has killed *all* that – including the fun bits that might have been worth keeping?'

'Well, I might be able to dig you out a pair of my old DMs, if you're that worried.'

'Oh, ha-ha. Look, I know this might sound like some sort of midlife crisis . . .'

'I didn't like to say, mate . . .'

'But all I'm trying to do is find something I can still get irrationally passionate about.'

'*Irrationally passionate*??!! Oooh, get you!'

'As opposed to celebrating when, I don't know, the bloody mortgage rate drops a quarter of a per cent, or I manage to park right in front of the house when I get back with a bootload from Sainsbury's.'

'Or Asda?'

'Oh, shut up.'

'Or Tesco's?'

'Look, I . . .'

'They deliver now, Tesco's, you know.'

'Listen, the point is, I reckon I've got a better chance with footie than with anything else. And a better chance with the Albion than with the Arsenal, simply because they're not so big and rich and . . .'

'Up themselves?'

'If you like. So surely even you can see what I'm driving at. It's not that complicated.'

'Course it's not. So, what, next time we meet up, I'm going to be looking at a rejuvenated Mike, am I? You'll have rediscovered your zest for life, thanks to watching Brighton and Hove pigging Albion?'

'That's roughly the idea, yeah.'

Andy just laughed. 'Oh, fantastic!' he exclaimed, scooping up our empties and heading back to the bar. 'This I must see! Same again?'

I've become like a kid in a sweetshop, albeit with marginally less inclination to shove sherbet fountains down my jumper. The way I'm acting, anyone would assume my real motive for splashing out £380 on that season ticket wasn't football-related at all, but that it would finally give me a legitimate excuse to purchase Albion novelties from the Seagulls Shop.

Oh, yes, the mighty, mighty Seagulls Shop. Not that mighty at all, to be honest, at least not on the scale of your bog-standard Man United megastore, but still offering a fairly impressive and curiously tempting range of goodies. I've walked past the place often enough – No. 6 Queens Road, a short downhill strut from Brighton station towards the sea, sandwiched between the BSM Driving School and the Lee Cottage Chinese Restaurant – and, all right, I admit it, I've popped in there once or twice, even before I had any valid reason to. Only to browse, you understand.

Well, OK, I did once buy a little Albion lighter. Just a disposable thing, back in the days when I was still on the Silk Cut Untastables. I didn't feel too bad about this, though; my excuse being – not that anyone ever asked to hear it – that I happened to need a new lighter in any case, and that this one (white, with a jaunty blue Seagull logo), was no more expensive than the regular sort they sold at the newsagent's just up the road. So there.

Or words to that effect.

But obviously I'd never felt able to indulge myself the way a proper fan could, by treating myself to something which openly implied a solid allegiance, such as an Albion T-shirt. And I certainly didn't feel I could stroll through town wearing the official replica top.

Up until a couple of seasons ago, mind you, I wouldn't have wanted to. I don't mean for football reasons, but because of the various sponsorships which the club had gone through. No disrespect, but I really didn't fancy strutting around with 'Donatello' (a local Italian restaurant) emblazoned in red italics across my chest, if only because I knew how soon I'd tire of the Ninja Turtle gags. Nor, in previous years, had I been hugely tempted by the prospect of having 'Sandtex' or 'TSB' strung between my nipples. As for buying an Albion shirt during the phase when the club was being sponsored by an office supplies company called Nobo, I've a hunch this would have ended up figuring in my top ten of Most Regrettable Purchases Ever, somewhere between the bondage trousers and the David Gray album.

But then, a couple of years ago, coinciding with all sorts of other key changes at the club – not least of which was the move back to Brighton itself – along came Fatboy Slim, superstar DJ. Also known as Norman Cook, or That Bloke Who Used To Play Bass In The Housemartins. (Or Quentin, if you want to call him by the name he was christened with and really piss him off.) When Norman's record label, Skint, took over as sponsors in 1999, a new hipness seemed to attach itself to all things Albion. Suddenly the kit was a style statement.

Norman is a huge local hero and has apparently been an Albion fan since approximately forever. He and his wife, TV and radio chirpy-person Zoe Ball, have a place on Hove seafront, complete with their own cordoned-off chunk of private beach. It's pretty impressive, if you ignore the fact that, from the back, it gazes over a mini industrial estate. Not that I'm jealous or anything.

Anyway, the point is, Skint – besides being an amusingly apt name to associate with a club that's no stranger to financial troubles – is a cool thing to have slapped across the front of your team's shirts. Or certainly cooler, I'd argue, than Donatello, Sandtex, TSB or Nobo. (And infinitely more hip, if you want to go way, way back, than Phoenix Breweries or British Caledonian.)

So all of a sudden, from my perspective, those replica kits became a lot more desirable. Added to which, the club shop began stocking a range of other Skint/Albion paraphernalia. The range of goodies seemed to multiply in a matter of weeks. I was becoming increasingly tempted. I'm nothing if not shallow, me.

So in a sense what I was doing ten days ago was buying myself a part of all this. Purchasing the right to show I belong. In fact, it occurs to me that maybe this is all I really wanted to do in the first place, which would be a bit of a worry. Obviously I'd always been at liberty to wander in to this oddly magical place and purchase what the hell I wanted, regardless of whether or not it made any sense. But now, thanks to my financial commitment – as if that's all it ever really required – any of this stuff can legitimately be mine. Like for *real*. I'm free to buy, wear, carry, watch, read, drink out of, set fire to, whatever Albion-related piece of gubbins I happen to fancy. And here's the most alarming bit: I'm genuinely thrilled by the idea. Totally exhilarated to think that I've now as much right as anybody else to indulge myself in these knick-knacks. At least I think I have.

There are obviously still a few grey areas. For instance, one of the goodies to which I treated myself today was an Albion car sticker, proudly declaring 'Champions'. Admittedly, I've not hesitated to attach this, slightly wonkily and still with one or two air-bubbles trapped underneath, to my rear windscreen, but I do feel a wee bit uneasy about it – as if I'm trying to grab a share of the glory associated exclusively with last year's achievement.

The end-of-season video (£16.99) I feel I can justify, if only for research purposes. *Championes!*, it's called, with reference to that strange Spanish-ish chant ('Cham–pee–oh–nayz! Cham–pee–oh–nayz!') now adopted, somewhat embarrassingly if you ask me, by just about any triumphant football team, whether they've proved themselves to be the cream of Europe or snatched a scrappy last-gasp winner in the West Sussex Gusset-Stitchers' Memorial Plate.

I suppose you could say I purchased this video (narrated by Albion obsessive Des Lynam and with a Fatboy-and-pals soundtrack) to try and get a feel for what I've bought myself into. It actually covers only the second half of last season, through to the promotion, followed by the title win itself, but that'll do. Don't want to go mad or anything.

Anyway, as I watched it I felt quite strange: an unsettling blend of envy, guilt and detachment. Envy for all the obvious reasons – watching the celebrations I'd not been a part of, knowing those hardcore fans were being rewarded for a loyalty which I could never hope to match. Guilt, because I could now be accused of trying to gatecrash on all this, albeit months later. And detachment? Well, yes, because, if I'm being honest, something was missing. Des kept implying that the hairs were going to stand up on the back of my neck, and they didn't. Now, obviously it had been assumed that I, the purchaser, would be an established Albion fan. But even allowing for that misunderstanding, the truth is that the video just didn't move me. Which is weird, because I can watch other teams, teams with which I have an even more tenuous connection, if any at all, and become genuinely emotional when I see them achieve something glorious. Show me a non-league side beating a Premiership club and you'll have me welling up.

So what's the explanation? I can only put it down to two factors. The first is that the guilt which I mentioned – and, OK, which I keep mentioning, because, God, that's how bloody *guilty* I feel – was even more oppressive than I'd first imagined, and that it kept gnawing away as I watched the tape. Had I been entirely neutral, I'd have probably just sat back and enjoyed it.

And the second? The second is that I think I'm suffering from AFS.

If you don't know what that stands for – perhaps because I've just made it up – then let me explain: AFS (I've decided) is Armchair Fan Syndrome, a twenty-first-century condition particularly prevalent amongst lazy arses who've come to rely exclusively on digital TV for their football, and who consequently expect to view every goal from 29 different camera angles, ideally accompanied by big whooshy noises and a chicken dansak. From an AFS-sufferer's viewpoint, a relatively low-budget video, however lovingly and professionally crafted, and even with Des doing the voiceover, lacks a certain edge.

As far as treatments for this condition are concerned, scientists have yet to conduct any detailed research into the controversial Shift-The-Fat-Fucker Technique, whereby the sufferer is repeatedly winched from his armchair over a nine-month spell and deposited inside a real football stadium. But, hey, I'll soon be able to save them the trouble.

Who Ate All The Pies? – THURSDAY 2 AUGUST

It's the first match of the season tomorrow, a friendly against First Division Sheffield United, and – gasp! – I simply didn't have a thing to wear.

Forget the replica shirt, though. The sponsor's name may be suitably cool these days, but that's no guarantee that, when I actually go and try one of these things on – as I did this afternoon – I won't look completely absurd. I picked out an XXL, slipped it off the hanger, tugged it over my head and – hey, presto! – Mr Hot-Air Balloon. I appreciate I'm not exactly Kate Moss, figure-wise, but who the hell works out the sizings on these things? Extra, extra large *what*, might I ask? Fucking leprechaun?

Still, I'm not too bothered. For one thing, I've never been that anxious to wrap myself in crackly man-made fibre. At best, I'd probably soon reek of sweat, and at worst I'm likely to turn myself into a fire-hazard.

Besides which, it's a bit naff, really. I know it's commonly accepted that to wear your team's shirt is an honour, the ultimate gesture of support, and that the only thing usually likely to dissuade you from doing so is a shortage of funds. But beyond your mid-20s – maybe 30 at a pinch – I can't help feeling you look a bit of a sad Muppet.

Added to which, it's a tribal thing. And part of my problem – one which I can't decide whether or not I'm looking to overcome this season – is that I've never been a tribal sort of bloke. I find it a bit scary.

I do realise that if every fan felt the way I do – introverted, understated, a bit of a wuss – then the atmosphere at matches would be roughly akin to an amateur bowls tournament. So I suppose what I'm saying is that I recognise football needs its tribal types; it's just that I don't want to *be* one. Or at least I don't think I do. I'll let the others get on with it – and when, come the next day of triumph, the manager acknowledges the fantastic role played by the fans, I'll just have to kid myself that he includes me.

I didn't leave the store empty-handed, incidentally. In the end I treated myself to a black cotton Skint T-shirt with 'Brighton Bloke' printed across the front in white lettering. Cool, adaptable, relatively understated – and, best of all, it fits me fine. It's only an XL, too. Work that one out.

For the record, I also bought an Albion mousepad and screensaver for my computer (old stock, featuring pictures of long-departed players wearing the Ninja Turtle kit, but it was all they had, and only a fiver), plus a mug (£3.99) and a key-ring (£1.99). I'm kind of easing myself in.

Sealions On A Shirt – FRIDAY 3 AUGUST

BRIGHTON 2 SHEFFIELD UNITED 3
(PRE-SEASON FRIENDLY)

Here come the teams. A mighty cheer goes up, or as mighty as you can expect when the ground's only half full. I look up from my programme, from which I've been trying to learn a few of the players' names, and – hang on, where the fuck are they? Oh, right. *That's* where the tunnel is. Oops, how embarrassing.

If only for a split second, I'd shown myself up. Or at least I would have done, in the unlikely event that anyone was more interested in my reactions than in what was happening on the pitch.

Still, I'll know next time, assuming nobody moves it for a prank; the tunnel, one of those foldaway concertina jobs, the sort designed mainly to deflect cash donations of the airborne variety, is at the far right-hand corner from where I'll be sitting, between the end of the North Stand and the tiny section set aside for away fans.

Besides, I don't know why I'm being quite so paranoid. It wasn't as if I'd stood up and yelled, 'Come on, you Sealions!' or turned to the bloke beside me and asked which team was which.

Being a pre-season friendly, the main purpose of tonight's match was obviously to allow the players to sharpen up, to move several steps closer to readiness for the new season, mentally and physically. But I suppose it was also a warm-up for the fans, still some way short of match-fitness themselves, in the spectating sense. One of them, of course, was a *long* way short of it.

With kick-off at 7.45 p.m., I figured I should leave the house just after seven. I realise this is an early contender for this book's Dullest Piece Of Information award, but I needed to work this stuff out. If I was going to get off on the right footing I'd have to allow myself enough time to arrive in relative comfort, soak up a bit of the atmosphere, grab a programme and, in what I assumed was still an important matchday tradition, treat myself to a crushingly disappointing burger.

Withdean Stadium isn't a football ground at all, by the way. At least, not a real one. Lying within one of Brighton's leafier, wealthier suburbs, it's actually an old athletics stadium – council-owned – which the Albion are being allowed to use until they find themselves a permanent new home. After the sale of the sadly crumbling Goldstone Ground in Hove – at a site on which there now stands the profoundly depressing Goldstone Retail Park (Comet, Burger King, Toys 'R' Us, Sofas 'R' Fucking Expensive These Days Aren't They, and a sports shop which doesn't even sell Albion shirts) – and following those two years at Gillingham, the council agreed to let Withdean be the club's temporary base. A lot of local residents initially reacted in the arsey manner in which local residents feel obliged to react in these situations, but the club eventually got the nod. That was in 1998, and the agreement has since been extended. As far as I can establish, the objectors have mostly stopped objecting now, or at least stopped objecting out loud.

Long-term, the club wants to build a flash new stadium, up the road at Falmer. But before there's even the vaguest prospect of that happening, there's a huge, dreary local planning process for it to wade through. Technically, this procedure isn't hugely different from the one you'd encounter if, for example, you wanted to convert your loft into a poky bedroom where you could repeatedly smack your head on the ceiling. In practice, I gather the stadium thing is on a slightly bigger scale, and likely to be tub-thumpingly tedious.

For the moment, then, it's Withdean or lump it.

On first impressions, I don't entirely hate the place, although I must admit the South Stand scares me a smidgen. It reminds me of one of those rickety-looking arrangements they erect for golf tournaments – or worse, the ones you see on harrowing TV news stories about foreign stadium disasters. The fact that, as I learned this evening, the fans also have a habit of stomping their feet to create an almighty rumbling effect, doesn't exactly put me at my ease. But, look, I'm sure it's absolutely fine. It's just me.

With its minimal protection from the elements, and its running track separating the crowd from the pitch, Withdean almost feels like an eastern European ground. One which, admittedly, may have seen better days. And which hasn't actually got any fans behind one of the goals. And, OK, one without crumbling stone terraces crammed with menacing militiamen clutching Kalashnikovs. But certainly a ground with its own slightly alien character.

The view my seat affords me isn't bad – or at least I assume it isn't, because when I arrived tonight it was already filled with someone else's buttocks. 'It's sit anywhere tonight, mate,' explained a burly, bearded steward, sporting what struck me as an unnecessarily fluorescent jacket for an August evening. It turned out that 'sit anywhere' was the policy whenever Withdean was substantially below full capacity for a match, which it sure as hell was tonight. With some relief, I noticed several other fans also questioning the arrangement as they filtered in, double-checking their stubs and quizzing the owners of the particular buttocks deposited on their own seats. So at least my ignorance hadn't singled me out.

To be honest, I reckon I'd have been well within my legal rights to have stood my ground and demanded the spot I'd specifically paid for, particularly if I'd been in one of those moods where I like to look a pompous arsehole. It hadn't come as part of my season ticket package, but I'd made a special point of requesting the same seat I'd be occupying all season, to allow myself the chance to, you know, acclimatise. To turn up and discover somebody else already occupying it – chatting merrily with their mates, clearly indifferent to the impact of what they'd done – well, I don't mind telling you, it had been a sizeable blow.

Still, never mind, at least my début snack hadn't let me down.

'And have you got any Diet Coke?' I'd asked the sad-looking lady, as she'd prepared me my quarter-pounder with onions. 'Yep,' she'd replied, handing me a warm plastic bottle of Diet Pepsi.

Drooling with anticipation and exactly four quid worse off, I'd carried my teatime treat into a relatively quiet corner – between a couple of bins and what looked like a generator – and taken a greedy bite. It had turned out, just as I'd expected, to be the sort of burger for which the description 'adequate' would be crazily generous. One of those in which the burger and the bun feel as if they don't really want to be a part of the same snack – the cold crumbliness of the catering-pack bap forming no sort of palpable partnership with the hot greasiness of the 'meat'. I gobbled it up in seconds.

It's a funny thing, me and rubbishy food, but there's something about it which I adore. I'm not talking about food which is obviously designed to kill me, or at least lay me up in hospital for several weeks. I just mean food, such as this burger, which scores a big oily zero on the scale of nutritional benefit and which doesn't even taste very nice. The fact is, I can't resist it. Julie finds this extraordinary, pointing out that at home we'll spend hours preparing decent, imaginative meals for ourselves, many of them as previously demonstrated by people wearing white hats on BBC2. To be honest, I think I probably find it quite extraordinary too. The only way I can even begin to explain my love of junk food is that it's fun. I don't mean so much the flavour, or even necessarily the physical process of consuming it, but just the fact that I'm allowing myself to do something I wouldn't normally do – or be expected to do – at home. The same sort of emotional release, I suppose – if we really want to move into amateur psychology here – as when I shout like a moron during the match itself.

Because, yes, I do shout. I remember now. I may not sing, or join in the chants, or wear the replica shirt, but individually I'm happy to yell. Provided everyone else is yelling at the same time, that is, and given the right circumstances.

Tonight's first real test for me came midway through the first half, when Albion conceded a corker of a comedy goal. A mix-up between their Dutch keeper, Michel Kuipers (I'm learning), and defender Andy Crosby (it feels a bit early for me to start saying 'our', although perhaps this is just because it was the sort of cock-up I'd rather not be associated with) allowed United's Somebody-Or-Other to sneak through and tap in the type of goal even my grandmother wouldn't miss. And she's been dead 20 years.

The interesting thing, as far as I was concerned, was how I'd instinctively react to this. Would I swear? Would I sigh philosophically? Would I – God forbid – burst out laughing? Or would I just do what I normally do when 'my' team concedes a goal – namely, just sit and stare ahead, kind of numbly? I was relieved to find myself doing the latter. It's not the most potent expression of disappointment, I grant you – not, for example, as visually impressive as bursting into tears like some fans I've seen on TV (although admittedly this is usually reserved for when their side has been relegated or lost a cup final or discovered the board has appointed Gordon Strachan as manager). But it was a steady enough start for someone keen not to draw attention to himself. Besides, I did experience a kind of sinking feeling at the same time, which had to be encouraging on the do-I-really-give-a-monkey's side of things. Unless that was just down to the burger.

The second goal, conceded just before half-time, was better in one sense and worse in another. Better in that it was a 'proper' goal, and therefore not half as embarrassing. Worse because, as the teams headed back to what I assume is a dressing-room, I was left to reflect on what I'd really let myself in for here. If it had just been a case of feeling twice as pissed off, now that the deficit had doubled, I wouldn't necessarily have minded. Again, it would have indicated an encouraging sense of commitment on my part. But it was more a simple case of wondering whether I was in for a season of frustrating shite. Three hundred and eighty quid could have bought me a half-decent stereo.

And then, five or so minutes into the second half, came the goal. The first significant milestone on my journey towards . . . well, towards whatever the hell it's meant to be towards. And yes, I cheered. Of course I cheered. Not the biggest, screamiest, most powerful release of pent-up emotion, but a not-bad reaction. Easily a big enough buzz to be going on with. Besides, exactly how mad are you supposed to go at friendlies? You'd have to be a bit nuts to cheer too loudly. Either that or concerned that what you've just witnessed might prove relatively rare in the months ahead.

The fact that, after Paul Brooker's effort had raised Albion hopes, United nipped straight down the other end and banged in a third, effectively putting the game beyond reach, was probably the night's most gutting moment. It was as if the visitors – the better side, although not by miles – were saying: 'Don't even think about trying *that* again, you sorry gaggle of mediocrities.'

As it happens, Albion did try it again – and succeeded – this time thanks to Paul Rogers, the captain. But it wasn't enough.

Still, pre-season friendlies are notoriously unreliable gauges of a team's chances for the season. Apparently. And if that's true, there was nothing tonight to suggest that the Albion should approach the coming campaign with trepidation. As for my own response, I'm sure I did fine. Not caring too much was a perfectly understandable reaction.

For now.

No-Score Drawers – SATURDAY 11 AUGUST

CAMBRIDGE UNITED 0 BRIGHTON 0

Marks and Spencer's ladies' lingerie department is probably not the sort of place where a bloke should really draw attention to himself. But it was only a mild expletive, and I'm pretty sure nobody heard.

Just before half-time in the match at Cambridge, with the score still at 0–0, Albion's captain Paul Rogers was sent off. Quite harshly, by all accounts. And there was me, not yelling abuse from Cambridge's away section, as were the Albion's travelling fans, but standing beside a rack of lacy thongs in Brighton's M&S, going 'Bastard!'

'What's up?' inquired Julie, inspecting a gusset. So I explained.

Up until this point, I don't think she'd even noticed the earphones, fed from the tiny radio in my trouser pocket. Nor had I really wanted her to. I didn't want her to think I'd become one of those husbands who spend Saturday afternoons being dragged against their will around a succession of shops, feebly feigning intense interest in every item which grabs their partner's attention while secretly longing to be at a footie game. Because, honestly, that's not how it is. There are times when I quite like shopping with Julie – preferably in small doses, I grant you, and ideally when no actual transactions take place. It's just that this was the first afternoon of the season, and I was meant to be showing some sort of commitment to 'my team'. So I had to make at least a token effort.

It wasn't Five Live who were covering the match (for some reason, the Albion are rarely top of their agenda), but our local-ish BBC station, Southern Counties Radio. One of the brilliant things about local radio, however – and an advantage it will always have over any national counterpart – is that it can be blindingly, bloody-mindedly, unashamedly biased. The co-commentator, an Albion obsessive called Ian Hart, virtually blew a gasket over Rogers' dismissal, and that's exactly how it should be, whatever the merits of the decision. Harty (it didn't take me long to pick up on the nickname) gave the impression he'd like to rip off his headphones, charge down to the pitch and sort out the official in person, and I suppose some of that incensed passion must have filtered through to me, as I stood in ladies' lingerie. So to speak.

Julie would have gone equally ballistic, however – or at least sulked in spectacular style – if I'd spent the entire afternoon with my earphones attached. So I satisfied myself with just shoving them in for a quick burst of commentary every five minutes or so. That way, if she wanted my opinion on whichever laughably overpriced garment had caught her eye, I was able to respond in the usual manner. Namely:

> JULIE: So what do you think of it then? Lovely, isn't it?
> ME: Hmmmm? Oh, yeah. Yeah, it's really nice.
> JULIE: Do you like it?
> ME: I do, yeah.

JULIE: Are you sure?

ME: Yeah. Honestly.

(30-second pause, while Julie holds the dress/jumper/indeterminate piece of cloth up against herself in the mirror, swivels a bit etc)

JULIE: So what do you think of it then? Lovely, isn't it?

This can go on for hours, as if on a loop, and it might, on face value, seem like a ridiculous waste of time. But we've been together for, what, 17 years now, and we both know what it's really about. My role in these situations isn't really to offer Julie an independent viewpoint, but merely to confirm what she's already thinking, or at least half-thinking. It's as if she's talking to herself, really. All I'm helping her to do is buy herself some thinking time.

It took a good many years for me to twig this, mind you, and for us to perfect the routine. For a while I genuinely used to imagine that she valued my opinion, so like an idiot I'd go ahead and give it.

She'd pick up some overpriced monstrosity, ask me what I thought of it and I'd go, 'Nah, it looks like the sort of thing the dog sleeps on.' Then she'd slap it back on the rail and storm out of the shop, purple with rage.

'What's the matter?' I'd cry, in all innocence, as I chased her down the street. 'Nothing,' she'd go. 'It's fine.'

'Nothing, it's fine,' I should explain, really means, 'Plenty's the matter, since you ask, but for maximum impact I'm going to keep you guessing for at least the next hour, refusing to acknowledge any problem, but at the same time making it patently obvious from my behaviour, body language, and the fact that I'm striding three paces ahead and not speaking to you, that I'm seriously pissed off.'

What I'd been consistently doing in all those situations, and it's obvious now, is questioning Julie's fundamental judgement. My response had implied a serious lapse of taste on her part, or at least a major gulf between her own tastes and mine. The most I should have done was hint at maybe the tiniest difference of opinion, so that, overall, we'd still be on the same wavelength. She'd wanted affirmation, not a full-scale debate. I know that now. Believe me, it's not a mistake I make these days.

Anyway, pretty soon we were out of M&S – Julie empty-handed, me just grateful that I wasn't being pursued by the Pant Police – and on our way to Sainsbury's. A wise move, I felt; Julie was hardly facing an imminent knicker drought, but our fridge and cupboards were in a serious state of Old Mother Hubbardness. Unfortunately, what I hadn't realised is that, once you're inside this particular store, you experience a sort of radio blackout, rather like Apollo astronauts used to face when they went around the dark side of the moon. So it wasn't until we got back home, more than an hour after the final whistle, that I was able to get the Albion result confirmed.

A goalless draw isn't too bad a start, I suppose, especially when you consider we played half the game with ten men. And, from a selfish standpoint, at least it means I may still witness Albion's opening goal for the season, assuming they can manage one at home to Wigan next Saturday. So that's something to look forward to.

I hope.

Plus, of course, this afternoon's big moment of controversy – the sending-off – did trigger some sort of response in me; surely that must be a promising sign. I didn't exactly explode, I admit, but you need to bear in mind where I was standing at the time. Middle-aged men going mental in knicker departments still tends to be frowned upon in this country.

If you likened my passion for football to a flat car battery – and, OK, there's no particular reason why you should – then maybe my reaction to that sending-off was like turning the key in the ignition and still hearing the tiniest whirr of life.

In which case, I suppose what I'm looking for now is a set of metaphorical jump-leads. Or something.

Separate Ways – SATURDAY 18 AUGUST

BRIGHTON 2 WIGAN 1

It really wasn't planned this way. In fact, it only occurred to me yesterday afternoon – but my season of commitment, for want of a less ridiculous expression, is likely to be getting me out of a number of family duties between now and next spring.

This afternoon, for example, was my nephew's birthday party, to which Julie, Em and I were all invited. Now, obviously I love little Oscar to bits, but when Julie made it clear that I wasn't expected to be there, well, frankly I could have hugged her. Come to think of it, I think I may have done. The prospect of a relatively compact house crammed with Oscar's fellow two-year-olds, plus various obscure grown-ups I'd no doubt have been expected to recognise – possibly even peck on the cheek – was not one I relished. Add to this the fact that the place would have been an ocean of discarded gift-wrap, and that at least 83 per cent of Oscar's presents would have required him to bash a button and hear some strangulated Yank voice croaking, 'P is for purrrrrrson' or 'Upper-raiderrr 911' and I think it might have done my head in within 20 minutes.

So I left it for Julie and Em to have their heads done in. I, meanwhile, psyched myself up for my first proper afternoon at Withdean.

And, yep, I was feeling quite upbeat. I can't pretend I've devoted extensive thought to the Albion since last weekend's season-opener, but then what has there really been to think about? No goals scored, none conceded, nothing much of consequence except that sending-off. It's almost as if that wasn't really the start of the season at all – just a final warm-up – and that the team wanted to wait until today to get things properly underway in front of us home fans. Specifically in front of me, even. Just humour me, OK?

So, what to wear – that was the first crucial question. I bought some combat trousers a couple of weeks ago – eight quid, from the cheapest clothes store in town, other than those which sell clothes already soiled by previous owners – and although I'm pretty sure Julie hates them (she certainly hates the store), I decided they'd be ideal for this afternoon: ticket, money and keys in the pocket halfway down my left leg; radio, mobile and miscellaneous crap in the one halfway down my right – and, bingo, no need for a jacket, or indeed anything else in which to cram all my clutter. It takes a bit of trial and error to get the balance right, I must admit, and to prevent myself walking with what appears to be an aggravated hamstring injury, but the arrangement on which I eventually settled felt just about OK. Having said that, and whatever the weight distribution, this whole combat trouser concept does take a bit of getting used to if you're 41 years old and you've never worn these things before. Physically, it just feels strange, as if you've developed enormous yet conveniently balanced growths down the side of each thigh. And mentally? Well, mentally, I suppose it could be argued that I'm too old to be wearing clothes like this, and that, to the neutral observer, I look a bit of an arse. A bit like pensioners do in denim. But I'm afraid that, for matches at least, I'm unlikely to find anything nearly as suitable. I'm one of these people who can never leave the house without carrying a whole heap of 'essential' bits and bobs which others seem perfectly capable of surviving without: in the case of the footie, I need my mini-radio to help me keep up with the other scores, the accompanying earphones, the mobile so I can ring Julie with the score at half-time (as if she gives a toss), the ticket, the cash, the extra cash because the first load of cash was never going to be enough, the keys, the wallet, the chewing gum, etc. etc. There will, I'm almost certain, come a time when I convince myself of the need for a

Thermos of piping hot oxtail and a couple of heavy-duty distress flares, just in case I take a wrong turning on the way to Withdean and end up stranded on Dartmoor.

And what did I wear on top? Just a plain blue shirt today, although, by the time I'd reached the ground, I have to confess I'd felt myself beginning to waver on the replica shirt issue – i.e. as to whether or not I should buy myself one after all. Always assuming I could find one to fit, that is.

En masse, I can't deny, it looked impressive, all that blue-and-white stripeyness sweeping towards the stadium. The expression 'solid sea of support' makes absolutely no grammatical sense, but it's the best way I can find to describe the sight which greeted me, and which, yes, made me feel quite emotional, as I filtered in from a side road to join the crowd.

If only those shirts looked more impressive close up; they're fine from the front, but the backs are a serious let-down. In the place where the number should be, there's a large unsightly plain blue square – theoretically allowing the buyer to choose which figure to stick on it. And then, between this square and the collar, there's a strip of plain white – obviously to accommodate whatever lettering you need to spell out the name of your favourite player. Unfortunately, if you look at the fans who've bought these bits of kit, only a minority seem to have taken up the numbering-and-lettering option; the rest walk around in shirts which look strangely, jarringly unfinished. Not only does this look slightly sad, but it also suggests that these fans aren't sufficiently convinced about any one Albion player. Not enough, at least, to have taken the plunge, labelling-wise. I'd expected to see loads of number 25s with 'ZAMORA' spelled out above them, seeing as Bobby is the closest the current side has to a star, but although these probably did outnumber the others, it wasn't to any mind-boggling degree. Not like, say, all the 'BECKHAM's you'd see at Old Trafford, or 'HENRY's at Highbury. But then maybe I'm reading too much into this; it could be that people are still saving up for the extra embellishments. Or maybe they just reckon embellishments are childish. Or maybe the machine's broken down.

Anyway, would I be any different, I wondered? Would I, if I did decide to buy one of these replica shirts, choose to stick my neck out and decorate it with one particular Albion player's details? Right now, bearing in mind that I'm still struggling even to remember who the hell they all are, I'd have to say I wouldn't. But what about long-term, once I've learned their names, numbers, positions and degrees of talent, or lack of? Will I warm to the idea? Or is it just something you should grow out of, at roughly the age when you're old enough to purchase solvents without arousing suspicion?

Towards the back of today's match programme – and every match's, I assume – there's an interesting double-page spread devoted to sponsors. Each member of the squad can have their kit sponsored by a local business, generous fan or whatever, both home and away. The sponsor then gets their name printed alongside the player's photo in the programme. It's hardly a revolutionary idea – I remember something similar appearing in the programmes when I used to make my odd trip to the Goldstone – but it's quite revealing in that, the way I see it, it spells out who's in favour, and in pretty clinical terms. Zamora, as the most obvious example, has already attracted sponsors for both his home and away kits. But then this is a guy who could probably attract sponsorship for his penis if the option were available. Keeper Michel Kuipers, by contrast, has currently only been sponsored for his Withdean games. And loyal defender Kerry Mayo seems to have attracted precisely fuck-all interest so far on either front, which seems a bit sad. OK, so this isn't exactly the definitive popularity poll, being based specifically on who's prepared to cough up actual cash to support these players, but it still paints quite a revealing picture.

Striker Lee Steele (sponsored at home by the A21 Supporters Club, and backed on away turf by the might of Windmill Kitchens) is one player who, if I did decide to stick my neck out on the shirt-decorating front, might be a strong contender. Firstly, because from what I can gather so far, he's a bloke who has yet to live up to his promise since joining the club – but who, judging from his reception when he came on as a sub this afternoon, is still a big hit with the fans.

And, secondly, because Steele's winning goal – a sweet strike, 12 minutes from time – marked a sort of watershed for me. It was a shame it happened at the far end of the ground, where I couldn't really see it that clearly, but what really mattered was how I reacted. The fact is, I leapt from my seat and roared my head off. I roared and I roared, and, realising this was quite a nice feeling, I roared some more. I roared till I was raw. Not a polite cheer, or generous applause, or any other phoney, feeble gesture of celebration, but an enormous, joyful release. With that single decisive shot, Lee Steele had reminded me why I was doing this.

When you also bear in mind that, for at least half the match, it had been peeing down with rain, and that I was soaked to the bones, and that I *still* couldn't have been much happier, then you begin to get some idea of how much that goal meant to me.

And it could hardly have worked out better. We – somehow it feels OK to say 'we' now (funny, that) – had gone a goal down midway through the first half, courtesy of a balls-up involving defender Nathan Jones (Family

Assurance Friendly Society, home and away), and I sensed an inky gloom descending over the ground. 'We've got a whole fucking season of this shit to look forward to,' I heard some bloke moaning behind me. At this stage, and until about five minutes from half-time, we really did look ropey. I won't say we looked shapeless, because that would imply that I have even the vaguest grasp of tactics, but we certainly looked overawed. Scared, even. It was as if, to a man, the freshly promoted Albion players had suddenly thought, 'Shit, we're playing decent teams now. I want my mummy.'

But then, just before the break, we won a penalty. I can't pretend I saw what happened or whether it was even deserved, but what the heck? It meant the Albion – and Bobby Zamora – could knock in the first goal of the season. And, once Bobby had successfully planted the ball in the net rather than the car park, the transformation was extraordinary. We could even have banged in a couple more before the interval, and that injection of optimism sustained us right through the second half. Sure, it was scrappy at times, and for every bit of skill on the part of either team there was at least one embarrassing mis-kick or cock-up to remind us (as if we needed reminding) that we weren't watching Premiership football here, but it was passionate and gripping and I absolutely loved it. By the final whistle, I felt exhausted and exhilarated – and, of course, drenched – but the buzz was the sort I hadn't experienced in God knows how long. It felt as if the medicine was already beginning to work.

As we filtered away from the ground, I decided to call Julie on the mobile. And that's when it hit me. As I began to give her a rundown of what had happened, I realised I was struggling to get the words out. Seriously. I was on the verge of tears. Don't laugh, but a 2–1 win in a bog-standard Second Division match between two sets of relatively unheard-of players – in a comedy stadium, and in front of fewer than 7,000 people – had just had the most extraordinary effect on me. I know, stupid, eh?

This early in the season, of course, my response didn't have much to do with the Albion securing three points, welcome though I'm sure they were. For the moment, it was mostly a selfish reaction. What had surprised me was that it had taken so little to get me this far. I'd expected to wait several weeks before I began to experience even the tiniest hint of emotion. Instead of which, a big dollop of it had been served up at the very first match. Of course, it's easy when you've just won. The long-term question will be, can I sustain it, or will it slip away, feebly and shamefully, once things don't go so well? That'll be the real test. That and finding out whether this feeling can become part of a collective thing – a sense of belonging – rather than just intensely me-orientated.

For the moment, all I can say for sure is that it feels pretty good.

As soon as I'd finished my call to Julie, out came those tears. Good job it was still raining.

The Drugs Don't Work – SUNDAY 19 AUGUST

And then come the days when I'm simply a miserable bastard.

Talk about a turnaround. If my mood today has been the result of coming down from yesterday afternoon's high, then I can see I'm going to have a problem here. If I'm looking to football – 'using' it, you might even suggest – to try and reacquaint myself with the euphoria of caring, then you could almost describe yesterday (and I know the drug analogy is as corny as hell, so I promise I'll try not to labour it) as my first real fix. Unfortunately, that meant today was always destined to be – yep, you've guessed it – the hideous comedown.

After a bit of a lie-in, we decided to spend the afternoon shopping – a hateful idea in itself, of course, but the more time I spend at the footie, the more I feel I should make up for it by spending at least the equivalent number of hours, if not more, doing stuff with Julie. Now, the way I see it we have a perfectly good range of shops here in Brighton. So where did we go? We went to the Bluewater flaming shopping centre in flaming Kent, more than an hour or so's flaming drive away. Even if you've never been to this place, you've probably still experienced it in every other sense: it's one of those echoey, undercover, could-be-frigging-anywhere places, packed with larger-than-average versions of mostly predictable High Street stores – Jigsaw, Gap, Virgin, Dixons, Hobbs etc – along with 578 zillion people. I'm amazed Julie likes it, but like it she most certainly does.

I could have just said no, of course – possibly should have done, on reflection – but if that was the way Julie wanted us to fritter away our Sunday afternoon, I felt I should go along with it. My only nagging concern, even before we arrived there to begin the frittering process – in fact, before we'd even set off, come to think of it – was that I'd woken up in the most spectacularly foul mood. And it wasn't showing the slightest sign of improvement.

It was as if I'd been invaded by the Misery Bug. Unlike your bog-standard foul mood, with this one I could almost step back and observe myself sounding like a horrible grump. Like an out-of-body experience, I could watch how it was poisoning my behaviour. Yet, frustratingly, there seemed to be no way I could step back in and overpower it. It wasn't so much that I disagreed with the ill-tempered utterings which the Misery Bug was forcing me to come out with; it was simply that I didn't need to say those things in the first place. I knew I didn't; I just couldn't stop myself.

It all came to a head in Jigsaw. Julie wanted a new suit for work, which was fair enough, and was trying on the jacket of one she'd taken a fancy to. On face value, it may sound like nothing more than another of our wifey-to-hubby 'what-do-you-think-of-it' situations, but this one soon developed an altogether more hostile edge.

As she paraded in front of the full-length mirror, it seemed blindingly obvious to me that this jacket didn't fit properly. Perhaps not to gangrene-inducing proportions, but enough to suggest that she might want to try the next size up. Now, I appreciate that by proposing such an idea in such a sensitive situation, I was straying onto tricky terrain. The words may well have left my lips as, 'Why not try the next size up?', but the likelihood, as I should have known, was that they'd reach Julie's ears as, 'My, but you ain't half a fat lass.' However, that wasn't the major problem here. The major problem was triggered when Julie replied, 'They're wearing them tighter this year' – a remark which, desperately though I struggled to fight it, sent me into Mr Sarky mode. Obviously what I should have said was, 'Of course they are, darling, and they're quite right to do so. It's perfect. Now, tell me, oh sweet apple blossom, by which method of payment should we hand this fine assistant our week's wages?' Instead, I subjected my poor wife to a three-stage interrogation. Firstly, I wanted to be reminded exactly who 'they' were. Secondly, I wanted to know why 'they' felt the average female body was, specifically in this year of 2001, somehow going to be better equipped than usual to cope with blatantly ill-fitting, uncomfortable clothing. And thirdly, just to round off my charm offensive in real style, I asked her whether, if 'they' were to announce that every woman in Britain should saw off her right leg with a rusty hacksaw, she would be equally prepared to go along with the idea.

By the end of which – would you believe this – Julie wasn't in the chirpiest of moods. We left the store, had one of those embarrassing everyone's-staring-at-us rows just outside, and then decided it might be best if we went our separate ways. I don't mean in marital terms; I mean for the next hour, on the basis that, in Julie's words, I 'clearly wasn't interested' in anything she wanted to look at.

It passed, of course, same as it always does, and Julie still ended up heading home with an outfit for work. Not the one she'd tried on in Jigsaw, but a black thing from a lesser known store, the precise name of which currently escapes me. I believe it was called something like Overpriced Suits For Suckers.

Two hundred and seventy-nine pounds, it cost – which apparently I should have been thrilled about, on the basis that this was 50 quid less than an outfit she'd spotted elsewhere.

Still, what right did I really have to argue? It was still a 100 quid less than I'd forked out to spend a season watching Brighton and Hove Albion. And when it comes to investments, at least Julie's don't usually prompt concerns for her mental well-being.

I Say, You Bounder – TUESDAY 21 AUGUST

BRIGHTON 2 WIMBLEDON 1
(WORTHINGTON CUP, ROUND ONE)

A couple of rows back from me, at every game so far, there's been a bloke I've privately nicknamed 'Teach'. I've nicknamed him Teach because – and be warned, you'll probably split your sides and ooze goo when you hear this – he sounds like a teacher!!! Ha ha.

OK, so I appreciate it's a rubbish nickname, making him sound like some fossilised, mortarboarded character from a 1950s issue of the *Beano*. But really that's my point. The semi-plumminess of the bloke's voice, and the stuff he actually says with it, conjures up this misty, musty image of a creaky old games master, barking orders from the touchline during an inter-school rugby fixture. Rugby, you'll note, not football. Teach just doesn't sound right at a football match. At least, not now that Stanley Matthews is out of the England reckoning. And yet he can't be more than about 50, this guy. We're not talking about some cloth-capped Mr Gummy.

'You're a disgrace, No. 11!' he'll cry. Or 'Welcome to the game, referee!' Or 'Did you get that flag for Christmas, linesman?' Or a plain but heartfelt 'Oh, you absolute berk!'

God alone knows why he speaks like this, but I'm actually quite glad he does. I'm already developing rather a soft spot for Teach, and so, it seems, are a lot of the other regulars, judging by how they grin, sometimes openly snigger, at his verbal contributions.

If ever we run a sweepstake on what he'll come out with next, I'm hoping I'll draw 'Away with you, you cad!'

Mind you, he'd have had every right to have come out with that line tonight, and to have aimed it directly at me, given my mood on arrival. I really *was* being a cad – and, I wouldn't mind betting, a bounder, too – turning up in the colours but, in truth, utterly indifferent to this match's outcome. Against a side with so much Premiership experience, defeat was a foregone conclusion, I'd decided. And big deal; it wasn't as if we were going to win this stupid cup.

On reflection, I was just being a coward, psyching myself into a negative frame of mind to soften the blow of what I'd convinced myself would be a trouncing. Instead, just as we'd done on Saturday, we humoured our opponents by letting them go 1–0 up, then turned it around with two goals from Bobby Zamora. This time it felt even more fun, though, because I really hadn't imagined we could do it. No faith, that's my trouble. Not yet, anyway.

Teach would no doubt suggest I start bucking my ideas up, Sunny Jim. Or at least show a little respect.

Just Lust – WEDNESDAY 22 AUGUST

I'm always deeply wary when Andy launches into his caring-sharing salt 'n' vinegar routine. Along with our topped-up glasses, he'll return to our table gripping a single packet of crisps between his teeth (it doesn't have to be salt 'n' vinegar, it just tends to be), which, once he's sat down, he'll proceed to rip right open – tugging open the top, slicing down one side, then finally prising apart the bottom seam, leaving the contents fully exposed for us both to dip into.

This, I'm afraid, is a sign. It's Andy's idea of matey intimacy, psyching me up for the fact that he's got something profound he wants to share with me. Other than his bag of Walkers, that is. Something a wee bit sensitive, perhaps. Something controversial, even.

Or, as was the case tonight, something like:

'You're having an affair, Mike.'

'I'm *what*???!!!'

About to take a slurp, I'd suddenly frozen in astonishment, my glass barely an inch from my lips. I must have looked like a third-rate soap actor, who'd dipped into his limited repertoire and, for the umpteenth time in his sorry career, pulled out this exaggerated gesture to indicate 'bewilderment'.

'Having an affair,' he continued. 'I was thinking about the whole business a couple of nights ago, and I suddenly twigged. It all makes perfect sense.'

'Really? I'm glad you think so. What the hell are you on about, Andy? I am not having a flaming affair. I don't even . . . '

'I don't mean an affair with a woman, you pillock.'

'Jesus, it gets worse.'

'I mean a football affair. An affair with another club. Listen, I've worked it all out, OK? Brighton and Hove Albion are your mistress, right, and . . . '

'Blimey, do people still use that word?'

'Sorry? What word?'

'Mistress. It sounds a bit '70s sitcom. A bit Felicity Kendall.'

'Er . . . I think so. Whatever. Anyway, listen, you're missing my point. What I'm trying to explain to you is . . . '

' . . . is that Brighton and Hove Albion are my mistress. I know. You just said.'

'Exactly! And that Arsenal, right, are . . . '

' . . . and that Arsenal are my wife.'

'Yeah! That's it! And . . . '

' . . . and you're going to tell me the spark really went out of our relationship a long time ago, but that we've managed to hobble along these last few years – until now, when suddenly I've found something new and different and exciting and blah blah frigging blah.'

'Er . . . yeah. Something like that.' For a moment, Andy looked deflated, as if he'd assumed he had some sort of copyright on half-baked analogies. Then he perked up again: 'Makes sense though, doesn't it?'

I paused, picked up a soggy beer mat, started peeling away at its layers – a gesture almost intended, don't ask me why, to spare his feelings, to give the impression that I was deep in thought, mulling over this amazing theory of his for the very first time. I wasn't really.

And then, having milked the silence long enough, I looked Andy straight in the eye. 'Yeah,' I went. 'I suppose so. More or less.'

I usually make it a firm policy never to agree with any of Andy's theories. It only encourages him. But tonight I made an exception.

'What?' he gasped. 'You're saying you agree with me?'

'I suppose I am, yeah. Although it's more a case of you agreeing with me. I'd already come up with virtually the same theory myself.'

'Blimey. That must be a first.'

'I know. Scary, isn't it?'

Before Andy got too carried away, I did point out there were certain differences between our theories. Mostly, though, it was just a question of degrees. Andy seemed to be implying that, having taken up with someone new, I no longer had the slightest interest in my old team. That isn't really true. I could never imagine severing *all* emotional ties with the Arsenal. Most likely, my interest will gradually fade.

I thought about debating this specific point with Andy, but then I thought better of it. It was getting late, and we'd already had way too much profundity for one night. For a few moments we just sat there, dabbing at the last few crispy crumbs. It was me who eventually broke the silence.

'Andy,' I said.

'What?' he replied.

'Erm, I don't know quite how to tell you this, mate, but I . . .'

'Go on.'

'. . . I bloody hate salt 'n' vinegar.'

Andy gazed up at me. It was his turn to adopt the soap-actor's look of bewilderment.

'Shit,' he went. 'Me too.'

Unlucky Dip – THURSDAY 23 AUGUST

The nurse dipped a little plastic stick into my pot of urine, then told me we'd have to wait two minutes. If it really did contain traces of blood, she explained, the tiny yellow square on the end of this dipper would develop green spots.

Oh, right. Fan-bloody-tastic. What a novel way to spend a Thursday afternoon.

You see, this sums up the whole problem. A couple of hours earlier I'd taken myself off for a routine health screening – just felt it was about time, really – and had emerged feeling . . . well, not terrified exactly, but hardly turning cartwheels. I was, they'd sternly informed me, three stone overweight. (Bollocks, I'd thought. Two, perhaps.) On top of which, they'd then added, my blood pressure and cholesterol levels were both too high, if not yet dramatically. Oh, and, yes, there seemed to be some blood in my urine.

Blood.

In my urine.

Lovely.

You can try all you like to recapture some of the spark of youth, the way I'm trying to do with this football thing. But whatever your mind chooses to believe, your body stubbornly sticks to its own pig-headed agenda. Especially if you're a pig, I'd imagine. Then one day something like this pops up, and the mind has to stop kidding itself. Suddenly it has to acknowledge that you're not remotely exceptional, biologically speaking, that you're ageing just like your father did, and his father before him, and that soppy abstract factors such as your attitude and your outlook and whether you're still young enough in your own head to get excited about frivolous fluff like football, well, they really count for nothing if your body's turned ropey. It's a bugger, but today I became officially middle-aged.

Nothing they told me this afternoon need be disastrous, but the matter-of-fact manner which, over the years, I'd complacently grown to expect from medical people had suddenly been replaced with something decidedly less comforting. I tell you, these people were wearing frowns. If they were trying to put the fear of God into me, then they did a spectacular job. My perspectives weren't so much shifted as rammed sideways and bounced off a brick wall.

I was so alarmed about the blood-in-the-wee thing, I left the screening centre and whizzed straight round to my regular GP's surgery. As fast as a 1996 Renault Clio is actually capable of whizzing, that is. The practice nurse was about to go off duty for the night, but she was kind enough to stick around so I could give her a fresh pot of my wee for a second test.

Two minutes, she was telling me. Then we'd see if those green spots emerged.

Ho-hum, twiddle your thumbs, been on your hols yet etc.

The time up, she squinted at the stick. 'I can't really see anything, can you?' she said. I leaned across and squinted for myself. 'Not really,' I told her. 'But then I'm not really sure what I'm looking for.'

The nurse opened her drawer and pulled out a little comparison chart, to show me, among a range of other potential colour-shifts, what form this speckled greenness should take. It looked like a Dulux sample sheet. I contemplated whether, if the resulting pattern proved sufficiently attractive, I could persuade Julie to have our bedroom decorated that way. Perhaps not.

We stared a little longer, then both wondered if maybe we could see just the faintest hint of apple-blossom spottiness emerging.

In the end we were stumped. We just couldn't be sure, so to be on the safe side they're going to send it off for analysis anyway. Wisest option, I suppose. Apparently I'll get the results when I go back to see my doctor a week tomorrow. At which point, she also promised to prescribe something for my groin fungus (Dhobie's Itch, apparently – a variation on athletes' foot) and for my recent unpleasant tendency to develop huge, unsightly boils on my inner thighs.

I've a feeling she fancies me.

Parasol Rage – SATURDAY 25 AUGUST

TRANMERE ROVERS 0 BRIGHTON 0
LEAGUE POSITION (now that these things start to make some sort of sense): 12TH

With the sun putting in a token appearance, we decided to spend the afternoon at the beach hut, Julie and I. Yes, *our* beach hut.

Call us uncool if you must, but we love it. Contrary to the common assumption, you don't need to be 108 and terminally arthritic to qualify for one of these places; the sole requirement is that you relish the prospect of a permanent little beachfront retreat of your own – somewhere to unfold your B&Q recliner, whip off your shirt and expose rolls of milky white flab to hundreds of passers-by.

Almost converted you, haven't I?

Well, I wouldn't have done at about three o'clock this afternoon, believe me, because that's roughly the time you'd have found me caught up in . . . Parasol Rage. My problem is that, while I love sitting outdoors, I can't stand direct sunlight – not just for the drearily well-documented health reasons, but because I find it brain-bakingly oppressive. (Yeah, I know, I'm such an old woman.) We already own a parasol, which we bought last summer from Homebase, but somewhat disappointingly it turned out to have been designed by a cretin. The little tubular sleeve on the base, into which the parasol's central pole has to slip – and which you then tighten to grip the contraption firmly in place – is fashioned from 100 per cent Fucking Useless Bendy Plastic™. So at the slightest gust – and, believe me, seafront gusts are rarely just slight – the whole thing buckles. Seconds later, the parasol is virtually horizontal.

So before joining Julie at the hut this afternoon, I decided to treat myself by splashing out on a lovely new replacement base. A decent one, this time. Yes, decadent, I know, but, hey, that's the kind of guy I am. Like a befuddled idiot, I began my search at Homebase, the store where I'd purchased the original heap of junk, as if naïvely imagining that, following some dramatic U-turn in company policy, they'd actually stock what I needed. But they didn't have any bases at all. Not even from the Cretinous Creations range. Nor any parasols, for that matter. Not in the entire store. Had I wanted a set of Christmas-tree lights, an inflatable Santa, or some kind of freaky ornament to display on the mantelpiece during Hanukkah, no doubt they'd have been able to whip me up a mouth-wateringly comprehensive selection, together with free next-day delivery; but what I'd done was commit the elementary error of searching for a summer item in, erm, summer. We had reached the 'end of the season', some acne-flecked assistant impatiently pointed out, addressing me as if I had learning difficulties. The next lot, he told me, wouldn't be arriving until next year.

I wasn't happy.

But it was my own silly fault. What I'd clean forgotten were the two fundamental principles by which large stores now appear to operate. Namely: (1) Avoid being left with unsold seasonal stock, as this can adversely affect in-store budgeting and re-ordering patterns; and (2) Remember to piss the customer right off.

Not that Homebase were alone. I spent two hours trawling every garden centre, hardware store and DIY shop in the neighbourhood, but without so much as a sniff of a parasol base. I even considered the possibility that, such is the refreshing diversity of modern retail, I might stand a better chance if I were to try a butcher's, perhaps, or the Carphone Warehouse. I finally headed to the hut empty-handed.

I was still determined to create myself a spot of shade, however, to allow myself to slump back in something approximating comfort while I listened to the Albion commentary via my earphones. So I gave our old parasol one last go. To its credit, it stayed upright for the best part of 20 seconds.

And then I flipped.

This isn't like me, it really isn't, but whether it was down to general weariness, the heat, my anxiety over that stupid widdle check, or simply because I fancied losing my rag in public for a change (and I think there's a lot to be said for that), the fact is I suddenly started attacking that poor, defenceless contraption. 'Fucking fucking stupid fucking thing!' I yelled, stomping up and down on its spokes, ensuring that there'd be no way this item of furniture would ever be usable again, other than as a brutally cunning device to poke out several people's eyes with a single thrust. Our hutty neighbours looked a bit alarmed.

'There,' I announced a few moments later, breathless and, to be honest, a teensy bit embarrassed. 'I feel better for that.'

I really did, too. Of course, it could just have been a way of releasing some pre-match stress, with the Albion about to go into battle at Tranmere. After all, I've already become quite acclimatised to the therapeutic process of letting it all out on a matchday. Perhaps I was just suffering from withdrawal symptoms.

That, plus the sense of helplessness you experience when you're unable to get to a particular game. When you're actually sitting in the crowd, you convince yourself that you can somehow help influence the match's outcome. (Or at least I do, but then I suppose I'm the sort of nut who shouts at umbrellas.) Listening on the radio, by comparison, leaves you feelingly frustratingly detached and impotent. I didn't mind so much about the away match at Cambridge on the opening day of the season, because that was before I'd really begun to care. The players, the team, they all still felt remote and alien to me. Now they feel a bit more real.

I have to confess, I switched off the commentary for lengthy spells this afternoon. I found it too uncomfortable, almost more so than the scorching sunlight to which I'd been forced to resign myself. Tranmere were clearly dominating the game. Like a coward, I told myself I'd switch back on for the final ten minutes.

When the whistle blew and Albion's backs-to-the-wall performance had earned them another handy away point, I let out a quiet 'Yes!' – impressively restrained compared to my earlier exclamations. I clicked off the radio, slumped back contentedly in my chair and gave Julie the good news. She smiled the smile of indulgence. I sensed the neighbours were pleased for me, too.

Seaside Special – MONDAY 27 AUGUST

BRIGHTON 4 BLACKPOOL 0
LEAGUE POSITION: 5TH

I hate Bank Holidays. I hate the way they expose the humdrum hollowness of our lives: the fruitless 50-mile excursion in search of the merest flicker of sunshine, the potentially lethal DIY botching, the ten-mile tailbacks, the piss-awful telly, the afternoon spent dragging your fractious family around some Godforsaken out-of-town furniture warehouse. Yep, I fucking hate Bank fucking Holidays.

Sorry, I had to get that out of my system.

Besides, how has it come to this? How come the banking industry determines when we get a day off, any more than we'd all down tools whenever, say, the nation's tobacconists fancied a lie-in? Beats me.

Anyway, I wasn't in much of a footie mood when I woke up. It wasn't so bad that I was considering giving the match a miss or anything quite so drastic, but it really didn't feel like the sort of day to be watching a game of football. It was too sunny, for one thing – the weather you so often seem to experience on the opening day of the season, when mentally you're still in mid-summer.

Also, if I'm being honest, I'm finding it desperately hard to sustain my interest between matches. Obviously I don't expect the victory buzz to linger for days – at least not on the same level, since I'd probably come across as a little strange – but at the moment it barely lasts more than an hour or two, like the transitory sugar-fuelled boost you experience after stuffing your face with a 400g bar of Dairy Milk. I may be rediscovering my passion for the game as a whole, but I can't say it's having a huge impact on my day-to-day life. I'm not living and breathing the Albion, checking on injury updates, pondering Micky Adams' likely tactical formations for the next encounter, wondering if I should maybe start attending reserve games. At the moment, each fixture exists in isolation, serving as a break from routine, a means of getting excited for a couple of hours – and then, erm, that's it.

Walking to the match this afternoon – grateful though I was to have something to do on a Bank Holiday which didn't involve motorways, rawlplugs or 0 per cent finance – I actually found my spirits fairly low. Could I really face going through this whole sodding process again? Watching each of the last two home games had been genuinely hard work. I'd longed for the final whistle, anxious that some last-minute cock-up might otherwise deprive us of the win. When that whistle eventually did sound, the feeling wasn't so much one of euphoria as one of relief. Phew. Job done. Just.

Now here I was, having to endure the agony all over again. The slate had been wiped clean, that last home win counted for nothing as far as this latest fixture was concerned. It didn't seem fair. It felt as if we should be allowed to pick up where we'd left off the last time I was here, a goal to the good. But it turns out they make you start from scratch, the bastards: another day, another team, another 90 minutes of pain.

I suppose that's one of the things I've never fully appreciated: that sense of the long haul, of enjoying each win but recognising that it's merely one step. Thanks to TV, I've grown mentally flabby about football, expecting it to deliver so much gratification but forgetting that, to experience real joy, something a bit more significant than just seeing your favourite Premiership team picking up a trophy on the telly, you have to invest a heck of a lot of emotional energy. More to the point, you have to keep drawing on your reserves of that energy, month after month after month.

Yet all the while, back in my own life, there are other factors which keep drawing on it, too. Helping themselves to whopping great chunks of it, in fact. I'm still desperately anxious about this health check business. And now I've got to find the best part of £1,000 for some spectacularly dreary repair work to the front of the house – the sort of outlay I always deeply resent, where you're forking out the kind of money which could buy you a home cinema system, or a week's break in the Canaries, and yet ending up with absolutely nothing to show for it. Other than a roof which doesn't let in several gallons of water per hour, I suppose.

Luckily, football can pull you back quite quickly. I feel different once I've actually arrived at the match, once I've made the effort. It's the emotional equivalent, I suppose, of dragging your slothful self to the gym – a struggle, perhaps, but one which, as often as not, brings its rewards. Five minutes or so after kick-off, I'm normally tuned back in.

Not that it was difficult today. The ball had barely picked up a scuff-mark before we witnessed the first big incident. A penalty. To the visitors. Bugger. Would this, I wondered, be the day reality kicked in, when I experienced my first bitter taste of competitive defeat, when the team began tobogganing down the table, when I felt my flimsy commitment starting to falter?

Nope, because Kuipers went and saved it, throwing himself low to his right and palming the ball away. We yelled our approval, and rightly so. My only concern was that the Albion players seemed more interested in rushing over en masse to congratulate our keeper than in concentrating on the resulting corner. They looked so chuffed – or surprised, maybe? – that I almost expected them to haul the guy onto their shoulders and parade him around the stadium for an immediate lap of honour, leaving a bemused Blackpool to tap the ball into an empty net.

Except I'm not so sure Blackpool would have managed that, even then. In fact, not even if the entire Albion team had marched straight off the pitch for celebratory pints of Carling in the pub next door. Because it turned out Blackpool had come with a special gameplan, namely to play like a bunch of wheelie-bins. Which, combined with the fact that the

Albion put on a display of the zingiest, pingiest football I've seen from them so far – especially in the second half, when Carpenter, Steele and Zamora added to a first-half corker from Oatway (I hope you're impressed, incidentally, by the way I've started to rattle off the players' names so matter-of-factly) – made for a perfect afternoon. I've never subscribed to the view that the most entertaining games of football are those which fly frenetically from end to end and finish up something like 6–5. At least, not if I'm supporting one of the teams involved, because it's just way too up-and-downy, emotion-wise. Show me a straightforward tonking any day, with my own team ruthlessly thwacking in as many goals as possible. A clean sheet is nice, too.

In that sense, this afternoon was football heaven. If you also throw in the fact that Blackpool had two sendings-off – one player (don't know who, don't really care) plus manager Steve McMahon, who became hilariously overheated at 3–0 down and was ordered from the dugout – then you're looking at the sort of entertainment that's nigh-on impossible to top.

I'd love to imagine I'll still feel this excited tomorrow.

Fat Chance – TUESDAY AUG 28

You may find this hard to believe, considering what I've been saying up till now, but today I went and tried on an Albion replica shirt. Yes, again. I'm still desperate for ways to make my support feel continuous and fluent, an integral part of my life, rather than just an occasional, isolated activity, but the only means I can think of so far involves heading back to the Seagulls Shop. I'd noticed they were now stocking the shirts in XXXL size – a whole X larger than the one which had made me look as if I ought to be attached to a large wicker basket and soaring over the South Downs – so I thought I might as well slip one on and see what I looked like.

I looked like an obese Andy Pandy.

It did at least fit me this time, but in every other sense it still looked ridiculous. I doubt if that polyester sheen would flatter even Naomi Campbell, but on a bloke who's just been told he should shed three stone of blubber, the effect is spectacularly awful.

If I were ever to wear this thing – slip it on, head to the match, casually attempt to blend in with 7,000 identically attired Albion fans – I know exactly what would happen: they'd halt in their tracks, aghast, guffawing, and all point at the stripey freakboy. They would. I know they would.

So instead, by way of consolation, I settled for another Albion T-shirt – dark navy cotton, with relatively restrained Seagull and Skint logos and a significantly more modest price tag.

Of course, if I were to lose all that weight, as the doctor has told me I should, then maybe the replica shirt would edge back into the picture as an attractive investment. Maybe I should make it a target, like Julie does with trousers.

Maybe.

By the time I stepped back out into Queen's Road, I'd also treated myself to an Albion tax-disc holder. Emily was speechless when she spotted this on my windscreen later. Extraordinary, isn't it, the way envy can affect some people?

Of course, a sceptic might argue that I'm trying way too hard here, over-compensating, even. A little like Greg Rusedski when he first began playing tennis for Britain rather than Canada and would turn up on court wearing that ridiculous Union Jack bandana – the sort of gesture you wouldn't dream of making if you were genuinely secure about your roots. Maybe the sceptics would have a point, too, but even in my current state of soppy souvenirmania, I think I'd draw the line at wrapping a Seagulls hanky around my head.

The beanie hat is tempting, mind.

It Lives – THURSDAY 30 AUGUST

What worries me about this whole doctor business is that it's no longer how it used to be. I've always been a mild hypochondriac, but until now I've been used to having the GP put my mind at rest. I'd privately fret over some perceived problem or other, finally pluck up the courage to get it looked at, and always kind of know that, the moment I did, she'd assure me everything was fine. That's the way it's always been. Or always used to be.

The moment I stepped into the surgery today I could tell from her look that it was no longer that simple, that this wouldn't just be a case of 'Nothing to worry about, off you go,' in that reassuring 'You're actually wasting my time, you twat' kind of voice. Not this time. I could see it in her eyes.

Nor, admittedly, was it a case of, 'Blimey, are you still alive? Behold, 'tis a miracle!' But she was certainly wearing her serious face, and she had good reason to. Or at least reasonable reason. I suppose she doesn't really see me as *me*, my doctor, at least not in the way I see myself. To my GP, I'm a 41-year-old male, three stone overweight, blood pressure too high, cholesterol likewise, who doesn't exercise nearly enough and who routinely drinks a fair bit more than the recommended maximum. Oh, and who still has blood in his urine. She's probably wondering if she should sign me up for one of those British Heart Foundation ads, where some middle-aged perspiring porker collapses with a massive coronary in the middle of Waterloo station.

That second urine test, she informed me this morning, had turned out to be negative. Whoopee, eh? Crack open the champers! Er, not quite. As if mildly hacked off at the new reading, she immediately asked me to provide a sample for yet another. More than a little dejected, I slipped next door, duly obliged, and returned with a fresh golden potful, still repulsively warm. Two minutes later, this one – and I'm convinced I detected a glint of sadistic satisfaction in her eye when she announced this – tested positive. It was a good job I wasn't being checked for pregnancy or I'd have been an emotional wreck by this point.

I'm not quite sure where all this is heading, but she's now asked me to go for a new set of blood tests, somehow different from the first, and also book up for a kidney ultrasound while I'm at it. Well, fine – why not, eh? Let's go kidney kerrrrraaaaaaaaaazy.

'Don't be alarmed,' she assured me. 'It's nothing to jump up and down about.' Apparently in most cases – 95 per cent, she explained – the blood in the urine turns out to be of no significance at all. 'So that's, what, a 1-in-20 chance of it having some greater significance which I'd rather not think about, then?' I replied, perhaps a wee bit abruptly.

She moved to the sink and began to scrub her hands. 'Let's just wait and see, shall we?' she said.

Oooh, yes. Let's.

NORTHAMPTON TOWN 2 BRIGHTON 0
LEAGUE POSITION: 2ND

Well, we had to lose some time. In fact, it's a good thing. Of course it is. Not just good for the team – the ever-reliable 'learn by your mistakes' philosophy – but good for me, too. Now I can start feeling less of a glory-seeker and more like a fan who'll be showing up at Withdean to watch my team – *my* team – through thick and thin.

Assuming I can be bothered.

The whole of tonight's match, in truth, passed me by. Southern Counties were broadcasting it live, but I didn't bother tuning in. It was Friday night, for God's sake – I could hardly subject my poor family to nearly two hours of local radio footie commentary. We're traditionalists, after all. Our tradition is to order a home delivery, slump down in front of the telly and pass out, horribly bloated and £25 worse off, midway through *Frasier*.

So when I did eventually find out the result, I just grunted. That was it. I hadn't been at the game, I hadn't been listening to the commentary and therefore, in my own tiny, selfish world, it was as if it barely mattered. Beyond Planet Selfish, of course, it mattered lots, just as much as beating Wigan had mattered in that opening home game, or hammering Blackpool four days ago. In fact, had we won tonight, we'd have topped the table – albeit probably briefly, with all the other weekend fixtures still to come – and I'd be retiring to my bed a contented man. But since we lost, and since the defeat was a distant, remote event, the result of a fixture into which I'd invested zero emotional energy, I've just shut down that section of my brain that's been learning to care again. Who the hell are Brighton and Hove Albion? Remind me, what division are they in?

Cynical and clinical, all in one.

It is, of course, a cheap, lousy way to behave, and only goes to show what a pathetic excuse for a supporter I really am. And yet a part of me – maybe it's the over-grown-up part, maybe it's not – feels that this is exactly how any rational, rounded adult *should* react: that you can't (and you shouldn't) force yourself to get wound up about something if, in the broader context of your life, it really, honestly, truthfully means stuff-all.

Besides, come on, what the hell sort of a night is a Friday for playing a football match? Monday nights I can accept, Tuesdays are commonplace, Wednesdays part of a long-standing tradition, Thursdays slightly weird but just about acceptable – but Fridays? Fridays are nights when, if your mind turns to footie at all, it's to the following afternoon's fixture list, when your team and most of its rivals are in simultaneous action. Action-wise, Friday nights are duffer nights – nights when the only teams playing football are those sludging around in the steaming mire of the lower divisions.

I really must try and get to one of these away games. It might do me a power of good.

Swede Dreams – SATURDAY 1 SEPTEMBER

MORNING

International football hurts too much. One of the attractions of workaday, bread-and-butter league stuff is that, even if your team cocks things up big-time – in a match, even in an entire season – the chance soon comes around to put things right. Even if, in the worst of all possible situations, your side is dumped into a lower division, there's nothing to stop them bouncing back 12 months later. In theory, at least.

Too much is at stake in international football. Way too much. Bad games, even relatively simple mistakes, can take years to redress. That's assuming the opportunity ever comes around. Look at Gazza's sob-fest in Italia '90, during England's semi-final defeat. There he stood, a brilliant young talent, The Future Of English Football – and yet that disaster of a match, where England went out on penalties to what was then West Germany, turned out to be the last he'd ever play in a World Cup finals. We failed to qualify for USA '94, thanks to a combination of below-par personnel and an over-reliance on *Mr Bean's Bumper Book Of Football Tactics*, and by France '98 our Gazza had become a balding, boozy blob, adjudged by manager Glenn Hoddle, probably quite rightly, to be mentally and physically unfit to make the final squad. So that was it. The end. Horrible.

As a fan it can be almost as bad. Put simply – if a wee bit morbidly – the older I get, the more remote the likelihood of my country winning a major football tournament before I die. And the more painfully aware I become of that.

Oh, I realise that's half the point. I realise the World Cup, even the European Championships, are such huge, prestigious events precisely because of their rarity. But that's no consolation. All it does is stoke up the tension.

Tonight we play Germany in Munich, in a World Cup qualifier which we need to win to stand any chance of going through automatically to next summer's finals. I thought, until I woke this morning, that the match hadn't been uppermost in my thoughts, but now I find I'm desperately uptight about it. I'd almost prefer not to watch, as if that were an option.

What's especially weird is that last night I actually dreamed about it. Subconsciously, then, it's obviously been playing on my mind. Normally when I can remember having dreamed about something, the dream itself has made no sense whatsoever: it'll have involved me rollerblading naked with the Duchess Of Kent, or fishing gherkins out of Sally Gunnell's ears. But this one was comparatively rational: it was Germany v England, as simple as that. Well, apart from the fact that, in a controversial move, I'd been selected to play for England in central midfield. Performance-wise, we soon went one up – but, silly us, we celebrated so excessively that the Germans had equalised before we'd even got back on the pitch. Shades of Albion v Blackpool there.

And then they scored another, possibly a volley from Boris Becker, and that was it. We'd lost 2–1. Worse, I'd barely had a touch.

I shan't read too much into it, however. If I were experiencing these dreams on a nightly basis, and the clues were turning out to be accurate premonitions, then, fair enough, I might make more of it. In fact, I'd probably make a lucrative career of it.

As it is, I think it's just a sign that I'm cacking myself.

England-wise, then, it's business as usual.

EVENING
GERMANY 1 ENGLAND 5

I want to watch it again, please. Like they do on the Teletubbies. Again, again! All of it, start to finish. This time I want to enjoy it.

I don't think any football result has ever meant this much to me. I have never experienced such shameless, unrestrained joy, such total euphoria. In physical terms, I have never bounced around a room so much, hugged a startled-looking spaniel so often, shrieked so loudly. I have never seen England 4–1 up and, with a striker racing in for a possible fifth, found myself inches from the screen, knees almost buckling, urging him, begging him, 'Pleeeeeeease!!'

I can't stop grinning.

Granted, these may be fleeting emotions. There are some aspects of what I'm recording here which, as a new day dawns, may read like adrenaline-fuelled, alcohol-stimulated, mad, ranty bollocks. But I don't care. I really don't. A result like this demands to be savoured, even if that means making a slight tit of myself. After so many miserable experiences, so many let-downs, so many cruel anti-climaxes, in so many competitions over so many years, I think we deserve a small celebration. No, tell you what, a bloody huge one. One with very big cakes.

I know it doesn't guarantee anything just yet, that we still need to win Wednesday's home tie against Albania, plus next month's at home to Greece, to make sure we top our group and qualify automatically, but it's the historical significance of this result which makes it so special. Whether we like it or not – and, personally, I wish it wasn't such a big deal – matches against Germany always have that extra edge. So to beat them in their own country, something we hadn't done since 1965 – and where I believe they'd only ever lost one World Cup qualifier (when I say 'believe' I mean I'm way too idle to go and look this up) – is a fantastic achievement.

And who deserves first pick of those cakes? Well, Michael Owen scored an electrifying hat-trick. The other two goals came from his Liverpool team mates Steven Gerrard and Emile Heskey (I promise not to call you a useless lumbering carthorse ever again, mate). But I can't help feeling it's really down to Sven. In his calm, simple, rational, professorial manner, the England boss seems to have taken all the promise, all the potential at which English players have hinted in the past, and finally shaped it into a team which, when the big occasion arrives, doesn't suddenly start playing as if the pitch is made of custard.

What's important now is that he keeps them focused for those last two matches. Another six points and, unless Germany miraculously make up the goal difference which we've now turned against them, we'll be through. How fantastic is that?

Almost too fantastic, perhaps – because I must admit I'm worried about a possible downside. Not from an England perspective, but from an Albion one. My feeble, couldn't-give-a-fuck response to Friday night's Northampton match seems even more disturbing now, up against my frenzied reaction this evening. Beforehand, it had felt like a minor setback. Now the implications seem a lot more serious.

Tonight I really don't fancy bread and butter.

ENGLAND 2 ALBANIA 0

Apparently my blood pressure is 140 over 90. I'm told this is less than ideal.

I'll take their word for it, but I do think I'd be a lot more focused on the problem if I had the faintest idea what this reading actually meant. One hundred and forty over ninety what, exactly? Go on, Doc, you can tell me. Pounds per square inch, is it? Or kilograms? Or chocolate trifles? Come on, give me a clue. 'Oh, it's complicated,' is all I keep being told.

If you'd watched me throughout tonight's match – steaming, ranting, all the old familiar stuff – you'd have probably concluded that it meant 140 tantrums per 90 minutes.

Logic had already hinted that frustration was on the cards, that the Albanians would park 37 men and a juggernaut between us and the goal, and that our lads would struggle to get past them, at least while retaining possession of the actual ball, a detail which can count for quite a lot at this level. But on top of that, like anyone who's watched England for so long – and who retains a fully functional memory – I'd convinced myself that we were guaranteed a massive anti-climax after Saturday's trouncing of Germany. So the longer it stayed at 0–0, the more profoundly those gut instincts kicked in. Those instincts which say: 'Yep, utter shite. This is more like it.' It's hard to stop yourself thinking this way, especially if lengthy experience has drilled it into you, year after frustrating year. This, you convince yourself, is our true level. This is all we really deserve.

This morning a nurse sucked another syringe full of blood from my left arm, which will now be sent off for further tests. The blood, I mean, not my arm. There'll be a second cholesterol reading, I believe, plus various other bits of probing around which might indicate whether or not my kidneys are seriously buggered. For somebody who, until very recently, has only really thought of kidneys in a pie-or-pudding context, it's all a bit unsettling. On Tuesday I'm going for that ultrasound scan, where apparently a nice man will smear jelly on my belly and then, by applying some sort of implement not dissimilar to a hand-held bar-code scanner, take a good close look. I'm told he's going to peep at my bladder, too. Lucky old him.

Every time I stop to consider the possible implications, I feel extremely jittery. I'm not sure if I really need to, or if I'm over-reacting. I just know I'm scared.

So I wonder, was it this scaredness which, until Michael Owen opened tonight's scoring just before half-time, had me fuming to such an alarming degree? Was it the fact that I've been trying to repress all that fear?

Or was my foul temper a symptom of my condition rather than a cause? God, do you suppose that's what it might be – that I've entered middle-age as the classic heart-attack-waiting-to-happen? If I have, why on Earth am I letting football get a grip on me? I ought to take up tapestry instead.

Dodgy Ground – SATURDAY 8 SEPTEMBER

BRIGHTON 2 QPR 1
LEAGUE POSITION: 6TH

Today, had I felt so inclined, I could have stroked Bobby Zamora's shorts. Not that he was wearing them at the time, I should stress. I don't think he'd have liked that.

Just after midday, there I was in the Albion dressing-room. And folded neatly on the bench beside me was – gasp! – Bobby's kit, laid out for this afternoon's match, along with those of the rest of the side. This was quite a moment.

The idea of taking the Withdean Stadium tour, once I'd found out that such a thing existed, was too tempting to resist. What the heck would they be able to show us, I wondered? This wasn't even a proper ground, for God's sake, just a makeshift arrangement knitted together with temporary seating, a smattering of Portakabins and a generously flexible attitude from football's powers-that-be. Surely we'd be talking ten minutes, tops?

Not according to the blurb. 'Now is your chance,' it promised, 'to take advantage of one of our superb stadium tours. As part of our exclusive package, you will be escorted by our guide to view the TV gantry, dugouts, police box/safety control box, Seagulls suite, boardroom, matchday office, dressing-rooms, press box, and PA box.'

Well, OK, make that 20 . . .

'The stadium tour,' it continued, 'takes between 45 minutes and 1 hour . . .'

WHAAAT??!!

'. . . and begins at 11.15 a.m. on a Saturday matchday. The tour is reasonably priced, at £5 per adult and £3 for Senior Citizens and Under-16s. Places are limited to 20 spaces per matchday, so please book early to guarantee your place on the tour.'

Well, I had to, didn't I? I just had to. If nothing else, I wanted to see how our tour guide managed to drag this thing out for quite so long; how he succeeded in making a poky hotchpotch of temporary structures feel like Division Two's Theatre of Dreams. I wanted to find out if this bloke came across like one of those uniquely talented QVC shopping channel presenters who can waffle on for hours about, say, a deluxe toenail-clipper or the David Hasselhoff novelty teaspoon collection.

So I rang the club, who put me on to a chirpy-sounding chap called Adrian. Adrian told me that he'd yet to run a tour so far this season – this was, to be fair, only the second Saturday home fixture – but that, yes, if he could get enough numbers we'd be on. I could, as I'm sure you'll appreciate, barely contain my excitement.

I mentioned the trip to my friend Liz, a proper born-and-bred Brightonian who's supported the Albion since she was an embryo. I assumed she'd already know all about the Withdean tour experience, and had probably already sampled it, but it turned out that it was news to her too. I suppose they must keep these things low-key to prevent a mad rush. Liz's boyfriend, David – a Spurs fan – fancied coming as well. As, rather amazingly, did Emily. 'Shall I wear my Man U shirt?' asked Em. My, what a wag my daughter is.

By the time we'd all congregated in Withdean's tiny car park – me, Em, Liz, David and eight others – it had started to spit with rain. As instructed, we'd arrived at 11 a.m., an earlier start than advertised, because apparently the tour now lasted 'slightly longer' than it used to. I hadn't dared ask how.

Adrian turned out to be a crop-headed, beer-bellied guy in a denim jacket. He also wore a replica shirt which bulged and strained so spectacularly that I began to wonder why I'd been so self-conscious the last time I'd tried one on myself. If he could get away with it, why shouldn't I?

He also turned out to be an excellent, engaging guide – a genuine enthusiast, without descending into nerd-dom. What a pity, then, that the same couldn't be said for a couple of the guys who'd joined us for this tour. From what I could make out, these two – both, I'd estimate, in their mid-30s – were engaged in their own private head-to-head smartarsery contest, the challenge being to determine which of them could most effectively piss off the rest of the party with his irritatingly meticulous knowledge of Dull

Albion Facts. Assuming the prize at stake was a meaty slap, I'd have been more than happy to declare it a draw and dish out the honours myself. I probably should have pointed this out.

They were at it more or less from the start, these two, but when Adrian took us inside the referee's dressing-room and began to deliver an anecdote involving an official at a Torquay match a couple of years back, the slightly smaller one seemed more desperate than ever to butt in. He was almost bouncing up and down and squealing, like a toddler in need of the lavatory. The reason, it turned out, was that he could actually remember the final score of the match in question and wanted to make sure we all knew this. 'That was the one we lost 1–0, wasn't it?' he eventually cried, seemingly unable to hold it in a moment longer.

'That's quite right, fuck-features,' I wanted Adrian to reply. 'But since the result of that fixture has absolutely no relevance to what I'm about to tell you, how about you do us all a favour and shut your frigging face?'

Instead, what Adrian actually said was: 'Yes.'

Smartarses One and Two reminded me of a couple of kids desperate to impress their teacher on a school outing – something which, when I was at school, could be achieved simply by having the good grace to use the proper ash-trays on the coach. Each time these blokes opened their mouths, Liz and I would exchange increasingly exaggerated raised-eyebrow glances, to the point where my own brows nearly ended up going over my head and halfway down the back of my neck. Liz is quite small and slight, but she looked as if she was seriously contemplating the viability of taking either of these guys quietly to one side and kneeing him in the nuts. I'm sure Adrian would have turned a blind eye. There are just some people – be they football supporters, music fans or beer mat collectors – whose degree of po-faced, weasely obsession seems designed primarily to discourage others from sharing the same interest. To meet them in the flesh is a sobering experience.

And then, like I say, you come across people like Adrian. Adrian told us that he used to be involved with Scars 'n' Stripes – which I assume refers to an Albion fanzine, rather than some sort of razor gang. But his obsession came across as a healthy one, the sort to which perhaps I should be aspiring; a serious commitment and belief, an understanding of what a fantastic, enriching thing it can be for a community to have its own thriving Football League team. Adrian saw the bigger picture, if you'll forgive the cliché. Or even if you won't.

He talked trivia, but it was good trivia. Astonishingly, given my initial scepticism, the tour ended up lasting two hours, and I came away enlightened and re-energised. No, seriously, I did. I also learned absolutely oodles.

I learned, for example, that Withdean's pitch-side Perspex dugouts, previously transparent, had to be coated in thick white paint in order to reduce the risk of crowd trouble. Apparently there'd been a number of incidents in which visiting teams' substitutes, taunted by the home fans sitting behind, had responded with somewhat unfriendly hand signals.

I also learned that the pitch suffered from phantom flooding last season: puddles would suddenly appear during the middle of a match, even when it wasn't raining, and the players would find themselves having to splash their way through them. It sounded like the sort of challenge which competitors used to have to tackle in Jeux Sans Frontieres, although presumably in the Albion's case the players weren't obliged to wear giant foam heads. It happened, explained Adrian, because earlier rainfall had seeped down into the valley in which the stadium stands, hit the layer of chalk beneath the surface and, with nowhere else to go, eventually risen again. When he went on to point out that they'd recently re-laid the playing surface and that we were unlikely to witness similar incidents this season, I couldn't help but feel a tinge of disappointment.

My favourite fact, however, concerned the trophy cabinet, newly built following the Division Three triumph and facing us now as we stepped inside the makeshift hospitality lounge. Adrian told us that this cabinet had been designed to the dimensions of the UEFA Champions League trophy – on the basis, quite seriously, that that's the largest piece of football silverware it's ever likely to have to accommodate. It was the loosest interpretation of the word 'likely' that I think I'd ever heard, but I admired them for it. While many clubs will trumpet their ambition with hot air and platitudes, the Albion were announcing theirs with fuck-off furniture. You had to respect that.

Other than that, the highlight was the trip to the dressing-rooms. They were terrible, of course – bog-standard, whiffy facilities in yet another temporary building – but just the idea of being there, with the kits already laid out under the appropriate pegs, and where the players themselves would soon be warming up for this afternoon's match, well, it felt mildly magical. This, by League standards, seemed about as functional and unromantic a setting as you were likely to encounter, and yet it still excited me. I decided to keep this excitement to myself, however. There's only so much enthusiasm you can display in a communal dressing-room without it being open to misinterpretation.

Ultimately, the message behind the Withdean tour – in fact, one of the reasons why it worked so well, contrary to my cynical expectations – is that the stadium is utterly useless. It's not a crumbling dump, just a frail, feeble skeleton of what a real football stadium ought to be. Adrian wasn't there to hide this fact, but to underline it. 'Here's what we have to put up with,' he was effectively saying, while clearly striving not to come across as too moany. It was, you might argue, a blatant propaganda exercise, part of the club's campaign for that new community stadium. But I didn't have a problem with that; if the Albion can't seize the opportunity to argue their own case, who the hell's going to do it for them?

Well, me, perhaps – because, at the end of the two hours, I felt surprisingly uplifted. After that hollow post-Germany feeling, I'd desperately needed something to put me back on track, to encourage me to care about the grass-roots stuff again, and this tour had done the job. Not despite its comedic value but almost because of it. For all the glory and exhilaration of that result in Munich, the national team is never going to touch my life directly. But the Albion might.

Adrian, I found out, belongs to a group called Falmer For All, a bunch of fans campaigning for the new stadium, and afterwards I waited behind for a brief chat. I'd like to help, too, I told him. I hadn't the faintest idea how – never having campaigned for anything in my life, or having felt even vaguely motivated to do so – but if there was any way I could muck in, I insisted, I'd really like to. Go on, mister, let me play.

What I really meant, although I didn't include this bit for fear of sounding deeply pathetic, was that I'd be thrilled to bits. Here it was, my first real opportunity to show positive commitment to this club, rather than just turning up once a fortnight for home matches.

Perhaps equally important, I owned up to the fair-weather fan business, right from the off. I felt I had to, otherwise it would just gnaw and nag away at me. If I do end up getting involved, it's anybody's guess how his fellow campaigners will treat me, the Bandwagon Boy. If they're OK with it, fantastic – it'll underline what magnificent, open-minded, positive individuals they are. And if they aren't, well, fuck 'em. But I did suggest to Adrian that if the stadium does get built, and assuming they'd quite like to fill it, then I'm exactly the type of fan the Albion will need to attract. I was quite impressed with myself, coming up with that one almost on the spot, especially as he kind of took my point.

And today's match? Fabulous stuff, topped off with a 90th-minute winner from a Paul Watson free kick. And, erm . . . yeah. That was it, really. Great.

You can probably see why I'm not a football reporter.

BRIGHTON 0 SOUTHAMPTON 3
(WORTHINGTON CUP, ROUND TWO)

The minute's silence was faultlessly observed, unless you count the rumble of the passing train. That, and someone's mobile phone playing 'Waltzing Matilda'.

We probably shouldn't even have been playing tonight, given this afternoon's events in New York and Washington. Thousands are dead, wiped out by an act of terrorism which defies belief. Two hijacked aircraft were crashed into the World Trade Centre, a third sent ploughing into the Pentagon. I'd say it felt like a scene from a disaster movie, but I've heard that said 100 times already. It's taken less than eight hours to create a cliché.

And yet here we all were, carrying on almost as if nothing had happened. The silence was moving, and more respectfully observed than any I'd ever witnessed, but once the referee had peeped his whistle to bring it to an end, that traditional post-silence roar had gone up – the one which seems to say: 'Thank God that bit's over, let's get on with the flaming game' – and it was business as usual. A football match. Brighton and Hove Albion against Southampton. In what I like wittily to refer to as the Worth-nothing Cup.

But then who am I to criticise? If I'd felt it was wrong for tonight's game, indeed all tonight's games, to go ahead after a day of such unspeakable horror, I was perfectly at liberty to give it a miss. I didn't, though. I didn't want to. I assume nobody else did either, considering Withdean was more or less full.

In fact, I'd have felt quite miffed if they'd called it off.

Is that a deeply shameful reaction, or an understandable one? I can't decide. On one level, it seems cold, selfish, almost inhuman. On another, it could be argued (in fact, it already has been) that the more we all carry on with our everyday activities – however mundane or trivial they suddenly seem – the more firmly defiant a message we're sending out.

On yet another level – and I think this is the closest I'm going to get to a rational explanation, even if it's not a particularly palatable one – perhaps it can be explained by the way in which football has always managed to detach itself from The Real World.

I must admit, I've always found this a huge part of its appeal – the regularity, the routine, the ritual, the sense that, no matter what else happened, football would always carry on. It was like a security blanket. I even like the way that in most football grounds – most of the proper ones, at least – you're within a fully sealed-off environment. The bulk of these places are built in such a way that you can barely catch a glimpse of the outside world. The stadium, for a couple of hours per fortnight at least, becomes a world within a world. It's a world with its own rules and values, and sod those which apply elsewhere.

I've even found myself disliking the way in which, in recent years, police officers have taken to coming onto the pitch to sort out flare-ups involving players, managers and officials. Deal with the crowd by all means, I've reasoned, but the other stuff is none of your business.

It's nonsense, of course, but that's how football gets you thinking.

Similarly, although my understanding of the commercial world is roughly on a par with Popeye's, I can't help wondering how many struggling clubs would have folded long ago if they'd been ordinary mundane firms. Firms making sink-plungers, say, or watch straps, or speciality soups.

But like I say, I'd be fibbing if I pretended I didn't like this aspect of the game. The truth is, I take great comfort from football's reassuring constancy, from its isolation and apparent detachment from even the harshest reality, the thought that it's always there, no matter what. I don't think this makes me a very good person, to be honest, but I'm not sure it makes me a bad one.

I remember being amazed after the Heysel disaster, back in 1985, that despite what had happened, despite the fact that 41 people had been crushed to death – not in somewhere distant and remote and really rather hard to get your head round, but *just over there, a few minutes ago at the side of the pitch* – the match still went ahead. But I wasn't appalled by the decision; I wasn't even angry. I still sat and watched the whole match.

Perhaps these are just classic examples of denial, where football allows us to remain oblivious to all that outside-world nastiness. But I don't think so. I think there's a separate issue here – namely, how much the human brain is able to take in and process the extent of these horrors. My own feeling is that our sense of scale and perspective goes haywire, leaving us to cling to something familiar and comparatively comprehensible. If we grieve, for example, over one person's death, does our grief multiply accordingly when we hear about the deaths of 10 people, or 100 or 1,000? It probably should, but I'm fairly sure it doesn't. I'm fairly sure it can't. On an immediate level, of course, we do grasp the enormity of an incident such as this afternoon's. We recognise its unparalleled awfulness; we voice an appropriate response. But if you were to imagine the distress you've felt over, say, the death of a close relative and then multiplied this several thousand times over, wouldn't your emotions overload? Mine would. So events like today's can leave you feeling desperately mixed up, clinging to normality not so much as a cold, insensitive response to what's happened but because, if you didn't – if you reacted on the emotional scale which the situation strictly demanded – you'd suffer some kind of mental meltdown.

And so, while we're struggling to make any sense of all this stuff, we'll go and watch some blokes playing football.

Now, this is going to sound a bit weird, but if there was one thing which really did appal me tonight it was the way the crowd treated the linesman. The one on our side of the pitch. Granted, the bloke was hopeless, but the level of abuse aimed at this poor clown struck me as far more distasteful then the actual decision to go ahead with the game itself.

Playing the match can be defended as an act of democratic defiance, whether or not you consider the argument a persuasive one. But I'd hoped that the mood tonight might be more charitable, more reflective, more . . . I don't know, just *kinder*. If you think that makes me sound laughably wet, then I apologise.

Actually, no I don't. If that's what you really think, you can go boil your head.

Tonight we should have been watching our football with some sense of perspective and proportion, aware of our priorities, a bit more tolerant towards other people's frailties. Maybe this poor bugger had other things on his mind.

At times, the abuse hurled his way – real throw-him-to-the-lions stuff – left me sickened. Perhaps that's hypocritical, since I've ranted at enough officials in my time, but tonight it just felt wrong.

I can't pretend the result was, though. We probably didn't deserve to lose by a three-goal margin, but we certainly didn't deserve to progress in this competition. We held Southampton off until late in the first half, but when they finally broke through, just before the interval, it was obvious this wouldn't be our night. Their second knocked the stuffing out of us. After that it became a bit embarrassing.

Even in simple, parochial football terms, however, I'm not too bothered. Southampton are a Premiership side – albeit a relatively lousy one – so nobody expected them to struggle against a team freshly up from Division Three. Other than the dent to the morale, this will have been a useful learning experience for the Albion players. Or at least it won't have done them any great harm.

I also believe, perhaps a bit bizarrely, that winning tonight could have backfired on us. As is traditional, Southampton have had a rickety start to the Premiership season; an embarrassing defeat here this evening might have meant the sack for their boss, Stuart Gray. And since the bloke they're known to have their eye on as a potential replacement is our own manager, Micky Adams – an ex-Southampton player and someone they've apparently approached before – it doesn't need a huge leap of the imagination to work out what could well have happened next. On top of which, they're also said to have their eye on Bobby Zamora. In other words, we could have lost both our star striker and our coveted manager in one fell swoop, for the sake of progressing one round further in a competition nobody really cares about.

So, yes, I'm really glad we got hammered and that Bobby played shit. Thrilled to bits, I am.

Just so long as we don't make it a habit.

For What It's Worth – THURSDAY 13 SEPTEMBER

Great news! You will, I'm sure, be delighted to hear that my kidneys are fine. I also have a splendidly functional bladder, thanks. The ultrasound results turned out to be normal, as did my latest blood tests, and although I've been reminded that I still need to lower my cholesterol and blood pressure, blah blah blah, and likewise my blubber content – mostly by cutting down on alcohol, it seems, and selecting nice sensible meals from Sainsbury's amazingly tempting Food That Wouldn't Feed A Sodding Flea range – the immediate panic seems to be over.

Actually, it's weird, but having fretted about this health business so much in recent weeks, I now feel crass and self-indulgent even mentioning these results, given what happened on Tuesday. It's that old business of proportion and perspective again. It's a sod.

WREXHAM 1 BRIGHTON 2
LEAGUE POSITION: 1ST

Yes, Brighton and Hove Albion are perched proudly on top of Division Two tonight. It'll only be fleeting – this was another of those stupid Friday-night away fixtures, with most of the other teams playing tomorrow – but it's still a nice feeling. With 14 points from 7 games, and with only one defeat, it's a more than decent start.

What's almost as significant is that we actually scored. Twice, in fact. Bobby Zamora's 68th-minute equaliser, followed by his penalty eight minutes later, were Albion's first away goals for months. Actually, Bobby should have had a hat-trick, only he fluffed his second penalty, awarded in the very last minute. Still, we all have our off-nights.

Useless git.

Obsessive Compulsive - SATURDAY 15 SEPTEMBER

Look, I'm not one for microscopic analysis of the league table, but it's worth noting that, even after today's games, we're still lying in a not unhealthy fourth place – one point behind the new leaders, Oldham. Bristol City and Brentford are second and third respectively, on the same points as us, but both with a better goal difference and each having played one game fewer.

Julie tells me I'm in danger of becoming a Brighton and Hove Albion bore. So that's good news, isn't it?

BRIGHTON 1 STOKE CITY 0
LEAGUE POSITION: 1ST

An Albion fan was killed last week. His name was Robert Eaton, he was 37, and he worked in New York. I know this because it was announced before tonight's game. Robert was working in the World Trade Centre last Tuesday morning.

Of course, it was absolutely right to stage a minute's silence in this guy's memory before tonight's game. And if you can have degrees of silence – which, grammatically, I'm fairly sure you can't – then tonight's silence was even more silent than last week's. All that broke it was a couple of isolated shouts, and even these seemed to come from beyond the ground. It was probably some blokes in the pub.

It still has me confused, though, this question of scale. Here we were, paying tribute to one lost life via exactly the same process by which we commemorated several thousand only a week back. That's not to imply that tonight's tribute was excessive – absolutely not – just that, in comparison, maybe last week's now seems even more pitifully inadequate. A few moments to reflect on the loss of one life, even if it's someone most of us in the stadium didn't know, seems manageable and fitting. We can handle that. But when you compare it to the identical tribute seven days ago, it does seem to underline the problem we have in grasping the comparative enormity of what happened. I certainly wouldn't criticise the decision to stage either of these tributes – it's what we do; it's what we've always done – but on a broader scale, it seems to highlight our helplessness.

For Robert Eaton, I'd imagine, an additional tribute – probably one he'd have preferred – would have been a fantastic game of football. A gripping, pulsating, end-to-end encounter, packed with goals, with Albion grabbing the three points thanks to a dramatic last-gasp winner, deep into stoppage time.

Well, we got that last bit. Unfortunately, the rest of the game was dire. Albion seemed jittery, on edge, unable to play their usual clever-clogs passing game. Stoke dominated possession, and if it hadn't been for their comical inability to actually kick a football on target, they'd have tonked us.

Instead, in the 94th minute, a scramble saw the ball run loose to Paul Watson and – blam! (or whatever the expression is) – he powered it into the net. There was barely time to restart the game. The three points were ours. We were back on top of the table.

Of course, it was desperately hard on Stoke. But who cares? I think we can say that one was for Robert.

Name That Seagull – WEDNESDAY 19 SEPTEMBER

All I need to do now is decipher the signatures. In front of me is a copy of a rather neat new book entitled *Albion: The First 100 Years*, for which I've happily handed over £29.99. Just as exciting is the fact that I've had it signed by several of the players.

Mildly disconcerting is the additional fact that one of them, if I can make out his autograph correctly, appears to be Nicholas Lyndhurst.

I'd been afraid this might happen. My first reaction, when I'd heard that several Albion players would be visiting a city centre bookshop this afternoon, scrawling their names on copies of this new publication, was that I simply had to be there. My second was the uneasy realisation that, being what could most politely be described as a latecomer to the Albion scene, I wouldn't have a clue who half these people were. In which case, what would happen if one of them started to engage me in conversation, reminiscing about the grim years in exile at Gillingham, perhaps, or the poignant final match at the Goldstone? How the heck would I respond? Would I be honest, and simply reply, 'Dunno what you're on about, pal. And while we're at it, should I know you?' Would I nod, smile and attempt to bullshit my way through it? Would I knot my brow quizzically and pretend to be a Polish tourist who'd popped in for directions to the pier? It was a worry.

I had a hunch, mind you, that I wouldn't be called upon to do any of these things. I'd been to the odd book-signing session before, and mostly it had been a clinical conveyor-belt kind of operation, with edgy shop staff urgently ushering people through as swiftly as possible. The last one I'd attended in this particular store, with Emily in tow, had featured two of the contestants from the first series of *Big Brother* – Nicola and Darren – signing copies of a spectacularly unreadable tie-in publication. The queue for that one had stretched halfway down the street, so the staff had had to get us in and out at almost breakneck pace. No time, then, for any incisive questions, such as asking Nicola whether she felt fortunate to be experiencing this level of adulation, given that she was so profoundly annoying. Still, we'd only gone along so that Emily could say hello to them, and she'd managed to do that OK. 'Hello,' Emily had said. 'Hello,' they'd replied. I don't believe they've kept in touch.

Today's wasn't nearly that perfunctory, to be fair, but the queue was still nudged along quickly enough to ensure that in-depth conversation would be out of the question. Probably just as well, as far as I was concerned.

When I reached the front, I found 11 people sat along a table with ball-points poised – including, first up, a trio of old-timers I'd have put in their mid-70s. Obviously these gentlemen's identities were an even greater mystery to me than those of the current squad, but they certainly looked very proud and, what's the word, *dapper*. Very few people bother to be dapper these days. I've a feeling dapperness died out in about 1964. Anyway, each of these old blokes directed me to a particular page in the book so that he could apply his signature to a specific photo. I took it, then, that they were ex-Albion footballers, these three, and that these photos were photos of themselves. But who knows? The whole thing may have been one enormous, elaborate prank, the perfect way for three mischievous old men to while away a dull Wednesday afternoon. In a way, I'd like to imagine it was.

Then came the current players. I really ought to have been able to put a name to every face by this stage of the season – after all, I've memorised all their squad numbers by now, about which I'm stupidly pleased with myself – but a couple had me stumped. I recognised Michel Kuipers, the keeper, and I'd have to have been blind not to identify star striker Bobby Zamora. Oh, and Welshman Nathan Jones (No. 15) I could spot, if only because he seems to have a remarkably tiny head, like a new potato. And was that Paul Rogers, the captain, sitting alongside him at the table? I thought so, only this guy seemed to have a startlingly red face, more befitting a prominent member of the local wino community. I concluded it was wisest not to ask. If it really was Rogers, I figured my inquiry might upset him. And if it really was Big Chief Wino, I figured it might earn me a glassing.

Which one was Robbie Reinelt, though? That was another mystery. Admittedly, Robbie was no longer with the club but, God, I ought to have been able to recognise him, of all people, given the key role he played in keeping the Albion alive. But of course I couldn't. I wasn't there at the time. Not that I don't remember the day quite clearly. On Saturday, 3 May 1997, the day Robbie scored the equaliser at Hereford which kept the Albion in the League by the skin of their teeth – and sent the home side plunging into the Conference – I was out buying some rather attractive floor tiles.

Having said that, the rest of this lot weren't there either. Nor were the final pair who decorated my book with their signatures this afternoon – assistant manager Bob Booker and top man Micky Adams. This was another team now. Another age.

By the time I reached Micky, he was chatting to a young fan about last night's win over Stoke. 'Great game,' chirped the lad, who could only have been about ten. 'No,' Micky corrected him, with a smile. 'Great *result*.'

And then it was my turn, and – gasp! – I actually found myself in conversation with the manager of Brighton and Hove Albion. Who'd ever have thought it? For want of anything better to talk about – I felt the circumstances didn't really lend themselves to a lengthy exchange on, say, the Middle East peace process or the eradication of foot-and-mouth – I told Micky how amused I'd been by his post-match interview, repeatedly played back this morning on the local radio sports bulletins. In it, he'd been informed by the interviewer that the Albion were back on top of the table. 'Oh, God,' he'd sighed, wearily, 'we're not are we?'

Micky seemed a tad concerned when I told him this had gone out several times on air. Perhaps, on reflection, he felt it had given the wrong impression. All he'd wanted to do, he explained to me now, was point out that sometimes it's best to be tucked in behind the leaders at this stage in the season, 'rather than out in front where everyone's gunning for you'. I assured him that I understood entirely. 'It's a sound philosophy,' I added. I sensed he was delighted to hear me say this. 'Great!' he was probably thinking to himself, 'I've just been given a vote of confidence by a four-eyed fatso. That'll do for me.'

Brief, functional and anonymous though it was, I kind of enjoyed my first face-to-face encounter with Micky and the Albion players. It made me feel just that teensy bit more a part of the whole thing.

For a while, at least. Now that I've come home and actually opened this book they've signed, my good mood has largely evaporated. It's not just because I can't work out who the hell's signatures are whose. Nor is it because, if one of them really is Nicholas Lyndhurst, I forgot to smack his face for *Goodnight Sweetheart*. And it isn't because there's anything wrong with the book itself. It's obviously been a labour of love.

But even a casual flick through its 243 pages has been enough to drive home one indisputable, dispiriting message. Namely, that I'm never going to be able to call myself a true Albion fan. Not a real one. Not a proper one. Not ever. No matter how passionately I'd like to do so, no matter how desperately, I've left it too late. Simple as that. You only have to look at the pages which detail the dramas of the last decade, most of them off the pitch rather than on it, to appreciate that there are hundreds, probably thousands, whose allegiance to this club is more deeply rooted than mine can ever be. People who put up with years of crap and who, in Albion's current performances, are finally being rewarded for their loyalty.

If I did have the chance to become one of these people, I blew it 15 years ago, when Julie and I moved down to Brighton. I could have made the decision, when we got here, to support my local side – already in decline, but not to an extent which seemed terminal – but other than the odd casual attendance at the Goldstone, I chose not to. So I had the chance and I rejected it. Even to come close to matching these people's loyalty and commitment, I'd probably have to support the Albion from now until I was 370. And if, along the way, I endured a few dozen relegations, only then would it really count.

Party Pooping – SATURDAY 22 SEPTEMBER

BRIGHTON 2 BOURNEMOUTH 1
LEAGUE POSITION: 1ST

Admittedly I haven't checked this, but I'm fairly sure the *Guinness Book Of Records* doesn't carry a listing for the all-time most pathetic rendition of 'Happy Birthday'. If it does, it's been out of date since four o'clock this afternoon.

It was 100 years ago yesterday that the club played its first game, but despite an outside risk of being prosecuted under the Trades Descriptions Act, the Albion advertised today's fixture as the official centenary match. And what better way for the club to mark the occasion than to ask a choirboy to stand in the middle of the pitch at half-time and sing 'Happy Birthday'?

Actually, just about any way would have been better. He made a magnificent effort, this lad – perfect pitch, if you'll pardon the pun, and faultless enunciation – and, to the credit of the 6,714 people in the crowd, nobody heckled. But it was so painfully twee, so toe-curlingly out-of-place, that it was all you could do not to burst out laughing. I can't remember when I've last felt so embarrassed at a football match. People were either staring at each other in open-mouthed disbelief, battling to suppress a titter, or just gazing at the floor, as if silently praying it would be over as soon as possible. 'Happy birthday, dear Seagulls . . .'

Jesus.

But worse was to come. No sooner had he finished than the guy on the PA announced that the poor sod would be singing it again. And this time – Oh. My. God. – he wanted us all to join in.

And did we? Did we fuck.

The response wasn't half-hearted. It wasn't even quarter-hearted. It was non-existent. The lad warbled on, but he warbled on as a solo artist.

I didn't know whose idea this performance had been, but they must have been quietly squirming.

Not that this was our only special treat to mark the centenary. At Tuesday's match we'd been advised to arrive a bit earlier than normal this afternoon so as not to miss the stuff before kick-off. They should really have added, 'But for God's sake don't come too early, or else you'll hear the band.'

Carnival Collective, this bunch called themselves, their mission apparently being to try and create some kind of pre-match party atmosphere. Now, call me a cynic, but when any group of people chooses to call itself a 'collective', it triggers alarm bells. If they've then combined this with the word 'carnival', I'm left with a chilling image of enforced jollity, of the sort you might witness under a brutal tinpot dictatorship. In reality, what we actually got was a couple of dozen people parping trombones, banging drums and blowing whistles, Brazilian-style – while wearing turquoise T-shirts, funny wigs and a hotchpotch of clothes which looked as if they'd been pinched from a kid's dressing-up box. I don't deny they could play their instruments. I just deny that we wanted them to. 'Bet they've got a bloody huge grant from the Lottery,' snarled a bloke standing next to me at the side of the pitch. So that was a comfort. It wasn't just me.

A wee bit more relevant was the bit which came next, in which lifelong Albion nut John Baine stood in the centre circle in his red-and-black away shirt and recited his special centenary poem. Despite not exactly being bestest buddies with the management under previous regimes, Baine – also known as ranting poet and punk veteran Attila the Stockbroker – had never wavered in his support for the team itself. These days – post-revolution, if you like – he's become, get this, Albion's poet-in-residence. How brilliant is that? It certainly beats having some twat dressed as a giant chicken.

A few minutes later came perhaps the most touching moment of the afternoon, as a giant blue-and-white Albion flag – apparently, at 64 ft by 32 ft, it's officially the biggest fuck-off football flag in the country – was unveiled in the middle of the pitch. Reportedly costing £2,000 (seems pretty expensive to me, but then I've not shopped around for flags much lately) this was paid for exclusively by fans. One suggestion, I gather, is to spread it across the grass bank at the west end of the ground (where there's no seating) for future home matches. Nice idea. Even nicer is that they've named it in honour of Robert Eaton, the Albion fan killed last week in New York.

Other than that, most of the rest was worthy presentations. Player of the Month went to the rejuvenated Lee Steele, last year's PFA Player of the Year trophy was belatedly handed to Bobby Zamora, and some other commemorative trinket was politely presented by chairman Dick Knight to his Bournemouth counterpart, seemingly just to be nice. Slightly confusingly, but with what I suppose was timely recognition of the club's heritage, the crowd were also introduced to the 91-year-old daughter of Charlie Webb, an Albion legend who played for the club from 1909 to 1915, and later went on to become manager. (Don't be too impressed that I can churn out facts like these, incidentally; I just fished them out of that book.)

Finally, as an inspired touch, we were treated to a desperately bad football match which we ought to have lost by triple figures but which we ended up winning thanks to a mis-hit cross and an own goal.

In all honesty, then, it hadn't been quite the grand occasion which the club had hinted at. But then, in their position, I'm not sure what I'd have suggested myself. I'm reasonably sure I wouldn't have suggested an Aled Jones soundalike or an over-jolly band of turquoise trombone-parpers, but you never know. It's easy to take the piss, and obviously hugely satisfying, but how exactly *do* you mark a football club's 100th birthday in a way which really stirs the fans?

I'm not sure you can. Football is so much about immediacy, about the buzz of the match itself, that nothing else can ever really match this. I'm sure the final game at the Goldstone must have been overwhelmingly emotional, but that was a genuine gut emotion, not a stage-managed one.

Obviously you have to recognise these occasions – out of a sense of history, respect and purpose. Even as the git who's muscled in from the outside, I've begun to understand how much this club means to people. But more often than not, it's small, dignified, understated ideas which connect most deeply.

It might be worth bearing this in mind for the bi-centenary celebrations. I may have even thought of one by then.

'So your kidneys are fine, you're saying?'

'Fine and dandy, Andy, thanks for asking. Tip-top. Couldn't be better.'

'Good. I'm thrilled for you. And your bladder? That's OK, too, is it?'

Sarcastic bastard.

'Perfect, yeah. More or less.'

'More or less?'

'Well, the bloke said there was still a tiny bit of urine in there after I'd emptied it.'

'Oh, lovely. Do I really want to hear this?'

'Probably not. Anyway, what they do is, they ask you to turn up at the hospital with a full one.'

'What, a full bladder?'

'No, no, a full suitcase. Yes, of course a full bladder, you berk. Then, once they've done the ultrasound test, they ask you to nip next door to the loo and empty it.'

'Great.'

'And then you go back in and they test it again.'

'Uh-huh. The point being?'

'Well, presumably to see if your body is, erm, evacuating everything properly.'

'And yours isn't?'

'Well, not 100 per cent, by the sound of it. But as near as damn it. This guy said it was nothing to worry about. He didn't seem too bothered.'

'Good. So it's just an old-man thing, then?'

'Sorry?'

'You know, just one of those inevitable side-effects of getting older. A minor waterworks defect.'

'Oh, thanks a bundle.'

'No, but seriously, it is, really, isn't it? You get to that age where, medically speaking, they just assume you're never going to be, you know, functioning at full efficiency again. They lower their expectations.'

'Look, I'm not about to sit here and wet myself, if that's what you're thinking.'

'Oh, go on. Please. I could do with a giggle.'

I suppose I should be grateful, at times like this, to have a mate like Andy to talk to. You always know where you stand with Andy. You know precisely how much sympathy he's going to heap upon you. Namely, none. He stops you from plunging into the deep, dark abyss of self-pity.

'Seriously, though,' I went on. 'Do you reckon this is it now? From this point onwards, do you reckon our conversations are going to be increasingly dominated by medical ailments?'

'Not if I can help it.'

'But that's my whole point. You can't. You're more or less the same age as me, so next time it could be you who's getting himself into a state over some condition or other. I mean, when was the last time you had a check-up yourself?'

'What the full going-over, you mean, like you've just had? Er, let me think now. It must be, ooh, about a month ago.'

'I'm sorry?'

'I had one about a month ago. Same kind of set-up as yours. Apparently I need to lose a bit of weight, and my cholesterol is slightly too high, but otherwise they reckon I'm fine.'

'You're joking?'

'No. Why should I be?'

'But you never mentioned it.'

'Nothing to mention, was there? Besides, who wants to listen to some bloke wittering on about his measly little medical complaints?'

'Oh. Right. Sorry. Point taken.'

'No, it's OK. I don't really mind you banging on incessantly about yours.'

'Because it means you can take the piss, you mean?'

'Ideally, yeah. But look, seriously, mate, it's fine to keep an eye on these things, but if you're not careful you can end up getting totally obsessive. You start convincing yourself that age has already taken its toll. You think yourself into that frame of mind.'

'And then I become a tedious prick, right?'

'Mmm, something like that. Still, what are mates for if they can't tell you these things?'

'Yeah, you're right. Nice of you to be so honest, really. I'd hate it if you felt you couldn't be direct with me.'

'And tactless?'

'Absolutely, yeah! Be as tactless as you like. Tell it to me straight, mate!'

'Good. I'm glad you feel that way.'

'I do, yeah. Definitely.'

'Because I've been meaning to have a word about that haircut.'

If The Kids Are United – TUESDAY 25 SEPTEMBER

WYCOMBE WANDERERS 1 BRIGHTON 1
LEAGUE POSITION: 1

I was busily preparing one of my home-made curries – strictly speaking, one of Ainsley Harriott's – when Julie shuffled into the kitchen.

'Was that Man United you were cheering?' she asked. 'Or Briny?'

(My wife, I should explain, has developed this peculiar habit of referring to Brighton – the team or the city – as 'Briny'. I assume this stems from the fact that the place is located beside a fairly sizeable quantity of salt water; even so, it's an utterly daft name which, outside this house, I've only ever heard used in the context of tinned sardines. She's a law unto herself sometimes, she really is. You have to love her.)

'It was Brighton,' I replied, rummaging through the cupboard for the Oxo veggie stock cubes I could have sworn I'd spotted earlier. 'One–nil. Nathan Jones.'

Like she'd know who the hell Nathan Jones was.

Once I'd finally located the Oxo, I went over to the fridge, grabbed the papery, sprouting remains of a well-past-its-peak garlic bulb, and tore off two cloves – that being the precise quantity indicated by Ainsley in this lamb dansak recipe of his. Then I tore off a couple more, on the not unreasonable grounds that I really like garlic, and that, as someone who sits at home and watches TV for a living, I'm rarely in a situation where I have to breathe on people (or, for that matter, get dressed). Admittedly, Julie has a job which requires her to mix with the outside world, but I've already thought this one through and, the way I see it, fuck the outside world.

Despite having found earlier radio commentaries utterly tortuous, I'd decided to tune our dust-caked kitchen stereo to Southern Counties this evening, just to catch the game's early stages as I prepared the meal. (As it turned out, I found myself coping with the tension of the game rather more comfortably than usual, probably because I also had this additional activity on which to focus my attention. The fact that this additional activity involved the deployment of large scary kitchen knives may also have helped.)

On the TV in the lounge, meanwhile, Man United were playing Olympiakos in a Champions League group match. Hence Julie's confusion from upstairs, unsure whose goal I'd just cheered.

But hold on a goddamn second there, you're thinking (or at least you might be, if you'd suddenly taken on the persona of a B-movie cowboy): Why would Julie expect me to cheer Man United? Don't say I've started supporting them as well, as a sort of glory-seeker's back-up option?

No, of course not. Credit me with at least a little self-respect. However – and you may find this confession very nearly as troubling – I do actually like them. Well, maybe 'like' is a tad strong, but I certainly don't hate them. Not in the sense that, if you call yourself a 'proper' football fan, I think you're meant to.

There, I've said it now.

I – Do – Not – Hate – Man – U – Flaming – Nited.

Blimey, eh?

But before you break down in despair, or feed this book to the waste disposal – or both – at least hear me out.

Actually, I can offer two main explanations for not hating Man United. And it's your lucky day, because I'm about to treat you to a full breakdown of each. You can, if you like, then decide which you consider to be the most pathetic.

WHY I DON'T HATE MAN UNITED: PATHETIC EXPLANATION 1

To be honest, I can't really bring myself to hate any football team. I wish I could sometimes. Hating at least one other team is really a basic requirement in any true fan, same as vowing to follow your own club no matter what, even to leaky away grounds with rancid toilets when they're lying 21st in a league sponsored by a glue manufacturer. Not to hate any other club, not to loathe that club's fans, their colours, their songs, their mascot, not to cheer with genuine delight at their every misfortune and setback, on and off the pitch, well, it singles you out as a bit of a wuss, really. A sorry excuse for a football supporter. As if you're missing some vital gene.

But, hey, that's me, I'm afraid. Sorry.

If we're talking about gut instincts, my own gut instinct, if the fans seated around me were ever to launch into a chorus of 'Stand Up If You Hate Man U', would be to stay firmly rooted to my seat, possibly even piping up with: 'Well, to be strictly honest, lads . . .' Not that I'd probably go ahead and actually do this, as I rather like my head the shape it is.

It's not just Man United I feel this way about. In my more committed

Arsenal days, I felt just as indifferent towards their 'bitter' north London rivals Tottenham. Possibly a lot of this stemmed from the fact that I'd never actually lived anywhere near north London, and so the full historical significance of this rivalry, assuming there was one, had always escaped me. I guess it can also be explained by the fact that I've never been part of any gang or tribe, football-related or otherwise, or been even remotely in touch with the game's sub-culture. In other words, I've never seen football as an excuse to get beered-up with a load of other blokes and pummel the shit out of a group of total strangers.

Why should I? It's silly. Why am I expected to feel such intense antipathy towards a load of people I've probably never even met, purely because they happen to support another football team, any more than I'd want to beat someone up on the basis of which TV programme they happened to like best (obviously I'd make an exception if it featured Jeremy Spake). Really, wouldn't it make a load more sense if football's 'hate' faction were to channel all that raw, primitive energy into something slightly more constructive, such as growing the fuck up? I think it would, you know.

So that's my first reason for not hating Man United. And if, as was the case tonight, they happen to be taking on European opposition, then I'm even happy to go one stage further, positively rooting for them as our British representatives. Well, British-ish.

Which brings us neatly on to . . .

WHY I DON'T HATE MAN UNITED: PATHETIC EXPLANATION 2

This time it's personal.

As I think I may have mentioned some while back, our daughter Emily is a Man United fan. She's never actually been to watch them play, I grant you, but that hardly makes her exceptional. The point is, she's glued to every televised game, owns three replica shirts and, most significantly, has pictures of David Beckham Blu-takked all over her bedroom wall. (And if you can think of a better way of spelling 'Blu-takked', incidentally, I'm very much open to suggestions.)

Now, I appreciate I could have sat her down a couple of years ago and talked her through this decision of hers. I could have put forward a very powerful case against it, arguing that this wasn't what being a football fan was really about – merely plumping for the richest, most successful, most fashionable team. I could have come out with that line about how, to appreciate the highs, you need to have suffered the lows. I could have suggested that her friends would have admired her individuality and independent-mindedness if she'd pledged her support to a less obvious club.

But I didn't.

I didn't because, if I had, she'd have raised her eyebrows and muttered, 'Yeah, right,' and I'd have been left feeling like a pitifully clueless fart.

So now, in our house, Man United has come to mean Emily. A Man United win means a happy Emily. A Man United defeat means a sulky Emily. It's an emotional barometer.

Which means I find myself, more often than not, wanting Man United to win just to keep my daughter happy. In fact, I suspect that's another reason why I've been happy to latch on to the Albion, two divisions down. Because it's safe down there. There's no clash of loyalties – whereas any enthusiasm I've shown for Arsenal, United's most consistent rivals in recent times, has made the atmosphere a bit tense.

But am I being over-indulgent? Abso-blooming-lutely. Ought I not to despair that my 13-year-old daughter has fallen for all that United-related hype? Quite possibly. Am I planning to try and change her mind? Not a hope in hell.

I may be striving to recover my own passion for football, to make it a central part of my life again, but it's never going to take precedence over my own daughter's happiness, is it? And for her, Man United *is* happiness. If only because, let's face it, they keep bloody winning.

Back in May 1999, on the night they clinched their historic Treble by beating Bayern Munich in the Champions League final, I was watching the match in a tiny, cramped bar in central Jerusalem. Seriously. I was over there for the Eurovision Song Contest, covering this musical feast for the *Daily Star*.

When, with only minutes remaining, it looked as if Fergie's men had muffed it, my feeling wasn't one of 'poor United'. It was one of 'poor Emily'. I visualised her sitting at home on the sofa in her favourite Man United shirt, weeping inconsolably. Or certainly having a spectacular sulk about it. So when Teddy Sheringham's equaliser sneaked in – in something like the 153rd minute, or however much stoppage time they'd managed to wangle this time – my resulting roar of happiness was for my daughter. And when Ole Gunnar Solskjaer stuck out a leg – his own, I seem to recall – and snatched that sensational winner a minute or so later, I was suddenly hugging the stranger beside me – with whom, by the way, I'd sat for the previous two hours without exchanging so much as a syllable – out of sheer joy for Emily's sake. She'd be so thrilled, I thought.

And then, for one horribly sceptical moment, I thought maybe she wouldn't. Maybe she'd have just expected all this. United have had so much success since Emily's been following them, she might just take this sort of thing for granted, almost as if it were scripted. From Emily's perspective, maybe it hadn't been about *whether* United would win, merely how.

But I rang her and it turned out she was genuinely delighted. Screaming with happiness, in fact. She could barely contain herself.

I'd say that's a pretty good reason, then, for not hating Man United. I'd like to hear a better one.

Language Lessons – SATURDAY 29 SEPTEMBER

CARDIFF CITY 1 BRIGHTON 1
LEAGUE POSITION: 2ND

This afternoon I shouted a rude word in the middle of a public park. Two words, in fact, although they did form part of the same expression. This outburst earned me a serious glare from an elderly woman walking some laughable excuse for a dog – but then she hadn't heard what I'd just heard, through my portable radio's earphones. Namely, that Cardiff had just equalised, ten minutes from time, denying us the three points which would have kept us top of the table. If she had, I've little doubt that her mask of suburban respectability would have fallen in an instant, and that she, too, would have screeched, 'Fucking shit.'

Quite by chance, my own dog, Barney, was unleashing that very substance against a tree at the time, so I didn't have much opportunity to wallow in my misery. Instead I had to fish the screwed-up Asda carrier out of my jacket pocket and wander over to scoop up his mound of soft, steamy poo. Then I had to walk around with this stinking package of plop until I came across one of the special bins which the council so thoughtfully provide. It really is great fun, owning a dog. I'd heartily recommend it.

As I learned while I was cooking the other night – the curry turned out great, by the way, thanks for asking – if I'm going to have to listen to a radio commentary to keep in touch with how the Albion are doing, then I need to be doing something else at the same time. Hence the dog-walking thing.

I'll just need to remember, if I adopt this tactic again, that as well as exercising Barney I also need to exercise a bit of restraint, reaction-wise.

It shows I'm beginning to care, mind. To the point, in fact, where I've been e-mailing the Falmer stadium campaign people, reminding them I'd like to help out in some capacity.

Nobody's replied yet, but I guess they have other priorities. Either that or they've heard the shocking news about my face. Two days ago, I came out in the most hideously ugly swellings you're likely to encounter this side of the bubonic plague. I'm going to have to see the doctor yet again, get some cream or something. So perhaps the stadium people are afraid I'd be a negative influence, especially if I were to campaign door-to-door. They're probably right, too. It wouldn't be the greatest of PR exercises, trying to elicit support while oozing pus on people's doorsteps.

Possibly beats yelling 'Fucking shit' at them, though.

The Pact – FRIDAY 5 OCTOBER

BRIGHTON 1 BRENTFORD 2
LEAGUE POSITION: 3RD

I was soaking in the bath when Julie rang. I'd reached that sorry stage, in fact, when the water was turning tepid and each of my fingertips had begun to resemble a tiny reproduction of Esther Rantzen's face – the point where you either resign yourself to the fact that the most enjoyable part of your bathtime is effectively over, or try and eke out an extra ten minutes by releasing a little of the lukewarm, murky liquid and replacing it with an extra couple of inches of the clear, fresh, piping hot variety.

I wiped my hands on the towel and reached over for the trilling cordless. It turned out Julie was stuck on the M25 and wouldn't be home for another half-hour. I reminded her that I'd be well on my way to Withdean by then – although I declined to add that this was to allow myself time for one of those greasy burgers which I'd promised myself (and Julie) that I'd given up.

'Nervous?' she shouted, hands-free, above the roar of the engine.

'No, not really,' I assured her. 'As long as I stick to the well-lit roads, I'll be fine. I'm a big boy now, and . . .'

'About the game, pillock-face.'

I love my wife so much.

'Oh, right. Yeah, I suppose I am, really. They're a really good side, Brentford.'

Dear God. Just listen to me: 'They're a really good side, Brentford.'

Brentford???!!!

Three months ago, I couldn't even have told you which division

Brentford were in, let alone whether they were 'a really good side'. Even a matter of weeks back, I wouldn't have known, let alone cared, if they were promotion challengers, mid-table mediocrities or relegation certainties. Or that Steve Coppell, ex-boss of Crystal Palace and Man City, was now their manager. Brentford meant nothing to me, other than via its mid-'70s association with the word 'Nylons' and a TV advert featuring Alan 'Fluff' Freeman. Yet here I was, Mr flipping Expert, suddenly offering an opinion on their prowess as a footballing unit.

'If they win tonight,' I added – as if that expression 'a really good side' hadn't painted a vivid enough picture – 'they'll go top.'

'Oh, dear,' shouted Julie. 'Tense one, then?'

I suppose it was, really, although I'd have been lying if I'd said I'd been on tenterhooks all day. I don't even know what a tenterhook is.

'Pretty tense, yeah. It's a bit of a test.'

'So, would you sacrifice it for a result tomorrow?' asked Julie. I could tell she'd moved onto serious conversational territory now because she'd taken the phone off its cradle and was – ummmm, naughty – speaking directly into the handset. The trouble was, I couldn't think what the hell she was on about.

'Tomorrow? We're not playing tomorrow.'

'Not Briny, you idiot. England.'

Good grief, how could I have let that slip my mind? She was talking about England versus Greece – tomorrow's final World Cup qualifying match. The one in which a simple victory – preferably a good sound tonking, but 1–0 will do fine if it has to – will automatically qualify us for the finals as outright group winners. Ahead of Germany, tee-hee.

I suppose I hadn't exactly forgotten it. How could I? It just threw me a bit, the way Julie suddenly brought the subject up. I hadn't expected the issue of World Cup qualification, via which England were hoping to come face-to-face with the cream of the planet's footballing talent, to crop up during a conversation about Brentford FC. No disrespect, you understand. Well, not much.

It was a good question, though. I mean, would I? Would I be prepared to accept an Albion defeat tonight – in what, after all, was probably our most important match of the season so far, against a side breathing down our necks at the top of the table – if I could be assured that this would somehow, as part of some magical deal with the Gods, guarantee England victory tomorrow?

I'd like to say I thought long and hard about this. In truth, I didn't need to.

'Of course I would,' I replied. 'It's no contest, is it?'

And it isn't. It never could be. As it happens, we went down 2–1 tonight, and probably just about deserved to. But even if we'd lost 15–0, it wouldn't have mattered *that* much. Admittedly, a 15–0 defeat may have dented the team's morale a smidgen. Micky might have wanted to give serious consideration to whether keeper Michel Kuipers was still up to the job, or whether it would be wiser to hand the keeper's jersey to, say, an enthusiastically agile Yorkshire Terrier called Poppet. And, yes, come the end of the season, we might have regretted having conceded quite that quantity, goal-difference-wise. But ultimately it would still only have meant sacrificing three puny points. We'd have had all season to make them up.

If England lose tomorrow – or even fail to win, seeing as the Germans are bound to flatten Finland at home – then it's all down to a two-leg play-off, against either Ukraine or Belarus. If we were to muff that, which wouldn't surprise me one bit, then that 5–1 triumph in Munich would count for nothing. The World Cup finals would go ahead without us. Again. Just as they did in 1974, after Poland had beaten us to it and I'd cried all the next day at school. Just as they did again in 1978, when I'd managed to save my tears until I got home. And just as happened yet again before the 1994 tournament, by which time I was mature enough just to shout 'Wankers' at the telly. It would be absolutely crushing.

But please don't mistake what I'm saying for tub-thumping, shaven-headed jingoism. I despise that stuff. I hate the crappy booing of other countries' anthems, and the poisonous bigotry often associated with 'supporting' England. It's just that, if forced to make a straightforward choice, I'd rather see England doing well than the Albion.

Is this simply because I've only followed the Albion for a matter of weeks – further evidence that my heart, soul, and any other relevant body parts still aren't truly committed to the club? In part, I suppose it has to be. But even if I'd been an Albion fan since emerging from the womb, I'm pretty sure I'd still be feeling this way. No, I'm convinced of it.

Success for the Albion can raise the spirits of an entire city, which is great. Success for England would raise the spirits of an entire country, which would be *bloody* great. Seems obvious, really.

Of course I wasn't forced to make that choice, between an Albion win this evening and England's automatic qualification tomorrow. It's just that, from the moment Julie posed this hypothetical question, it's been feeling that way. As if I've only been allocated a limited quota of football-related luck this weekend, and if I'd chosen to use it up tonight, well, I'd have had to live with the consequences.

So I walked back from Withdean in a weird mood. Hacked off about the defeat, naturally, yet unable to fight off the daft, superstitious, wholly irrational notion that, as the first part of this pact, the Albion had just done their job to perfection.

Never In Doubt – SATURDAY 6 OCTOBER

ENGLAND 2 GREECE 2

Julie made a very wise decision this afternoon. Not on a par, of course, with the one she made 15 years ago when she agreed to marry me, but pretty damn close. This afternoon she decided that, rather than stay in with me and Em to watch the England match, she'd take her mum shopping. Not because she – or her mum, for that matter – actually *needed* to go shopping. They rarely do. But just to get out of the house.

'I'm sorry,' she said, 'but I don't think I could stand it.'

On reflection, this decision illustrated just how clued-up Julie can be, football-wise. While virtually everyone else – fans, writers, bookies, TV pundits, celebrity chefs – had been banging on about this match all week as if it would be party time, as if a thumping England victory were a foregone conclusion, Julie had sensed it would be anything but. If, indeed, it were to be a victory at all. Had I questioned her further, she may well have been able to predict this afternoon's events with an even more uncanny degree of accuracy – adding that, just five weeks after the Germany match, England would revert to the type of shapeless, clueless, headless-chicken performance which any English supporter of my age – reluctantly, but with a weary sense of the inevitable – has come to expect.

She'd probably have pointed out that we'd freeze. That the likes of Gerrard and Scholes, in particular, would be about as effective in central midfield as Atomic Kitten. That, Beckham aside, the rest of the team would barely be able to string two passes together. That, true to our national character, the significance of the big occasion would weigh like a ton of lead (or a ton of anything, I suppose – the effect would be much the same) on the players' minds, while the Greeks would approach the game with that chilled-out fluidity which you so often see from sides with stuff-all to lose.

All of which would mean that, once again, I'd be utterly unbearable to share a room with.

Julie knows what the England team can be like. She knows what her husband can be like. Mix the two together, ladle in a way-too-large helping of tension, and what you're left with is completely unpalatable.

Midway through the game – after a brief burst of ludicrous optimism, triggered by Teddy Sheringham's equaliser, had made way for yet more despair, with the Greeks re-establishing a lead almost at once – I actually told Emily it might be best if we lost. Best, in fact, if we lost the play-off as well. I meant it, too. I really did. At the time. Because, like I've said a million times before, watching England is torture. Even the Germany game I only found enjoyable for the last ten minutes or so, once their uncharacteristic ineptitude had finally convinced me that they were unlikely to pull back four goals even if we'd let them play all year. So did I honestly want to suffer another World Cup finals with England taking part? Wouldn't it be more enjoyable for us if they just stayed at home and played golf, or whatever it is footballers like to do, and we viewers/fans could simply savour top-quality international football without having our souls torn out? I appreciate we'd never get quite as excited, potentially quite as euphoric, as we would if we were watching our own side – but, by the same token, at least we wouldn't face yet more of the sort of agony we had to endure this afternoon.

Julie rang from the High Street with five minutes to go.

'Are we winning?' she asked, chirpily.

'No, we fucking aren't, we're fucking losing,' I barked, perhaps offering a hint as to why I've never been asked to become a guest pundit on Sky Sports. 'We've fucking fucked it.'

'Oh,' went Julie. 'Right. Well, I'll leave you to it, shall I?'

She didn't even wait for me to reply.

For the next few minutes – the dying minutes – I was a disgrace. Eighty-eight minutes. Eighty-nine minutes. Ninety minutes. When I wasn't thumping doors and kicking the sofa, I was kicking doors and thumping the sofa. Ninety-one minutes. Ninety-two minutes. I was ranting, cursing, steaming. The anger, the despair, the sheer bloody frustration. Year after year after sodding year. God knows what this was doing to my already dodgy blood pressure. 'PLEEEEEEASE NOT AGAIN,' I kept yelling. 'Not a-bloody-gain.'

And then I'm crying. But these aren't the tears of defeat.

In the 93rd minute, Teddy Sheringham has won a free-kick – a questionable one, but what the heck? – fractionally outside the Greek penalty area. There's still just the tiniest glimmer of hope. The England players don't know it, but the whistle has just sounded in the Germany game: the home side has been held 0–0 by the Finns. Incredibly, a draw for England will be enough after all. If we score now, we'll be through.

Becks steps up to the ball. Please, God, make him do it. He's already had about half-a-dozen free kicks from similar positions, but so far, although he's been the sharpest England player on the pitch by an absolute mile, it hasn't been his day, shooting-wise. Only one free kick has even hit the target, early in the first half, and that one's been parried away by Greece's sod of a keeper.

Please, God, I'll be good forever. I'll go back on that low-cholesterol diet – OK, *start* that low-cholesterol diet. Whatever. I'll cut down on the booze. I'll exercise properly. I'll stop moaning about being middle-aged. Or just stop moaning, full-stop, if you insist. Yes, even about Highway Code Rule 198 and economy bin-liners and the bloke in the Gillette Mach 3 advert. I'll do lots of other worthy stuff which I can't even think of right now. Tell you what: do they still need volunteers for Meals On Wheels? Fine. Sign me up.

Just let him score.

Please.

Emily grips my hand. Her absolute hero (bedroom wall picture count now approaching stalker levels), the guy pilloried by merciless morons three years ago when, so they reckoned, his sending-off got us knocked out of the World Cup, suddenly has the country's footballing fate resting in his hands. Or in his boot. Surely he can't do it? Surely it's too much to ask of one player? Surely we're about to witness yet another horribly flat anti-climax? He's going to scuff it into the wall, I know he is. Or belt into the 25th row of the Stretford End.

PLEASE LET HIM SCORE. PLEEEEEEEEEEEEEEEASE!!!!!

Becks takes a short run-up and swings at the ball. Up he whips it, over the wall. Over, not into. That's good. It's curling, too, perfectly, sweetly, exquisitely . . .

OH.

MY.

GOD.

It's not going into the 25th row. It's not even going over the bar. Or wide. Not this time. It looks as if it's heading for the top left-hand corner. The keeper's stretching at it, but . . . fucking hell, the net's rippling!! It's *in*! He's flaming done it!!

Emily screamed. I screamed. I tore the lining from the back of my throat, screeched myself hoarse with the joy. The sheer joy which only a great football moment can bring. Ecstasy and relief, rolled into one and multiplied a millionfold.

We hugged. We danced. And then Emily rushed over and kissed the screen.

Seconds later, that was it. The final whistle blew. By then, the news from Germany had obviously filtered through to the England players. Thanks to this moment of football magic, the jammy buggers had actually made it. Never mind how, they were through.

And on came the sobbing.

Emily grabbed the phone to make an important call. When Julie answered, Em didn't say a word. She just yelled.

'YEAAAAAAAAAAAAAAAAAAAAAAAAAHHH!!!' she screamed. Which I felt summed things up rather neatly. Then, having calmed down a fraction – and filled Julie in, with slightly more attention to detail, on what had actually happened – she handed me the receiver.

What a waste of time *that* was. I tried to construct a coherent sentence in something close to English, but I could barely speak. 'Are you crying?' asked Julie.

As if.

In one extraordinary afternoon I'd been reminded of the very worst that football can subject you to. I'd almost convinced myself I couldn't stomach it any more. Almost. And then I'd been reminded of the very best, of the out-of-this-world euphoria that it can spark, and I'd realised that of course I could, stupid. Of course I could carry on torturing myself, because it's these fleeting, blissful moments which make the years of torture worthwhile.

Julie had bought herself some socks, by the way.

Darkest Before Dawn – WEDNESDAY 10 OCTOBER

It was bound to happen sooner or later. Later would have been nicer.

Six o'clock in the morning – when, if I'm awake at all, I'm fumbling my way through a mental fug, still struggling to figure out what day it is – can hardly be the ideal time to hear that your team's manager has quit. But then I don't suppose an ideal time exists. Not when you're talking about a bloke who, arguably more than anyone, has been responsible for making that team halfway decent again. Three-quarters-way even.

To be strictly accurate, Southern FM's news bulletin didn't say for certain that Micky had gone. At that stage, nothing official had been announced.

It just made it abundantly clear that his departure was imminent – that the man who took us to the Third Division title (OK, took 'them', as the Albion still were at the time) would be packed and gone before the day was out.

Yesterday, Micky collected his Manager of the Month award, at a celebration lunch in a local Italian restaurant (not, for some reason, the one which used to sponsor the club), and while that particular honour is traditionally seen as a harbinger of doom for whoever receives it – second only to the grimly portentous 'vote of confidence' from the chairman – this time it's proved to be a lousy omen for the recipient's club.

The station's news reader, Albion-worshipper Richard Lindfield, who'd attended this presentation, said the lunch had 'felt like the last supper'. Unless he's a whole lot older than he looks, I'm not sure how Richard felt able to make such a comparison with any degree of first-hand authority, but I could understand what he was driving at. It was the news we'd all dreaded.

The rumour sweeping the restaurant – one which has now turned out to be horribly accurate – was that Micky was on his way to Leicester City. Or soon would be, once he'd wolfed down his tiramisu and left a nice clean plate. Not as top man – that role would be taken by Dave 'Apparently I Used To Be Quite Good But God Alone Knows When That Was' Bassett – but as assistant manager. The number two. The idea being that, once Dave stepped down in a year or so, Micky would automatically take his place. In other words he was, to coin a horrible expression which I really feel should be applied exclusively to horses, being 'groomed'.

And in many ways you can't blame him. For one thing, Leicester City are a Premiership club, at least for the time being. For another, Micky's salary will look a fair bit healthier. And since he's already been treated pretty poorly by a couple of his previous clubs – Fulham and Brentford – it's not surprising that his own personal ambitions have become his immediate priority these days. If only to a small degree, his rotten experiences are bound to have left a few scars.

But *Leicester*?! I mean, really.

As for my own response to the news, I'm delighted to report that I'm gutted. Genuinely, no faking. Other than my reaction to each of the Albion's results so far this season – which, since we're only in October, can only really be of limited significance – this has been my first serious test of loyalty. And since I've spent today in a don't-even-bother-trying-to-speak-to-me kind of sulk, I'd say my response has been commendable. Had I felt indifferent to Micky's departure, or even just mildly miffed, it would have cast serious doubts over the authenticity of my commitment. Instead of which, I feel miserable and deflated. It's great news.

Throughout the day I've been casting my mind back, trying to remember what this feeling reminds me of, beyond football. And this evening it's finally dawned on me. Of course! It feels like the day I got dumped by Sally Kershaw.

I was 21 at the time, and Sally (obviously, out of respect, that's a pseudonym; she wouldn't want you knowing that her real name was Mary) was the first proper long-term girlfriend I'd ever had. We dated for nearly three years, all told, until one day, entirely out of the blue, she announced she'd had enough, and that – get this – she was going back to her old boyfriend.

Her old boyfriend! That was the vicious twist. Mary – sorry, 'Sally' – wasn't simply declaring that, in her opinion, our relationship had run its natural course, that she'd had a great time, but that it would do us both good to meet new people. Oh, no. She'd effectively done her own little product comparison, had Sally-Mary, just as you might do if you were weighing up the relative merits of Whiskas, Kit-E-Cat and a dismembered mouse – and concluded, after sampling each at some length, that she preferred the original. And please let's not be in the slightest doubt as to what sort of 'original' we're talking about here. We're talking about a bloke – to protect his identity, let's just call him Total Shit-head – who wore towelling underpants. Yes, you read that correctly. Not towelling socks, but towelling *underpants*. I know this because I used to go and play squash against Total Shit-head and, well, you can hardly help noticing that sort of thing. Can you?

Yes, towelling underpants. Go back and read those words as many times as you wish; they won't change. And anticipating your other question, I seem to recall that one pair was purple and another a sort of slime green. Sorry, but when you encounter something quite that unsettling, the details remain lodged in your memory, even 20-odd years later. Especially when – and this was the other reason I was so offended that she wanted to crawl back to this guy – the person who wears the towelling underpants also happens to stink. I mean, really, really reek. Like compost.

Micky, I grant you, has never managed – or assistant managed – Leicester City before, so the point about comparison tests doesn't really apply. But he must know, deep down, that he's leaving behind a bunch of people who really value and appreciate him, and taking up with another lot who surely won't. Not to the same extent anyway.

Before every home game this season, I've always made a big point of applauding Micky as he's trotted across to take his place in the dugout. As hard as I possibly could, until the palms of my hands would sting. Call me mad, but a part of me genuinely believed – and I'm serious here – that the louder the applause, the happier and more appreciated Micky would feel, and hence the more likely he'd be to stick around, at least until the end of this season. Yes, I honestly believed that a 39-year-old man's long-term career strategy might be influenced by how loudly some myopic chubbo in Block B (admittedly in tandem with several thousand other fans) managed to thwack his paws together. It's amazing how stupidly football can make you think sometimes.

Anyway, it's obviously done no good whatsoever, because Micky's off to join a club which, if you want to reintroduce my analogy here, wears towelling underpants.

Oh, well. It's his loss.

Not that I'm prepared to criticise him for lacking loyalty (as if I'm in any position to). Loyalty is one of those daft, overworked words which dimmer fans (but ones who, unfortunately, are just about bright enough to get through to radio phone-ins) like to bandy about at every opportunity – as if there's some sort of primitive tribal morality thing going on here, as if loyalty should forever be expected of anyone even briefly associated with that supporter's club. With all due respect, these people are spouting guff. Micky might deserve some flak, perhaps, if he were a born-and-bred Brightonian, or if the club had rescued him from the managerial scrapheap, or if the chairman had once snatched him from the path of the Gatwick Express. But he's just a bloke who's come along, done a more-than-decent job, and now has the chance to step up. As far as I'm concerned – and, from what I can make out, most Albion fans feel the same about this – the very best of luck to the guy. He's done the club proud.

It won't be forgotten.

Bring A Friend – THURSDAY 11 OCTOBER

Micky Adams has apparently advised Dave Bassett to buy Bobby Zamora. Bastard.

HUDDERSFIELD TOWN 1 BRIGHTON 2
LEAGUE POSITION: 3RD

There can't be that many occasions when the expression 'I wish I'd gone to Huddersfield' has passed my lips. But it did today. I really wish I'd been there.

With this afternoon's team selection – and motivation, more to the point – left jointly in the hands of Albion's assistant manager, Bob Booker, and the club's youth development person, Martin Hinshelwood, the players could conceivably have gone to pieces. Not because these two aren't up to the job, but purely because of the destabilising effect of Micky buggering off. Instead, by all accounts, they held it together like stars. Bobby scored a bit of a classic, too. I expect that means he's worth a few hundred thousand more than he was worth at breakfast time.

But I didn't even get to hear the commentary. Julie and I had driven off to a wedding reception at a hotel in Hampshire – in some bland sort of nowhere land between Southampton and Portsmouth – and, frustratingly, Southern Counties' signal doesn't stretch that far. The first I knew of Albion's success – against serious promotion rivals, too – was when we dumped our luggage in the hotel room shortly before 5 p.m. and I made an immediate dive for the TV's 'on' button. As fate would have it, the Albion result was the very first which flashed up on the *Grandstand* teleprinter, just as I was throwing myself onto the bed and kicking off my DMs, and I cheered it probably more loudly than any of our away results so far. Given what a rotten week it's been, it was a fine achievement – a sign that, while Micky may have headed northwards for a taste of football's towelling underpants, there's plenty to stay cheerful about. It made my day.

It was just as well something did, because the actual wedding reception ended with Julie and I having an absolute stonker of a row, albeit after we'd marched huffily back to our room.

What triggered this row was my dancing. Or rather, my lack of it. Not once throughout the evening had I joined her on the dancefloor. I hadn't wanted to. I hate dancing. I always have, except for a mid-to-late-'70s punk phase, when dancing really meant jumping like Zebedee, and I gave that up the night I accidentally knocked out Geoff Moore's tooth.

Proper dancing I just can't do. I dance like a person who's taking the piss out of someone who can't dance. I'm agonisingly self-conscious, and I've every reason to be.

So what had we discovered, when we'd arrived at this do, was to be the central element of the evening's entertainment? Corrr-rect. A fucking disco. I was only amazed the organisers hadn't gone one step further, by draping giant banners over the front of the hotel itself, reading: 'Half-man, half-whale! Come and see it trying to dance! Free bottle of house wine.'

The baffling thing is, I'd assumed Julie was OK about me sitting it out. These were workmates of hers, so she'd looked happy enough as she'd headed over to join them on the dancefloor for some stupid leg-kicky arm-flicky thing. It was only when, at around 1 a.m., we decided to turn in for the night that she suddenly threw a complete wobbly. Apparently I'd embarrassed her. All evening.

I argued, calmly and politely at first, that I hadn't. I pointed out that I'd not actually been rude to any of these workmates of hers – I'd chatted whenever I'd had the chance, and spent the rest of the time either quietly nursing my drink or sneaking back up to the buffet to shovel more grub into my face (I'd recommend the deep-fried prawny things). But she insisted I'd let her down. I'd 'sneered' at people, is how she put it.

Bollocks. I hadn't sneered at anyone. Why should I? I think what she was getting mixed up with was me taking the piss, to which I readily and unashamedly admit. Not out of anyone on a personal basis – they seemed like really nice people – but simply when confronted with the generally appalling sight of Blokes On A Dancefloor. Any blokes, any dancefloor, it matters not a jot. I'm afraid I can't bring myself to be apologetic for this. These guys have got it coming. Whenever anyone asks me why I choose not to dance, I simply point out a man who's already doing it – any man will do – and go: 'There, that's why.' Blokes dancing look like arses.

'Oh, but you shouldn't be so self-conscious,' someone will invariably argue. 'Nobody's watching.' But this is missing the point entirely. The fact is, I *should* be self-conscious. People *are* watching. Just as I was watching people tonight. I was watching blokes dancing and in each case I was thinking: 'You look absolutely fucking ridiculous, mate. Haven't you got any self-respect?'

Yet a part of me admires them. Wants to *be* like them, in fact. I don't necessarily want to be able to dance properly; I just want to be able to dance badly and not care.

This is exactly the same self-consciousness which haunts me at matches. It's why I've yet to chant, 'Sea–gurrrlls!' or 'Albee–yurrrn, Albee–yurrrn, Albee–yurrrn' – even once – when really I'm desperate to. It gets me down sometimes, being so uptight. Most times, in fact.

Maybe the answer is just to take the plunge. If I were forced onto a dancefloor – probably by means of one of those tranquilliser guns they use for sedating rhino – I'd be left with no option but to fight my way through this horrible, stupid self-consciousness barrier. Once I'd done that, maybe I'd emerge as a happier, more relaxed human being, reducing the threat of future dance-orientated marital conflicts. Similarly, if I were to force myself to join in one of those Albion chants – arm movements optional – I'd probably be taking a major step towards loosening up all round. Maybe that's something else football can do for me.

In fact, I might even try it at next Saturday's match. The chanting, I mean, not the dancing. It's Oldham at home – another biggy – and the first game at Withdean since Micky left. So why not? Why don't I go ahead, cast aside the stifling emotional constraints of a lifetime, and actually join in with a football chant – loud, proud and bursting with unbridled passion?

I'll think about it.

Over The Wall – MONDAY 15 OCTOBER

Maybe I shouldn't be making a big song and dance about this, but I do feel quite a sense of achievement tonight. Shortly before seven o'clock on this soggy autumn evening I finally made The Big Breakthrough: I penetrated the Albion's inner sanctum. Sort of.

This wasn't, let me stress, some underhand – or undercover – piece of snooping. Nor was it a case of jemmying my way into the hospitality hut – sorry, 'suite' – clambering inside, and making off with the Third Division championship trophy. (For a start, they don't keep it there on weekdays.) It was just that, after a lengthy silence which I'd huffily interpreted as a snub, I'd found myself invited to attend – and I hope you're sitting down for this bit, in case your knees buckle at the sheer magnitude of what I'm about to tell you – a meeting of the stadium action committee.

Phew, eh? Rock 'n' roll.

Admittedly, they're not actually *called* the stadium action committee; that's just me trying to inject a little excitement. What they're really called

– what *we're* really called, since, amazingly, they've let me become a member tonight – is the Falmer For All committee, Falmer being the place up the road, remember, where they're hoping this new stadium can be built. Keep up.

So, yes, I've joined the group which, over the next however-flaming-long-it-takes, will be co-ordinating this whole campaign. And, OK, I know I may have used the expression 'tub-thumpingly dull' but that was before they let me in to play.

Yes, *me*.

Less than three months after setting out on this whole weird adventure – less than three months after I'd decided to try and make myself give a monkey's about Brighton and Hove Albion FC – here I was, parked two seats away from its chairman, Dick Knight, and its chief executive, Martin Perry: not some couple of pompous suits, despite the traditional stuffiness of their job titles (although, admittedly, Martin was sporting a particuarly nasty pinstriped number this evening), but two key figures responsible for preventing the Albion from crumbling into oblivion. Attila The Stockbroker, poet-in-residence, was there too. I was mixing with the big boys. And girls, for that matter.

Mind you, I still wasn't too sure, when I arrived for tonight's meeting, whether these boys and girls really wanted me to play. One or two looked curious – if not downright suspicious – as to the identity of this speccy stranger who'd shuffled in out of the cold, although it seemed they were half-expecting one or two new faces. 'Are you Leo?' asked a man with luxurious eyebrows.

'Er, no,' I replied, a little edgily. 'I'm Mike.'

Of course, had I been in a more relaxed mood, I'd have wittily snapped back with, 'Nah, I'm Taurus, mate.' I just lacked the necessary confidence at this stage.

Once I'd explained that I'd been invited by Adrian – the bloke who did the stadium tour – this man with the eyebrows, who turned out to be Paul, the group's chairman, seemed happy enough. 'You understand I just have to check these things,' he said. 'In case you're a mole.'

'I'm sorry? A *mole?*'

'In case you're from The Other Side,' he explained – presumably referring to the stadium's opponents, rather than suggesting I might be a poltergeist.

To be honest, I didn't contribute an awful lot during the two hours of the meeting itself. In fact, I said precisely nothing, other than nervously introducing myself to the 18 people who'd gathered around the table and explaining, when politely asked whether I had any specialist skills which I could bring to their campaign, that I was 'just a fan'. Of course, I could have been a little bit more honest at this point. I could have told them '*only* just', for example. Or I could have said, 'Well, to be truthful, chaps, I'm a shameless glory-seeker, so I take it we'll be getting this nice new stadium officially approved and constructed within the next three or four days, and that I'm going to be given all the credit for it, because otherwise, frankly, I'd rather fuck off home and watch *Corrie.*'

But I didn't say any of that. I wasn't sure it would have been appropriate.

Indeed, I couldn't think of *anything* worth saying. Literally. Not a grunt. At least, not a grunt which wouldn't, I felt pretty certain, already have been grunted at one of their countless previous meetings. I was a bit overawed.

What did feel quite exciting, though, was listening to Dick Knight – the Albion's charismatic, grey-goateed, Silk Cut-puffing chairman – as he filled us in on the latest developments in his search for a new manager. He wasn't really telling us anything that he hadn't already revealed in public – namely, that his shortlist had been whittled down to four candidates (none of whom he'd reveal) – but somehow it *felt* as if he was, as if those of us sitting with him around this table were the privileged few. The in-crowd.

Not that 'search' seems quite the right word to describe what he's been up to, considering potential candidates have reportedly been hammering at Dick's door, at least in the metaphorical sense. I can't say for certain who any of these people are, but names which have been mentioned include Peter Taylor, the former Leicester City boss (and one-time England caretaker manager) who was stupidly sacked a few weeks ago after a poor start to the Premiership season; Gordon Strachan (who recently parted company with Coventry City), Jim Smith (dumped by Derby), Joe Royle (sacked by Manchester City) and Bryan Robson (with whom Middlesbrough finally ran out of patience in the close season). Steve Claridge and Nigel Clough are getting talked about, too. Oh, and there's also the Albion's current assistant manager, Bob Booker; I think Bob's a bit of a low-key hero myself, but I doubt he'll get the job.

Despite the fact that most of these guys have become available as a consequence of having screwed up elsewhere, it's still quite a mouth-watering list. Assuming that at least some of those names are genuine contenders, what it means is that, blimey, this is a club which Famous People want to come to. Maybe not famous people in the global sense – I doubt we've had an application from Madonna – but certainly famous in a football way. It looks as if I've chosen my bandwagon well.

My own favourite – and most of the fans', by all accounts – would be Peter Taylor. My only concern is that, having experienced the big-money, squeaky-clean sophistication of the Premiership, he won't fancy dropping into Division Two, which, comparatively speaking, is poor and smelly.

It would be funny, though, if the Albion ended up with the former manager of Leicester, while Leicester ended up with the former manager of the Albion, albeit as their number two. Funny as in 'ironic', that is, not as in 'rib-tickling'.

The other thing is, I've come away from tonight's meeting having made rather an alarming commitment. Despite having only just muscled in on this stadium campaign, and despite the fact that I've got absolutely no idea what they're on about, I've volunteered to help man a table at Saturday's match, dishing out campaign leaflets and glossy information packs. As I'd sat in almost complete silence for two hours this evening, I felt I ought to make some sort of positive gesture, if only to assure them that their new recruit wasn't clinically dead. And, well, this seemed the ideal opportunity. My worry now is that, being so blindingly ill-informed at this stage, I could make a stupendous prat of myself. What if an aggressive sceptic marches up and starts to interrogate me in detail, throwing in expressions such as 'transport initiative' and 'infrastructure' and 'are you making this up as you go along, or what?' I may have to feign some kind of seizure.

Vroom Flipping Vroom – TUESDAY 16 OCTOBER

SWANSEA 1 BRIGHTON 2
(LDV VANS TROPHY, SOUTHERN SECTION, ROUND ONE)

ARSENAL 2 SOME TEAM FROM GREECE 1
(UEFA CHAMPIONS LEAGUE, GROUP C)

The Arsenal were on TV. The Albion were on the radio. A familiar clash but one which, by recent standards, prompted a slightly unfamiliar reaction on my part. Tonight, just like the old days, I cared more about the Arsenal winning. Or, at least, less about the Albion losing, which I think is pretty much the same thing.

It's not because I'm wavering. It's not because I'm tempted to go back to what Andy would no doubt call my 'ex' – even though, a couple of days ago, I did become a bit misty-eyed when I spotted one of my old Arsenal T-shirts poking out from near the top of the ironing pile. ('Gunner Till I Die' proclaimed the peeling slogan. I tugged it out and shoved it to the bottom.)

No, it's just the nature of this latest tournament the Albion are competing in.

I have absolutely no idea what LDV Vans are, but I doubt it would make a lot of difference if I did. With the greatest of respect to the no doubt hugely generous sponsors, it sounds suspiciously to me like The Cup Designed Exclusively For Teams Who Stand Bog-All Chance Of Winning Anything Decent. In that sense, I think I'd rather we got knocked out. Thumped, even. Surely the longer you're associated with this type of tournament, the longer your club's name remains linked with measly lower-league ambitions.

Since our caretaker management duo rested several key players, I got the feeling they felt equally uninspired. In their position, I'd have gone further, putting out the youth team, or sending Michel Kuipers out in a pair of Mickey Mouse ears. Then I'd have left them to get on with it while I went back into the warm to watch the Arsenal match.

Sometimes you need to make a point.

Christmas Comes Early – WEDNESDAY 17 OCTOBER

I can hardly believe it. It's Peter bloody Taylor! Dick Knight has persuaded the ex-Premiership man, the ex-England man, the man behind (and let's not underestimate the significance of this) one of Britain's most highly acclaimed Norman Wisdom impressions, to become our new boss.

The announcement came at half past four, at a press conference held in the hospitality hut. We knew something big was about to break, because Southern Counties interrupted their usual weekday afternoon show, *Tunes For The Dying*, to broadcast it live. Such was the size of the press pack which showed up, the local station's reporter was apparently squashed behind a door, his own microphone lead perilously close to throttling him. He sounded quite miffed about this.

I'd been pacing the kitchen nervously for several minutes before the news was confirmed. Em was with me, possibly because she was quite excited as well, possibly to offer me moral support, or possibly because, having just arrived home from school, she felt an urgent need to raid the fridge for Crunch Corners. I'd even made a special point of rinsing out my Albion mug, wiping it dry with a scrap of kitchen paper and making myself what I hoped would be a celebratory Ty-Phoo.

When, after the inevitable kerfuffle, they finally told us it was Taylor, my eyes began to prickle. Emily seemed a little surprised by this. She wasn't alone. I'd expected to be emotional, but not *this* emotional.

'Are you *crying?*' she asked, peeling the lid off one of those vanilla-flavoured ones with the tiny chocolate beads, and seemingly uncertain whether or not to tease me. '*Again?*'

''Fraid so,' I sniffed, moving across the kitchen to hug her, as much to distract her from the widescreen view of my weeping as through any sudden rush of paternal affection.

And then it occurred to me: the significance of that word 'again'. The last time I was moved to tears by football – plump, salty, pear-shaped tears, that is, not just the temporary golf-ball-in-the-throat sensation – was when that emotionally debilitating World Cup qualifier had finished in such dramatic circumstances. But that was England, the team I'd instinctively cared about since birth, so I was bound to get a bit choked up. Today it was just Brighton and Hove Albion, some team I'd cared about since, what, late July. Hardly in the same league, devotion-wise.

Of course not.

The very idea.

God, I can't wait for Saturday.

Sign On The Line – SATURDAY 20 OCTOBER

BRIGHTON 3 OLDHAM ATHLETIC 0
LEAGUE POSITION: 2ND

Dear Council Bloke(s),

With reference, so I'm told, to the 'second deposit draft of the Local Plan', whatever the fuck that is, I am writing to express my unreserved support for amendments SR25 and SR19a. I have absolutely no idea what these are, what their numbers refer to, or even what those initials SR are meant to stand for (Spaghetti Rings, perhaps? Salman Rushdie?), but I was handed this letter this afternoon, by some speccy fair-weather fatso from my football club's Falmer For All campaign team, and promised that if each supporter signed a copy of it, to indicate their backing for whatever it is these SR things happen to be, it would significantly improve the chances of Brighton and Hove Albion getting their new stadium built. So consider it done.

I understand, of course, that I could be the victim of a cruelly elaborate wind-up, and that, in putting my name to these obscure amendments, what I may actually be doing is inadvertently giving you written permission to break into my house at dead of night and pinch my hi-fi. But, hey, I'm a trusting type, the fatso sounded authentic enough, and, to be honest, the hi-fi's sod-all use unless you get the CD-player fixed.

Anyway, do keep in touch. Lots of love etc.

Some people, it seems, will sign anything. What you've just read isn't really the wording of the standard pro-forma letter to which I was trying to persuade fans to put their signatures this afternoon. But it might as well have been. Between 1.30 p.m. and kick-off, 651 people wandered up to one or other of the wobbly makeshift stands we'd set-up (mine was between the burger stalls, just beneath a loudspeaker through which Attila was broadcasting highlights from his punk collection) and each happily scribbled their name, address and signature. I'm not suggesting that, given a tediously microscopic run-down of all the facts, they wouldn't still have gladly done so. I certainly didn't *force* anyone to sign. Nor, it goes without saying, did I threaten anyone with violence. A lot of them were bigger than me.

No, the main point is, they *wanted* to sign it. Strip out all the bureaucratic guff, and the important message you were left with – the one nobody was in any doubt about – was, 'we'd like to stop having to play in this dump, please'.

The other point is, these Albion fans trusted me – trusted *me* – to be on the case; they assumed that, if I told them this letter was important, it must mean this letter was important. So that was nice. Weird, but nice.

My biggest fear – to the point where I'd actually been swotting up on the relevant facts and figures as I sat in the bath last night – had been that I'd be forced into a discussion with some mouthy smartarse. Obviously I'd have respected his right, within a democratic society, to *be* a mouthy smartarse; I just didn't want to show myself up. Or I didn't want my ignorance advertised in 20ft-high neon, put it that way.

Luckily, it wasn't. Nobody argued. It was a sound start. I'd done something positive, a real we're-in-this-together thing, and I'd got a major buzz out of it. More important still, I'd got my very own stadium pass: it was only a temporary thing, a slip of yellow card, valid for today only, but it had Access All Areas stamped above my name, and obviously that gave me an enormous thrill. Never mind that there weren't any areas I actually wanted access to, the fact was that I could have had access to them if I'd wanted it. To all of them. That's what it said.

Ideally, I'd have liked my photo on it as well. And one of those little clear plastic sleeves to slip it into, with the metal clip at the top, so that I could wear it on my jacket and walk around looking Officially Dead Important. But I figured maybe it would be pushing my luck to beg for those extras, at least the first time around. Besides, they may have thought they were dealing with an imbecile.

Actually speaking to people, too – that was a whole new experience. Other than the general rubbish I've shouted during the games themselves, I've a feeling my longest matchday conversation, before today, consisted of:

> THEM: 'D'you want onions with that, mate?'
> ME: 'Yes, please.'
> THEM: 'That'll be £2.80.'
> ME: 'Really? My, what splendid value for such a tasty, nutritious treat.'

And even the details of that one may have become a little hazy.

I must confess, I was a tad disappointed that the bigwigs – Dick, perhaps, or even Peter Taylor – didn't pop by to see how we stall-holders were getting on this afternoon. Still, maybe they had other things on their minds.

Either that or they may not have spotted us. For all our enthusiasm, we did look a bit amateurish: no fancy banners, no T-shirts, none of that screamingly high-profile stuff you might expect from a campaign like this. Just letters and brochures, stacked on hastily erected trestle tables. To a casual passer-by, we probably looked as if we were holding a small car-boot sale. Maybe one or two of those whose signatures we managed to procure had originally popped over in the hope of picking up a rusty Teasmade.

But never mind, we're bound to sharpen up. We're bound, for example, to remember to bring enough sodding pens next time. And somewhere safe to put the completed letters once people have handed them over, rather than shoving them into the same crumbled, third-hand Asda carriers I carry round for collecting Barney's poo. Little details, but kind of important, I feel.

And yes, there will be a next time. There'll be loads of next times. There'll have to be. This is just the start.

It was also just the start, of course, for Peter Taylor. I was mildly miffed that, since we were collecting signatures right up until kick-off, I wasn't able to take my seat in time to contribute to the welcoming applause for our new manager. But I think the other six-thousand-seven-hundred-and-whatever-it-was fans more or less made up for my absence. He may not even have twigged that I was missing.

The result, I hardly need add, was fantastic. Admittedly, the second half stank, but that was OK. We'd stormed to our 3–0 lead within 29 minutes.

So an exhilarating day all round – marred only by the fact that, moments before Paul Rogers opened the scoring, half my face fell out. Well, perhaps not quite, but I did lose an enormous chunk out of one of my teeth – which felt like pretty much the same thing. This wasn't the result of a fellow supporter failing to match my level of commitment to the stadium campaign, but, rather bizarrely, the consequence of chewing on a piece of gum. Wrigley's Orbit, if you must know – the brand that's sugar-free and therefore supposed to be good for your . . . well, I'm sure you're already chuckling at the irony. Ho ho.

This chunk of tooth – bottom row, right-hand side, halfway back, whatever that one's called – actually managed to crumble off and lodge itself directly into my Orbit, so the first I knew of the problem was when I encountered a slightly crunchier texture than I usually associate with this product, other than when I pop in some gum after eating a Snickers.

Obviously from a medical point of view, the only sensible option was to leave the ground at once and seek emergency dental treatment. After all, I could have been on the verge of a complete molar meltdown. By half-time, my entire mouth may have been awash with chunks of chipped tooth and dislodged fillings. And these things can have a knock-on effect, can't they? Next, I could have lost an ear, or stood helplessly as one of my eyeballs suddenly plopped out of its socket and started bouncing down the steps to the running track. Either way, my courageous plan to burst into song this afternoon was obviously going to have to be put on hold – what a shame – for fear of showering the people around me with fragments of fang. Zipping off to get immediate help had to be my priority.

I left the ground at 4.55 p.m.

NOTTS COUNTY 2 BRIGHTON 2
LEAGUE POSITION: 2ND

There are moments in life when a wave of creative inspiration can sweep over you so suddenly, so unexpectedly, so forcefully, that it leaves you gasping for breath. Exhilarating, electrifying, more than a little frightening, it's as if a mystical energy, a supreme force, way beyond your comprehension, is pulsating through your very being, powering you, urging you, ever onwards, ever upwards, towards the zenith of artistic self-expression.

And then there are times when you dream up shitty poems in the bath.

Tonight I found myself doing the latter, inspired partly by the impressive way the Albion had fought back this evening from 2–0 down (thanks to Hart and Zamora), but largely as yet another means of trying to make my presence felt within the club's inner sanctum. It may sound a barmy way to go about this, but don't forget that poetry has become central to Albion folklore, thanks to the way Attila, for God knows how many years, has used it as a means of chronicling the club's fortunes. And its misfortunes. You can buy his latest anthology in the Seagulls Shop, very reasonably priced at £3. All profits to the youth scheme.

So when my very own wave of poetic inspiration suddenly hit me this evening, I obviously had little choice but to succumb to it. And quickly, before it vanished down the plughole. I clambered out of the bath, towelled myself down, and ran to grab a pen and paper. Seemingly from nowhere, it had suddenly come to me: a poem about our stadium campaign (yes, I know – quite), complete with lots of handy rhyming bits. If this was how these things came to Attila himself, he must have permanently soggy carpets.

An hour later, I'd typed it up, tweaked it a little, and e-mailed all six verses to my fellow campaigners. I felt sure they'd understand. More optimistically, I suppose what I really wanted was for at least one of them, someone of influence, to be utterly bowled over, to consider my creation worthy of publication in Saturday's match programme, or maybe reading out over the PA system, somewhere between 'Babylon's Burning' and 'Peaches'.

So really I'm being horribly pushy. And manipulative. And cynical. The sentiments in this poem may be genuine, but it's also, let's face it, another cheap, calculated attempt to link my name with the Albion's, another way to convince myself, and others, that I belong. It's as if, by having a poem printed in the programme, or hearing it crackle over those cruddy speakers, I reckon I'll have sunk a few firmer roots.

Not that either of those things looks likely to happen. Skimming through this effort again now, I must admit that two obvious weaknesses occur to me. The first is its sheer blinding hypocrisy, given my Nouveau Seagull status. And the second? Well, just take a look:

FALMER FOR ALL

It sounds a tall order
A mighty big deal
But we're off on the road now
To making it real

A home fit for heroes
Sounds clichéd, I know
But it's not just the Seagulls
Who'll flourish and grow

Our town's now a city
With all that this means
With confidence, style
And a whole host of dreams

But dreams count for nothing
Without words and deeds
And this is our moment
To sow the next seeds

So put pen to paper now
Falmer For All
Where everyone wins
Where a city walks tall

It's your voice that matters
As loud as the last
Take pride in a future
As proud as our past

Our past?! Christ, I wish I hadn't sent this bloody thing now. I'm squirming.

That second weakness, as you'll have spotted, is that it reads like a greetings card message, albeit quite a long one. Da-diddly diddly diddly-dee. Da-diddly diddly diddly-dee. God almighty. When you care enough to send the frigging best, eh?

This isn't entirely surprising, mind you. For years, my parents ran their own card shop, a temple of tat which was stocked to the ceiling with exactly this kind of stuff (although admittedly very little of it related to football stadia). I grew up immersed in bad verse, some of it *so* bad that it's a miracle we were never raided by the Crap Poetry Police.

And yet I also found it strangely fascinating, probably in the same slightly twisted way that people like to take picnics to the scene of fatal road accidents. I was especially mesmerised by those verses – and there were hundreds of them – where the writer, while presumably still happy to pick up the pay cheque, clearly couldn't be arsed to do their job properly:

Congratulations! Raise a toast!
This is your happy day
May all your dreams come true, on this
Your burr-urrr-urrr-urth-day

Even back then, it struck me that if you were seriously thinking of buying anybody such a lazy, disinterested card, you may as well just send them a big sheet of paper saying, 'Fuck right off.' The message would amount to the same.

But obviously the influence has rubbed off on me. While some people, depending on their age, would cite, say, The Beatles, or The Clash, or Nirvana as having shaped their personalities from adolescence into adulthood, obviously my own artistic temperament has been moulded by a bunch of anonymous, ham-fisted, ditty-mongering hacks. Because, now I think about it, I could bash out this sort of shit almost on demand. Once I start, I can't stop. It just floods out. I mean, here you go, here's one I've just made up for a sympathy card:

I'm sad to hear your husband's dead
He was a quite good bloke

Still, never mind, he's buried now
So have a Diet Coke

See what I mean? I've been poisoned.

So, no, I don't think the Albion will be using my Falmer poem.

On the other hand, if Attila ever needs a couple of weeks off, I could always offer to step in as holiday cover. It's not as if I'd be a threat. I'd just be there in case something dramatic happened at the club while he was away, and an emergency poem needed to be rushed in at short notice.

I'm sure it must happen.

Highly Strung – SATURDAY 27 OCTOBER

BRIGHTON 1 COLCHESTER UNITED 0
LEAGUE POSITION: 2ND

She hasn't yet come out and voiced this directly, but I sense that Julie is beginning to lose patience with this whole Albion thing. Today, once again, I abandoned her just after midday so that I could arrive at the ground early, help set up a rickety table for the Falmer campaign and begin collecting more signatures. Julie, meanwhile, was at home cleaning the oven. I guess it's not exactly her idea of a soaraway Saturday.

Over breakfast, as we'd sat scoffing boiled eggs and Marmite-smeared bread (not cut into soldiers, mind), I'd tried to get her excited by showing her the fabulous new bargain clipboards I'd picked up at a local stationery shop for a mere £1.25 each, perfect for gathering signatures with the maximum of efficiency. Julie hadn't seemed interested. Nor had she shown much enthusiasm when I'd pointed out the bargain pack of ten ballpoints I'd managed to find for just 99p. As for the ball of string – can you believe this? – not so much as a flicker. Not even when I'd explained the ingenious thinking behind this purchase: namely, that it would stop the buggers fucking off with our pens.

I'd toyed with the idea of involving her in my last-minute preparations – say, by asking if she'd like to chop the string into the necessary lengths (40cm each), or tape a pen to one end of each chunk. But I'd decided against it. She hadn't seemed remotely interested in this campaigning business, full-stop. She'd just given me a succession of funny looks. Perhaps she was trying to decide whether to phone for the doctor.

It was either that or, entirely unrelated to anything of an Albion nature, she was just in a stinker of a mood. We did manage, quite impressively, to squeeze in three separate rows, all money-related, in the two hours before I had to leave the house today – the first stemming from her frustration (and I may be giving you a slightly biased picture here) that we couldn't afford some stupid, ugly, witchy-poo house she'd spotted in an estate agent's window; the second resulting from my reluctance, in stark contrast to hers, to spend as much on tarting up our bathroom as many Third Division clubs would spend on a new keeper; and the third because I told her I didn't want to take a week's holiday in April.

Actually, that holiday one wasn't really money-related at all. It was merely because the week which Julie had in mind was the week in which the Albion would be playing their last home game of the season, against Swindon Town. I thought it wisest not to admit this, though.

On the other hand, if they play like they did this afternoon than maybe seven days in Majorca will be the more tempting option. It really was dire. Zamora flicked one in from a free kick after 15 minutes, but for the rest of the match we played clown football, with only Kuipers keeping us ahead. Colchester's boss reckons his side deserved five. I reckon he's being harsh on them. Despite the win, I left in a lousy mood. Not as lousy as Julie's this morning, obviously, but lousier than a match has left me feeling for some while.

As predicted, the buggers didn't print my poem.

Van With Ample Legroom – TUESDAY 30 OCTOBER

BRIGHTON 2 WYCOMBE 1
(LDV VANS TROPHY, SOUTHERN SECTION, ROUND TWO)

I couldn't resist it. Twenty minutes in, I had to ring Andy on the mobile. 'Guess where I am!' I cried. Andy responded with a grunt of crushing indifference, almost as if to suggest, imagine this, that he'd rather I'd not interrupted *Holby City*. 'How the hell should I know?' he replied. 'Out with the dog?'

'Ha!' I exclaimed, chuffed to find him as hilariously wide of the mark as I'd hoped. 'Not even close.'

'Really,' he sighed.

'Yeah, really! I'm at Withdean!'

'Right.'

'And we're a quarter of the way through a game. Can you hear the crowd?'

'Nope.'

'Exactly! It's like a funeral.'

It was, too, albeit without an actual corpse. Barely half the regular number had turned out for this evening's game, leaving gaps so vast in the South Stand that I half expected to spot clumps of tumbleweed scuttling between the seats. Atmosphere-wise, it made the pre-season Sheffield United game feel like the UEFA Cup final.

Not that it didn't have its advantages. For one thing, I had so much room I could have stretched along the adjacent seats as if they were my sofa. And so flat was the game itself, initially at least, that this wouldn't have seemed an inappropriate thing to do. All I'd have lacked was the cushions and the box of Maltesers.

The LDV Vans Trophy is not a tournament to set the pulse racing. I'd sensed as much the first time around, after that 2–1 win at Swansea. But I had no idea that the degree of sheer couldn't-care-bloody-lessness was quite this extreme. Even the club itself seemed to have a take-it-or-shove-it attitude to the fixture. I could understand Peter Taylor's decision to rest a few senior players – Zamora being the most notable absentee – but when you turn up at a match and discover that the official programme, normally a pleasingly plump 48 pages, has shrunk to an anorexic eight (and they still expect a quid for it), you can't help but wonder why we're all bothering.

Except, of course, I had to. In my bid for credibility, it was arguably more important that I showed up for this utter turkey of a fixture than for any of the league games so far. It bolstered my claim to having become a truly committed Albion supporter. In fact, I even made a point of parking myself in my regular seat, when I could have chosen from thousands of vacant ones, many in far more favourable positions.

What I was really doing, patting myself smugly on the back in the process, was playing the loyalty card. And I know this for sure, because it wasn't just me who said it. The fact that the 3,000-or-so fans who bothered turning up tonight were the real hardcore faithful was also pointed out by Ian Hart on the radio commentary.

How do I know that? Because I was listening to it. Yep, during the actual game. Kind of strange, I know; I regularly jam in my earphones on the way to a match, but wearing them throughout most of the play was a definite first. Shortly after I'd called Andy – and, come to think of it, that was also the first time I'd made a telephone call during a game – I decided what this fixture urgently needed, short of an earthquake just big enough to give them an excuse to abandon it, was an extra human dimension. With none of my regular neighbours mouthing off around me, I felt lonely. I was missing that relentless, opinionated soundtrack I've come to take for granted. So on went the radio, in went the earphones, and suddenly I was experiencing this match from a completely fresh perspective. No need to squint to see who was getting yellow-carded on the far side of the pitch. No need to query who'd scored – or, more likely tonight, who had catapulted the ball 50 yards over the bar. No need to crane my neck to appreciate the bit where the linesman was sent crashing hilariously into the running track following a collision with a Wycombe attacker. All the hard work was being done for me. It was like watching on TV.

Like watching on TV, that is, on a night when I've left all my windows open, sending the temperature in my lounge plunging to about minus 40. Boy, was it cold tonight. And, boy, had I stupidly turned up in just a T-shirt and denim jacket. Well, that and some trousers.

The trouble is, when you treat yourself to £9.99 worth of Bobby Zamora T-shirt – navy blue, with a giant 'Z' dramatically slashed across the front in Zorroesque fashion – then you're bound to want to show the damn thing off. Unfortunately, I hadn't paid much attention to the weather forecast – I never do – so I hadn't considered how hopelessly unprotected this get-up would leave me. Not that it took me long to find out. Without the natural wall of insulation normally provided by the mass of fans squashed in all around me, I soon began to shiver. This wasn't turning out to be the most enjoyable of nights.

At the campaign table, business had been sluggish. One fan had tried to engage me in small-talk as he flicked through the apology of a programme. 'Nice to see we've got one of our ex-players refereeing tonight!' he'd quipped, pointing to a 'Paul Armstrong' heading the list of officials. 'Hahahahahahahahahaha!!!!!!!' I'd exclaimed, with exaggerated mirth, thinking: 'What the frigging hell's he on about?' I'd assumed there must have been a Paul Armstrong who'd once played for the Albion, but obviously I hadn't asked for confirmation of this. Likewise, when this same guy had made a joke about the excessive amount of steam rising from one of the nearby burger vans, comparing it to some apparently hilarious steam-related incident at a Third Division stadium last season, I'd forced myself to chortle accordingly. I'd felt like one of those prisoners of war who headed for the Swiss border at the end of *The Great Escape*, agonisingly aware that the tiniest slip-up would instantly blow his cover.

Mind you, I was sorely tempted to tunnel out of Withdean by the time we reached the 45th minute. By now almost rigid with cold, and having made a mental note to alert the club statistician first thing tomorrow, to update his entry for Biggest Fucking Waste Of A Tuesday Night, I seriously toyed with the idea of calling it quits.

And then we scored, and everything changed.

The second half was hardly football nirvana, but suddenly we were heading for a win. It would be a win, I grant you, in a tournament which I'd insisted I didn't care about, but one which, I now realised, would have a certain cachet: it would mean we were in the quarter-finals, which always sounds nice. Admittedly these would only be the *southern-section* quarter-finals, with as many teams still surviving in the north, but it still implied significant progress. It sounded good. Nationally, we'd be in the last sixteen, three wins away from a trip to the Millennium Stadium for the final.

I'd warmed up a little now. It sounded as if the other fans had, too. The game had a focus.

And then, bugger and shit, it had another goal – a Wycombe equaliser, courtesy of a Nathan Jones Cock-Up™. And that's the way it stayed until the 90 minutes were up. Which meant we were looking at extra-time. Which meant, even worse, that we were looking at a Golden Goal fiasco. Who Scores Wins.

It was so nearly Wycombe, who launched an attack right from kick-off, as if their coach driver had refused to hang around beyond quarter to ten and they'd all have to hitch back. But Kuipers chose this moment, bless his wooden clogs, to pull off his most spectacular save so far this season.

Seconds later, the ball was down the opposite end. My end. At the feet of Steve Melton. And Steve was obviously longing for his cocoa, because he didn't hang about. Whoooomph! Straight past the keeper. We were through. Hypothermic, but through.

So that made it three firsts tonight: the first time I'd made a phone call during a game, the first time I'd listened to a match's live commentary while watching it at the ground, and the first time a Golden Goal had gone in favour of a team I was actually supporting. So not such a shite night, I suppose.

Come to think of it, make that four firsts. It was also the first time I'd felt excited about a tournament with a mode of transport in its title.

I might give Andy another ring.

BRISTOL CITY 0 BRIGHTON 1
LEAGUE POSITION: 2ND

It's vaguely ironic, I suppose, but I actually hate seagulls. It beats me how anyone can find the squawking, scavenging bastards even remotely cute. Seagulls are filthy, vicious, thieving bastards. Don't let anyone tell you otherwise.

A few months back, I was treating myself to a late breakfast on the sun-drenched terrace of a Brighton café – just me, the morning papers and an ill-advised full-English – when one of these little buggers swooped down, paused momentarily to look me straight in the eye (seagull body language, I assume, for, 'Wanna make something of it, pal?'), snatched the buttered toast from my side-plate and soared off. I say 'little' buggers; up close, the average seagull is, in fact, alarmingly huge. It was a bit like glancing up from last night's match report to discover that, say, an Alsatian has just landed on your breakfast table. An Alsatian with an extremely large wingspan, I grant you. And, OK, a beak. And feathers. Anyway, look, my point is, you wouldn't argue with one of these things. Or if you did, it would only be the once.

Yet I suppose I'd miss them if they weren't here. In their rightful place – over the actual sea, several hundred feet up, safely out of toast-thieving distance – they're welcome to squawk to their hearts' content. Seagulls are, after all, an integral part of the traditional Brighton picture, up there with the pebbly beach, the Pavilion and the 1.5 piers. This is, of course, the touristy picture; as with any city, the day-to-day image of Brighton conjured up in the minds of people who actually live here is a less romantic one, more likely to feature the towaway squad or someone slumped by a cashpoint, asking if you can spare any change (here's a tip, by the way, for anyone who does that: cashpoints give out *banknotes*, not change. If it's change you're after, hang around the pay-and-display in the NCP).

Sometimes, mind you, we all like to be tourists, even if we're here the whole time. Now and then, I like to amble down to the shore just to remind myself why, for all its faults, I love this place. So that's exactly what I did this afternoon. I went down to the seafront. I *ambled* there.

I thought it might be a good way to cope with the tension of the match commentary. I thought right. A perfect autumn's afternoon, the beach just busy enough to give it a buzz, moist pebbles crunching beneath my leaky Doc Martens, the sky almost cloudless, the light casting its delicious caramel glow across the peeling seafront buildings (shall I carry on like this, or would you like to slap me right now?), it helped me put the whole thing into a suitably chilled perspective.

It was almost better than being at Bristol City.

Because, seriously, I do love this place. It's my home. My adopted home, admittedly, but more of a home than anywhere else has ever been, or ever will be. I never want to leave.

So maybe that's one of the things which is helping me learn to love the Albion. The fact that it's the natural, obvious thing to do, that it's part of the same package. When the Albion win, it's about more than just some soppy position on a league table. It's a home win in a far bigger sense.

As the whistle blew, I was gazing way out to sea, thinking of nothing in particular but feeling remarkably good about it. My shoes were sopping by now. I'd drifted too close to the edge. If I'd thought about it I'd have taken them off and walked barefoot instead, letting the gently foaming water trickle across my toes.

Sorry, I'm off again.

For Robert – FRIDAY 9 NOVEMBER

BRIGHTON FANS 4 CRYSTAL PALACE FANS 4 (I think)

When tragedy can turn to comedy you sense there's still hope.

I turned up tonight, along with several hundred others, to celebrate the life of Robert Eaton, the Albion supporter killed in the 11 September terrorist attack on New York. I left with a £30 voucher for Rug World in Hove, 13th prize in the half-time raffle. I hope Robert would have found that at least slightly hilarious. I know I did.

The setting for tonight's charity kickabout, raising funds for a footie school for New York youngsters, wasn't Withdean but Southwick FC, a lower league set-up about five miles up the road. The weather was bitter, the tea bar doing a roaring trade. The cheeseburgers were £1.50 each, and surprisingly tasty. The chips, 80p a cone, were crisp if a wee bit oily. I was in my element.

Or, strictly speaking, other people's. So far I've been thinking of Withdean, with its temporary stands, its hotchpotch of Portakabins and its capacity of under 7,000, as the real grass-roots stuff. It isn't, of course. It's not even close. The likes of Southwick FC, tucked away on a '60s housing estate and with only one small section under tinny cover, *that's* grass-roots stuff. It was fun tonight, but I couldn't stomach it every week.

The strips were familiar, as were the chants: 'We hate Pal-iss and we hate Pal-iss,' even on a night like this, when they'd come down to do us a favour. But if ever you wanted an illustration of how lean and fit and sharp the typical professional footballer has to be, even in Nationwide Division Two, here you had it in abundance. There was lots of running, some not-bad little touches and flicks, but even a complete outsider could have twigged, from one glance at these guys, that they weren't real footballers. Some were too slight, scrawny even; others, though significantly trimmer then I've personally been since the middle of the last decade, carried far too much flab for athletic purposes. The strips hung loosely or clung accordingly.

The raffle tickets cost £2 for a strip of five, and for some reason I had a good feeling about the numbers I bought: 46 to 50 on the orange. I'd no idea how many of these things the organisers had sold, but I was careful to note which of my countless stupid pockets I was stuffing these tickets into. I had this weird hunch I'd be needing them later.

Which is bloody typical really. I have Premium Bonds, I buy lottery tickets, I do the pools each week, I ring our local radio station on a regular basis, coughing up 50p a time to register for the chance to play their Name Game – identify a mystery voice and win thousands – and never have I scooped so much as a penny. Not from any of these things. I've always consoled myself with the thought that, sooner or later, everyone gets that lucky winning break if they keep plugging away, that the moment eventually arrives when some sort of prize comes everybody's way. So, great, when it finally *is* my turn, when my share of good fortune *does* come along, it goes and happens in a flaming local raffle, where the top prize – and I'm not making this up, I promise – is a weekend for two at a hotel in East Grinstead. (For two what, I wonder? Masochists?)

I don't know if Peter Taylor bought a ticket, but apparently he was there tonight, in the exclusive club officials' bar to which the rest of us weren't allowed access. Through its steamy window, I was able to make out the unmistakeable balding head and goatee of Albion chairman Dick Knight, gabbing away to God knows who. I also spotted the woman who presents the local BBC radio breakfast show. I didn't spot any real players, but I guess they were getting an early night. Tomorrow is a big day, at home to Port

Vale. If things go our way, we could go top again.

I also bumped into the man with the giant eyebrows, who I now know fairly well and actually have a heap of respect for. Paul Samrah, who chairs our Falmer For All group, was sporting a less than fetching brown cloth cap, as if he'd dashed straight here from a mid-'50s Accrington Stanley match. 'Hello, Mark!' he called, from behind a cloud of what smelt like Bovril steam. I'd obviously made an impression.

I was too cold to make conversation, however, other than a feeble, 'Nippy, isn't it?' Paul seemed to feel likewise. 'All ready for the morning?' was pretty much the extent of it. I told him I was, that I'd be there, on the dot of nine, at Hove Town Hall, £1.25 clipboard in hand, for our stadium committee brainstorming meeting.

With this in mind, I didn't hang around after tonight's final whistle, despite the promise of a bar remaining open till 11. I fancied an early night. I'd paid my entrance fee (£2), bought the raffle tickets, even donated £25 to sponsor one of the matchballs, though I dare say it was the one which, in the 23rd minute, flew out of the ground and bounced to oblivion down Old Barn Way. Conscience-wise, I'd ticked off all the boxes.

Before heading back to the car, though, I had to go and fetch my lovely prize. And that's when I learned the astonishing news: it turned out I hadn't won a raffle prize at all. I'd won two. My orange number 46 had also come up trumps: I'd won a pair of day-members' passes for Plumpton Racecourse. I was positively reeling.

Being the sort of night it was, when the good cause was central to the whole exercise, I realised I should hand one of these prizes back, allowing them to raise even more cash by raffling it for a second time.

Then I thought, naah, fuck it. It's years since I've been to the races.

And I quite fancy a jazzy little Persian weave to slip under the coffee table. Who wouldn't?

One Man's Meet – SATURDAY 10 NOVEMBER

BRIGHTON 1 PORT VALE 0
LEAGUE POSITION: 1ST

Marbles muesli washboard watermelon Dale Winton. I was scribbling down any old bollocks, just to make it look as if I was taking notes.

Hat-wise, it's a fashion free-for-all at the
Albion's victory parade, Saturday, 27 April 2002.

Victory parade, Saturday, 27 April 2002. It's a bit hard to make out, but the lady pictured below is wearing a seagull hair clip. I forgot to ask her where you can buy them.

Fans at the Albion victory parade, Saturday, 27 April 2002. That isn't the real trophy in the picture above, by the way. It's just a foil.

The two Liz's, both lifelong Albion nuts. Below is fan club superwoman Liz Costa. Right, reading *The Argus* in that totally unconvincing way people do when they're posing for photos, is Liz 'The Trumpet' Fleet.

Adrian 'Ground Tour' Newnham (above) and fan club chairman Tim Carder, pictured at Withdean, Saturday, 13 April 2002. Minutes earlier, the Albion had clinched the Division Two title. You'll notice they look quite pleased.

Fans invade the Withdean pitch to celebrate the Albion's title win, Saturday, 13 April 2002. A fortnight later, at the victory festivities, Attila (below) is delivering another of his poems to mark the achievement.

Above: These pro-stadium lapel badges were all my own idea. I knew you'd be impressed.
Below: Our campaign banner spells out its message clearly enough, despite a slogan which sounds as though it's been translated from Korean.

Above: Lee Steele lifts the Division Two trophy at the Albion's victory parade, Saturday, 27 April 2002, while Richard 'Jurgen' Carpenter looks on. Below: With the festivities over, the players seem unsure what to do next to entertain the crowd. Kerry Mayo, far right, has one idea.

I'm not good at sitting in meetings. I never have been. Intense expressions, metaphorical flagpoles, 'windows', 'loops'. I'm either bored senseless or struggling not to laugh. But it was years since I'd had to sit in one like this, so I'd forgotten.

Look, I'm totally behind this stadium campaign, I really am. I've been manning those tables at each match, badgering fans (and non-Albion-supporting friends) for signatures, e-mailing my half-baked ideas to fellow committee members. I mean, come on, it was me who came up with that inspired clipboard idea. And the poem. This week I even sent a letter to the *Argus*, our local paper, responding to some ill-informed anti-stadium piece of correspondence they'd published the previous day. I do feel I've been doing my bit. Or a bit of my bit.

But brainstorming sessions? They're really not me. I'm afraid. My brain just flatly refuses to be stormed. I said virtually nothing today. Yep, again. Considering we were there for well over three hours this time, as opposed to two, I felt exactly half as bad again as I did the first time.

Sitting next to me for a lengthy chunk of the proceedings was a guy called Steve Bassam – or Lord Bassam, as I believe he's officially known these days. Steve – I'll call him that today as it's a Saturday and he was wearing a leather jacket – obviously felt in his element, being a councilly-type person through and through. 'Yes, yes,' he kept mumbling, whenever he heard a suggestion he liked the sound of. 'Good idea,' he'd go. Which was fine, except I couldn't help wondering whose benefit his mumbles were for. The layout of the council chamber – and I think we'd been given use of the main bit, by the look of it – was such that, without the microphones switched on, he couldn't possibly be heard by anyone except me, sitting right beside him at the back. And since he didn't actually converse with me directly at any stage, I don't think he was specifically intending his mumbles for my ears. So presumably this is just what you're meant to do on these occasions. That and some nodding.

Actually, nodding makes slightly more sense, because at least people can see you doing it, even from the far side of the room. It's a way of indicating, as far as I can establish, that you're a Serious Person giving Serious Thought to Serious Issues. It gives you an aura of earnestness, implying that you're making a valid contribution, if only by visibly agreeing with what someone else has just said.

But I just couldn't do it. With respect to all these genuinely decent people, it looked silly.

Just as I do at the matches, I felt an uncomfortable detachment. All I could do was sit and watch, registering not so much what people said and did but how they said and did it. A part of me – a huge, aching part of me – longed to be able mentally to muck in, to thrust my hand in the air, to offer some valid point about the campaign, about this or that tactic or detail, not to give a damn if I was shouted down or contradicted, not to worry what the seasoned campaigners might think of this clueless wassock. I just wanted to join in. But I couldn't. I'd brought my clipboard, even inserted a fresh pad of paper, as if preparing to make tons of notes, but I knew from the start that even if I did write down anything of significance I'd never actually look at it again.

Paul Samrah, in the chair, seemed very much into Doing Things Professionally. He did it as if it was the natural thing to do, as if there was nothing remotely absurd about it; I could only admire him for that. People like Paul are why campaigns like this one succeed. I gather he's an accountant, which would explain a lot: his comfort with the overhead projector and the flip charts, his enthusiasm for splitting us into little groups midway through the morning, then getting us to report back later with our fresh ideas.

My ineptitude, my total unsuitability for procedures like these, was best illustrated when we were sent away to our various different rooms for these mid-morning sessions. For starters, I got lost. Physically, first of all, then mentally. My group, I'd been told, was going to gather in Committee Room One, but while I'd been hanging back in the main chamber, just so as to grab a quick coffee and a sticky bun, the rest of my bunch had buggered off. It was obvious that I was one of the few people completely unfamiliar with the layout of this place, and I spent the next ten minutes wandering up and down its coldly municipal corridors, wondering where in hell's name I was supposed to be going – the only amusing consolation being that I bumped into an equally baffled-looking Dick Knight along the way. With spectacular dumbness, I managed to stumble into the rooms being used by each of our other four specialist sub-groups (Communication, Events, Council, Student Liaison) before stumbling upon the one assigned to my own. Paul had put me in a group headed 'Role-play and Businesses'. Bless him, but fuck knows why he'd done that.

What made the next hour even more dispiriting is that my group was being chaired by Martin Perry, Albion's chief executive. Now, I like Martin a lot, not least because he frequently likes to butt in with the odd attempt at a gag to break the ice, but here I found his presence daunting. 'I could play the role of someone who doesn't know what the hell this is all about,' I suggested to him, as, somewhat breathless, I finally tumbled in and took my seat. He looked at me as if he'd been saddled with Sam Dingle, the village idiot from *Emmerdale*.

The thing is, I wasn't kidding. The more this meeting had gone on, the more depressingly bewildered I'd become. Obviously I knew the basic idea: there were two possible sites for the Albion's new stadium – one at a place called Village Way North, the other at a place called Village Way South – for either of which a whole load of persuading would need to be done. Councillors, especially the dozen who made up the planning committee, would need convincing. The arguments of the anti brigade would also have to be addressed. There'd probably be a public inquiry, too. I didn't doubt that the bulk of the people here were well clued-up, knew the case thoroughly and, kind of importantly, believed in it with all their hearts. But until I could match their clued-upness – and they'd had a good couple of years head start, this lot – I couldn't see how I had the right even to open my mouth. There was nothing I could suggest to the likes of Martin, in particular, which he surely wouldn't have heard a zillion times before.

Or was it just my typical over-cautiousness? I can remember being like this when I first went to stay with a family in France, aged 17, on a school exchange trip, the purpose of which had been to brush up on my French conversational skills. Instead of just trying my luck with words and phrases, loosening up, seeing how I got on, I'd pretty much verbally frozen for a fortnight. I'd been so afraid of getting it wrong – of wanting to say, perhaps, 'May I have another slice of cake, please?' but instead coming out with, 'Your mother has the face of a baboon' – that I'd finished up saying more or less nothing. I hadn't wanted to make a fool of myself, so I'd opted to stay virtually silent. Yep, for *two weeks.* I'd figured it was safer that way.

You'd think, a quarter of a century on, that I'd have evolved at least a little as far as conversational risks were concerned. Judging from today, I've gone backwards. But it doesn't deserve sympathy, this state of mind. It deserves a punch. How fucking arrogant, to act as if my utterances are *that* significant, to assume that those around me would want to dissect them in microscopic detail.

I slipped out into the November sunshine feeling mildly depressed. Fuck me, what was all that about? It had all felt so complex, so grown-up, so flipchart-clipboard-nod-and-mumbly. I didn't understand the rules, or didn't want to. It was chess, whereas, me, I'm more of a snakes-and-ladders man. I realised I'd reached my limit, that I was never going to play an influential role in this thing. I'd still play my part, of course I would, but three or four years from now, when, fingers crossed, this stopped being a stadium campaign and became a stadium for real, I wouldn't be the one who'd made the difference. Not even close. More likely, I'd be the one who'd made the sandwiches.

The town hall clock was showing half past 12. Surprisingly, so was my watch, give or take five minutes. In little more than an hour I'd need to be at the ground – not to collect signatures this time, but to help dish out a fresh set of leaflets. These would explain to fans that they now needed to write to the council in their own words, not once but twice, in support of each planning application. Lucky them.

I was told that, as before, there'd be a pass for me at Gate 21. A couple of weeks back I'd have felt dead excited about that. Today I felt numb.

I headed home, made myself a coffee, flicked on Sky Sports. It was showing Dagenham and Redbridge versus Northwich Victoria, in the Who-Gives-A-Flying-Fuck League. I watched it till the end, not because I had the slightest interest but because I didn't want to be at Withdean dishing out leaflets. Not today. I was Falmered out.

By the time I reached the ground it was 2.20 p.m. Head bowed, collar upturned, I took a shifty, circuitous route through the crowd, keen to avoid my fellow campaign members, half a dozen of whom were milling around, thrusting these green sheets into supporters' hands. Mine was a cowardly strategy, but it worked. I managed to sneak through unnoticed and, with over half an hour still to go before kick off, decided to take a lazy walk along the athletics track in front of the South Stand, as far as the stewards will let you. A clutch of kids had brought a tennis ball and were having a kickabout in front of block F. They looked as if they were looking forward to the match. I wanted to do that, too. Just enjoy the game.

By five o'clock my wish had been granted, if not in spectacular style. Bobby's glancing header in the 49th minute was apparently his 50th goal for the club, but what mattered more was that it had taken us back to the top. Brentford had lost 3–2 at Stoke, so we'd leapfrogged them.

Up at Old Trafford, meanwhile, England had drawn 1–1 with Sweden in a traditionally pointless friendly. Given its insignificance, I'd been happy to miss the live TV coverage of this match, but Emily had been there in person, taken up to Manchester as part of a birthday treat for her cousin, Oliver. Gloriously for her, Becks had scored a first-half penalty. Better still, he'd scored it at the end where she was sitting. She'd been ecstatic. I envied her.

BRIGHTON 1 SHREWSBURY TOWN 0
(FA CUP FIRST ROUND)

By the time Bobby stepped in to join us, he already had his coat on. He'd done his job for the day – scored the first-half goal which, despite another scrappily unconvincing performance, had put us through to the second round of the cup – and he looked like a bloke who wasn't planning to mingle for too long. Just long enough, it seemed, to satisfy the bunch from Barclays Bank plc, today's match sponsors, plus an assortment of individuals who, for one reason or another, had been granted one-day-only permission to taste this smoky, lagery fug of post-match hospitality. Mascots, mascots' mummies, people like that. Plus Liz.

A few hands shaken, a few smiles smiled, a few polite words exchanged. 'How's the leg, Bobby?' 'Leg OK, is it, Bobby?' 'Hey, Bobby, what happened to your leg?' 'Hello, Bobby, I have nothing of the remotest consequence to say to you but I rather like the sound of my own voice.' The inevitable series of photographs, rattling through all the permutations of people who'd either purchased or earned the right to be pictured with the man himself – swift, functional, adequate. A succession of wonky grins.

And then it was Liz's turn.

Liz stepped forward and pecked Bobby coyly on the cheek. Bobby returned the favour. She looked quite excited. But only quite.

The trouble was, it hadn't been Bobby she'd wanted. Liz had wanted Gary Hart – loyal, hardworking Essex boy, number nine, prone to occasional flashes of brilliance, signed from Stansted in 1998. She'd even turned up with her picture of him, temporarily taken down from her bedroom wall. (She's 32, but who am I to pass judgement?) For safe keeping, Liz had put this photo – an A4 action shot, purchased from the official website for £9.99, featuring Gary in the black-and-red-striped away kit – inside her Albion centenary book, itself wrapped inside a polythene bag, ready to whip out for her hero to sign. But Gary, we were then told, wasn't in today. Sorry, he'd got the flu.

So she'd have to make do with the superstar.

Even so, Liz seemed pleased that I'd helped fix up this fleeting encounter. It had been Emily's suggestion, actually – a way of cheering Liz up after an operation which had forced her to miss the last five home fixtures. It had also presented me with a fine opportunity to go, 'Yeah, no problem, leave it to me,' as if, within three months, I'd developed some sort of smug special relationship, a unique bond, a formidable influence within the upper echelons of Brighton and Hove Albion FC, allowing me, casually and effortlessly, to pull whatever strings needed pulling. In short, I was showing off. What an absolute prick.

All it had really taken, in truth, was an e-mail to the Albion's commercial manager, the almost very famously named Kevin Keehan, mentioning two vital chunks of information: firstly, the fact that Liz had been a season ticket-holder for years, was the person who'd been invited onto the pitch to parp the 'Last Post' before the final game at the Goldstone, and therefore richly deserved some sort of post-operative boost (implying, 'Unless you want to look like ungrateful shits . . .'). And secondly, that, hey, I'm on the stadium committee, me, so this isn't just any old bloke you're dealing with. What an absolute arsehole.

It had actually been a cinch to arrange. Kevin had kindly agreed to it without hesitation. But I wasn't going to tell Liz that. I'd wanted her, a proper Albion fan for more than 20 years, to be impressed by what I'd done. What an absolute tit and three-quarters.

Bobby draped his right arm around Liz's shoulder, pulling the necessary face at the camera. Liz swivelled round to do likewise, slightly less comfortably. She still had her Albion scarf on. Bobby's coat, no doubt cripplingly expensive and chic, reminded me of school, of the drab navy regulation mac we were obliged to wear each winter. The big fat knot in his shiny blue tie took me back to the same era, the way it left the tip sitting about six inches above his navel.

Flashety-click. Flashety-click. And one for luck.

Customer seemingly satisfied, Bobby gave a half-smile. 'I have to shoot now,' he announced. 'Well,' I piped up from the wings, 'that's your job, mate!' He can't have heard me, though, because he didn't collapse in hysterics.

'Sorry it was over so quick,' I commented to Liz as we nudged and excused our way towards a couple of vacant seats in the corner. It was a line I hadn't spoken to any woman except my wife for 15 years. 'That's OK,' Liz replied, thankfully choosing to ignore my unintentional double entendre. 'It was really exciting!' I think she meant it, too.

We were having to hang around for another half-hour or so. Kevin had told us the picture, snapped on a digital camera, would be printed more or less at once, in the office out the back, ready for Liz to take home. While we waited, I nipped up to the bar and bought us a couple of bottles of Becks. Peter Taylor was stood there, already swigging from his own, but I couldn't think of anything to say to him. It struck me he looked a bit lonely, not quite fully a part of things, but it hardly seemed the moment for a total stranger to butt in and ask him if he'd had a bust-up with Bob, or if he was missing Leicester, or if, just out of curiosity, pardon me for asking, he happened to be wearing slime-green towelling underpants. I wasn't even sure whether to ask him for an autograph. Was I allowed to? I'd not seen anyone else in here doing it, not even with Bobby, so I figured that perhaps, without prior arrangement, it was against hospitality-hut etiquette.

Through the fumes I spotted Dick Knight and Martin Perry. I hoped one of them might smile in my direction, acknowledge my presence, possibly even pop over to say hello. Liz would have been *so* impressed by that. But they ended up going over and talking to some big, crop-headed bloke who kept banging his beer bottle on the table, as if demanding silence for the Best Man. Lee Steele – the closest we'd got to that role, after being voted Man Of The Match (against his former club, too) – wandered in next, and he, too, went straight across and started chatting to this bloke. For some crazy, arrogant, screwed-up reason, I found myself feeling a bit jealous. Everyone seemed to be smiling at the fat guy. Laughing and joking, all pally. I concluded that appearances really were deceptive, that whoever this bloke was, he was obviously a profoundly respected figure, even though, from looks alone, you might mistake him for the sort of football supporter you traditionally see being tear-gassed by Belgian riot police. Either that or, who knows, maybe they just liked the guy. I dare say he was perfectly charming once you got to know him, and provided he wasn't sitting on you at the time.

Liz and I sipped our beers in relative silence and gawped vacantly at the wall-mounted TV, muted since *Grandstand* had finished. By the time Kevin re-emerged from the office, photograph in hand, a special celebrity edition of *Friends Like These* was silently underway – presented by ex-Arsenal and England hero Ian Wrong, and featuring teams from *Ready Steady Cook* and *Changing Rooms*. Carol Smillie was doing something strange with a basketball.

Kevin, we then noticed, wasn't just clutching a photograph – he was clutching a *framed* photograph. A proper A4 thing. I was impressed. What a nice touch. The little extra which shows you really care. He edged towards our table, then took a last-minute left-turn and handed the picture to some guy at the bar.

Five minutes later he came back with Liz's – standard sized, unframed, slightly curled. Bobby's eyes were half shut, making him look as if he'd just been coshed. We said our thank-yous very politely, keen to convey our gratitude.

I asked Kevin if we could maybe leave him with Liz's picture of Gary, ready for the flu victim to sign once his prescription-strength Lemsip had kicked in. Kevin had a better idea. 'Why don't we do this again when he's better?' he said. 'Then you can come and meet him after all.'

Nice touch, I thought. Liz almost bit his hand off.

Back home I couldn't wait to tell Julie about our little adventure. She seemed in a good mood, too. 'Arsenal drew 1–1,' she told me. 'I know,' I replied. 'Guess what! Liz has just met Bobby Zamora!'

Julie smiled indulgently and planted a welcome-home kiss on my lips. Then she reeled back, her face crumpled in distaste.

'Uggggh!' she cried. 'You've been smoking.'

Smoke Detector – WEDNESDAY 21 NOVEMBER

BRIGHTON 1 PETERBOROUGH 1
LEAGUE POSITION: 1ST

'I see you've started smoking again.'

Andy was clearly gunning for maximum points in the observation round.

'Oh, God,' I groaned. 'Don't you start.'

'I won't,' he promised. 'I'm just surprised, that's all. What's brought this on?'

I suppose it was a reasonable enough question. 'I haven't a clue, to be honest,' I told him. 'It just seemed to happen.'

Andy didn't seem wholly convinced by this.

'What, you mean you just woke up one morning and there was a Marlboro Light already smouldering away between your lips? Blimey, that could have been pretty hazardous. You wanna watch that.'

'Yeah, yeah, OK. But you know what I mean. It seemed like an obvious thing to do. A sort of natural evolution, after getting back into the other parts of the matchday routine. You know: stroll to ground, buy programme, shove nasty burger in gob, smoke fag.'

'So it's only on matchdays then?'

'Well, yeah. It was.'

'Was?'

'Well, you know how it is . . .'

'Nope.'

' . . . the way you tell yourself you'll only have the odd one . . .'

'Which, granted, you probably needed tonight, seeing as I gather they were a dollop of steaming shite.'

' . . . and then it kind of . . . develops.'

'Go on.'

'Well, say I've bought a packet of ten . . .'

'Oooh, you devil, you.'

' . . . and I have a couple before the match, two or three during, a couple more after. It means when I wake the next morning I've still got three or four left. And it seems a pity to waste them, so I think, right, I'll just have one of these with my coffee – and then, perhaps an hour later I'll think . . .'

'That you might as well puff your way through the rest?'

'So then it gets to lunchtime, and I've smoked the three I had left, but by then it's effectively become A Day When I'm Smoking – I'm into the swing of it – so I go and buy some more. And that's pretty much all it takes. I'm suddenly back into the habit again. I'm lighting up regularly throughout the day. And do you know what's really annoying and stupid?'

'No idea. The new series of *You've Been Framed*, with Lisa Riley?'

'No.'

'*No?*'

'Well, yes – obviously that's annoying and stupid, too. But what annoys me with the fags is that I don't even enjoy them.'

I stubbed out my latest, still only burnt halfway down, as if to emphasise my point.

'Really? What, not at all?'

'I don't think so, no.'

'You don't *think* so? What the hell's that supposed to mean?'

'Oh, I don't know. I suppose once or twice I've had a fag and it's just momentarily hit the spot, triggered some chemical release in the brain which made me feel pleasantly relaxed for a few seconds. And all the rest – 99 out of every 100 probably – have just been a doomed attempt to get that same effect back.'

'And I take it they don't?'

'You've never smoked, have you? Trust me, mate, they don't. Not if you're anything like me. You just keep lighting up in the hope that one of them will do the job, but it's almost certain it won't.'

'So what effect *do* you get?'

'Sickness, basically.'

'Sickness?'

'And queasiness.'

'Oh, right. Well, I can see why you've got back into the habit again. You make it sound *so* appealing. And how has Julie taken all this?'

'Well, she didn't really know until Saturday. When I got back from the Shrewsbury game. I'd had a few with Liz in hospitality afterwards . . .'

'Oooooooh, get him!'

' . . . oh, fuck off. And, anyway, Julie smelt them on my breath when I got in.'

'Oh, dear. Not best pleased, then?'

'Not exactly. And what's even more embarrassing is that she sussed my gum trick too.'

'Your gum trick? Why, what have you learned to do with your gums?'

'*Gum*, not gums, you prat. As in chewing gum. She twigged that I'd shoved my gob full of Wrigley's Orbit to try and hide the smell.'

'Oh, you sad prat. What are you – 14 years old?'

'I know, I know. Mind you, it's actually even sadder than that. I even use the gum to try and get the smell off my fingers.'

'Er, dare I ask how?'

'Well, what I do is, just after I've shoved a couple of fresh pieces in my mouth – it always has to be two at a time, by the way – I stick the two fag-holding fingers of my right hand in there too . . .'

'Oh, tasty.'

' . . . and then I sort of rub the gum along them with my tongue, so they get coated in the minty flavouring. Isn't that ridiculous?'

'And does it work?'

'It usually seems to, yeah. The only problem is, those fingers are then left all horrible and sticky, with bits of semi-chewed gum all over them.'

Andy began to look ever so slightly sick. 'You know, Mike,' he said. 'I think I preferred it when we talked about your urine.'

SWINDON TOWN 1 BRIGHTON 1
LEAGUE POSITION: 1ST

How the pigging hell was I supposed to know the way to Muswell Hill? I'm hopeless with directions. Julie knows that. Directions stink. They bore the pants off me. Optimum route between one place and another? Couldn't give a stuff. We'll get there in the end. We always do. And we rarely travel more than 400 miles out of our way.

Besides, angrily chucking her A–Z into my lap wasn't really going to help us much. Not this afternoon.

'It's either Woodgrove or Woodside,' I explained, flicking to the index and running a forlorn finger down the Ws. 'Woodgrove Drive,' I think. 'Or Woodside Avenue.'

'You think?'

'No, I'm sure it is. One of those two.'

Julie turned a funny colour. 'You're telling me you don't even know their fucking address?'

I was telling her I didn't even know their fucking address.

Or rather I wasn't. Not directly. But that's what I meant. This was the first time we'd visited these friends of ours, Nick and Karen, since they'd moved to this new place – and, yes, OK, I suppose, on reflection, it might have come in handy if I'd scribbled down a note of where they actually lived.

'Why don't you just put that fucking phone down, Mike, and concentrate?'

With my usual ear for subtle detail, I happened to notice that Julie was saying 'fuck' quite a lot. This usually means she's a bit cross. In this instance, I think she was a bit cross because, in the absence of a Five Live update on the radio, I'd spent the last ten minutes fiddling around trying to get the Albion score on my WAP phone.

But I also think there could have been more to it – that Julie's display of anger was just the latest symptom of what's become a more worrying problem. I think, on reflection, that I was wrong to suggest she dislikes all this

Albion stuff. I don't think she does. I think she hates it. I don't want to give the impression that we spend all our time bickering – we really don't, we love each other to bits – but last night we had another billy-belter of a barney, this time over the amount of time I've started dedicating to club-related activities. 'You never told me it would be like this,' she complained. And she was right: I hadn't. Although, in my defence, nor had I told her it wouldn't.

Having to leave so early for matches was bad enough. Having to attend these stadium campaign meetings, even if only in a metaphorical sandwich-boy role, didn't help either. But in the week ahead, I told her, I was going to be out three nights, all on stuff connected with Brighton and Hove Albion. Monday was the official campaign launch at Hove Town Hall. (Big one, that: Des might be there.) Wednesday was a meeting of our media committee (just six of us, I think, and probably no celebs) at Adrian's house in Shoreham.

And then there was next Saturday.

Next Saturday will be my very first Albion away match. And for reasons which now escape me, I've gone and picked the game at Bury. I mean no disrespect to Bury itself; it's just the small matter of where it happens to be, map-wise, in relation to where I am. Even as a self-confessed dork when it comes to directions, I can reliably inform you that the distance between Brighton and Bury is precisely 832 squillion miles. This means the coach which brings us home probably won't pull in till about March. If Julie has a tether, I sense she's getting close to the end of it.

'Why don't you just ring Nick and ask him for directions?' I suggested, offering her the mobile. What I was really attempting, of course, was subtly to alter my phone's role in this argument from a negative to a positive one, and therefore remind Julie that I hadn't got my priorities pathetically upside-down after all. Admittedly, this noble sacrifice of mine was rendered a little easier by the fact that I'd already managed to get hold of the final score. A 1–1 draw was a let-down, but I'd figured it best to keep my disappointment to myself. She'd only have gone off on one.

'I can't bloody phone them, can I?' she snapped. 'I'm driving. You'll have to do it.'

Shit. What was their number? Why hadn't I programmed it in to the phone before we left?

'Well, go on. What are you waiting for? I'm driving around in sodding circles here.'

I was just trying to figure out how best to own up when the phone began vibrating in my hand. I pressed the fat green button.

'Hi, Mike,' went the caller. 'It's Nick. Are you lost?'

Ten minutes later, there we were, safely arrived in Woodland Rise. Karen was at the door, cradling baby Joe. 'Had a good journey?' she called. 'Not bad, thanks,' I lied.

Nick squeezed past her and trotted down the steps to help us with our luggage. 'Nice T-shirt,' he commented, spotting my navy blue number with the Seagulls strung across the chest. I think perhaps he was being sarcastic. 'But I thought you were an Arsenal fan.'

Oh, here we go.

'It's a long story,' I replied, feeling that now was probably not a great time to begin telling it.

'Don't listen to him, Nick,' snapped Julie, grabbing her coat from the back seat before prodding the door-lock button on her key-ring. 'It's not a long story at all.' The VW lights gave a brief flash, followed by a reassuring clunk from the central locking. 'It's a very short one. Mike's going through a little Albion phase,' Julie explained. 'You'll just have to humour him.'

I'm sure we'll be speaking again by the morning.

On With The Show – MONDAY 26 NOVEMBER

If nothing else, I could be proud of the badges. They'd been my idea, those, and everybody seemed to be wearing one: assistant manager Bob Booker, club captain Paul Rogers, right-back and free-kick supremo Paul Watson, midfielder and all-round good-egg Charlie Oatway, every one of these guys had pinned a Falmer For All lapel badge to his jacket. So had Dick Knight, Martin Perry, Adrian Ground-Tour, the usual bunch. I may not be offering much in the way of a heavy-duty strategic contribution to this campaign – and, frankly, I'd done bugger-all towards this launch night – but if it was silly gimmicks you were after, obviously I was your man. I might suggest Falmer pants next.

I suppose what I really liked best about these badges, other then the way they doubled as both a neat promotional tool and an easy-on-the-pocket fund-raising novelty (a bargain at just 20p to the standard punter, and probably free to this lot) was that they meant that I – yes, me! – had directly influenced the actions of several Albion team-members. If it weren't for me, these players wouldn't have gone through the process – albeit a simple, almost sub-conscious, seemingly mundane one – of pinning this badge to their clothing.

Now you may mock, or assume I've gone mental, but think about this. Huge developments in history can be affected by the tiniest, most trivial of incidents. If you've ever listened to one of those discussions about the plausibility of time-travel, the one argument to which the sceptics always return is the don't-kill-a-fly thing. Their point is, during your travels back in time you might casually, almost without thinking, splatter a bluebottle – one which, had it survived, may have gone on to poo on the supper of a brutal murdering despot, leaving him with a fatal dose of food-poisoning. But because you splattered this thing, its killer poo was never deposited, the brutal murdering despot survived, his timetable of brutal murdering and despotting went ahead as scheduled, and history followed an entirely different route. So different, in fact, that, generations later, your parents never met, you never ended up getting born, and now, somewhat inconveniently, you don't actually exist. Or something.

This is probably quite an extreme example, but you never can tell. If one of these badges had been a bit rusty, and if one of the Albion players had accidentally stabbed his thumb with it and contracted lockjaw, I'd have been able to say that his lockjaw was all thanks to me. It's nice to have influence.

Slightly less excitingly, I could also congratulate myself for even bothering to turn up tonight. I'd spent the whole of the day in bed, my throat feeling as if someone had popped in to sandpaper it before applying a double coat of Ronseal Five-Year Woodstain. I was coughing my chest up, too. I felt like a packet of crap.

But I couldn't miss the big night, even though I knew what to expect: a slick, twenty-first-century presentation at Hove's aggressively twentieth-century town hall, where the bigwigs would officially be announcing what they'd unofficially been saying for months – namely, that we desperately needed this new stadium, that the club would be in deep doo-doo if it didn't go ahead, that the objectors were talking out of their bottoms. I still had to be there to witness it, no matter how familiar the script.

If only I'd arrived earlier, I could have bumped into Fatboy and son. Norman Cook and 11-month-old Woody apparently turned up at the start of the evening to show support. Unfortunately, they soon had to pootle off home again, as it was way past his bedtime. Woody's, I mean.

I did catch a brief glance of Des, but he seemed to be on castors. It was midway through the evening – a 20-minute pause for the imbibing of liquid refreshment and the flogging of Falmer badges, T-shirts and car stickers – and the man looked very much exit-bound. He was edging his way through the crowded first-floor bar in the manner which famous people often have to adopt when mingling with mortals – gazing rigidly ahead, a determined gait coupled with a fixed expression, seemingly anxious not to linger or make eye contact. But I may be doing the man a disservice; it was good that he'd joined us in the first place. Maybe he was just desperate for the loo.

The second half of the evening felt like a repeat of the first, but I don't suppose that did any harm. There were about 750 fans in the hall (or, more likely, 744 fans and half-a-dozen spies from the opposition camp) and the obvious aim was to drill the main messages home as clearly as possible: Write to the council on all the dreary-but-necessary points. Grab a petition form and fill it with signatures, preferably of a non-Disney-related nature. Buy the stickers, wear the T-shirt, pin a badge to whatever part of your anatomy you like to pin badges to. Do your bit.

I didn't really feel I'd done mine tonight, but I made sure I said at least a brief hello to some of my committee chums, many of whom had been toiling away since mid-afternoon, setting up tables, lights and such like. Partly I wanted to assure them of my continued support and commitment, and partly I wanted to make sure they heard how croaky I was.

Then I handed over £20 and grabbed a couple of T-shirts – one for me, one for Em – before heading back to the car. I couldn't imagine Julie wanting one, although obviously I'll offer her the option at a later date. Hell, I might even treat her to one for Christmas.

Before starting up the engine to set off for home, I clambered into the back and slapped the new sticker – white lettering, green background, with the curiously clumsy slogan 'Stadium Yes' – in my rear window. By placing it directly above my Champions one, I realised I was probably obstructing my rear view in a constabulary-displeasing fashion. But, hey, fighting for your cause means you sometimes have to buck the system, right?

To be honest, I was still more excited about the badge. *My* badge. I'd even bought some spares to give to friends.

A pity Peter Taylor couldn't make it tonight, but I expect they'll leave him one on his desk.

BURY 0 BRIGHTON 2
LEAGUE POSITION: 1ST

There must have been, what, 15 of them. Probably nearer 20. Marching defiantly towards me, most in replica shirts, chanting over and over, 'Bu-reee! Bu-reee! Bu-reee!' And there was me, heading alone towards the ground, having carelessly become separated from the rest of my fellow Albion supporters, and – worse – decked out in £6.99's worth of brand new, feel-free-to-kick-my-head-in Seagulls scarf. I was a sitting target. There was nowhere to hide.

I think I'd have felt even more scared if the average age of this bunch hadn't been about ten. And more impressed if half their replica shirts hadn't had Vodafone stamped across the chest, indicating their affinity with a slightly more fashionable club just up the road. I don't think they were even heading to this match, to be honest. They just happened to be passing, had spotted a load of Southern nancies stepping off a coach and had realised that this was a priceless opportunity to take the piss. Little sods.

It was just gone 1.30 p.m., and after a six-hour journey, punctuated only by a 40-minute stop at a Not Very Welcome Break in Don't Ask Me Where, we were relishing the chance to stretch our legs. The rain had finally eased off, thank God, and a weak, watery sun was filtering through the cloud.

Our driver had pulled up about 200 yards from the ground, which meant our first proper sight of Bury, other than through a rain-speckled window, had been a majestic view of the local cemetery. Of the 100-plus passengers who'd filled our two coaches – the official supporters' club transport, laid on by Brighton and Hove Bus Company – I'd felt sure at least one person would leap at this chance to contrive a pun-based quip, hilariously linking the word 'burial' with the name of this town. If they did, I must have missed it.

There was nothing remotely significant in the choice of Gigg Lane for my first Albion away game, other than the fact that the date was free. I'd already warned Julie that I fancied a taste of away fandom – just occasionally, not regularly, I'd promised her – and, apart from last week's temporary tantrum, she'd adjusted to this idea surprisingly well. Possibly because she wanted to get on with the Christmas shopping, where there wasn't much to be gained from having me in tow, other than to remind her, on a once-every-five-minutes cycle, what a miserable, soul-destroying experience it is.

But it wasn't until the other day that I began to realise just how far Bury is from my front door. '*Where* did you say you were going?' Andy had asked.

'Bury,' I'd told him, still not entirely sure whether I was meant to pronounce it 'Berry' or 'Burry' or 'Boo-ry'.

'Fuck me,' he'd replied. 'You've got it bad. You know that's about six hours each way, don't you?'

'Of course I do,' I'd replied, not having had the slightest clue.

Yesterday, as if to underline Andy's remark about how scarily obsessed I'm becoming, I did something else which, for pure football-related nerdyness, is likely to take some topping: I programmed an Albion ringtone into my phone: 'Sussex By The Sea', the creaky old song to which the team still runs out.

In my defence, you might argue that a football club ringtone isn't that unusual these days. To which I'd say: 'Thanks for trying to make me feel better about this.' Unfortunately, that's not the half of it.

The scary bit is that my particular phone, a Siemens (like Bury, I'm still not entirely sure how I'm meant to pronounce that), doesn't take the standard ringtones which you can get from websites, newspaper ads etc. If you want to give it a new one, rather than selecting one of the 40-or-so perfectly adequate options with which it comes ready-programmed, you have to key it in yourself.

Every. Single. Note.

One. By. One.

Then you have to adjust each one for length, pitch etc. It's a lengthy, time-consuming labour of lunacy.

And then, shortly after we'd climbed on to the coach, I suffered a minor panic attack. My original intention, naturally, had been to impress my fellow passengers if, sometime during this journey, my phone were to ring. 'Wow!' I wanted them to think, as it bleeped out its electronic update of the club anthem. 'There's a true Albion fan/sad fuck, and no mistake.' But suddenly an appalling thought struck me: what if I'd got the bloody thing wrong? My interpretation was, after all, only based on the crackly old tape I'd heard over the PA – that, plus the crowd's attempt to chant it during play – so what if I'd misheard the tune? I'm no musician, so it was more than likely. One piffling note out of place and it'd be the *Great Escape* giveaway all over again. Cursing my own complacency, I switched to vibrate-only, making a mental note to double-check the correct sequence of notes when, as I figured was fairly likely, the Albion fans launched into it this afternoon.

At about 2.30 p.m., with about 900 of us gathered behind one of the Gigg Lane goals, I received the confirmation I'd been after: 'And we're go –ing – up – to – win – the – cup forrr Sussiiiix Byyyyyy The Seeeeea.' It still sounded strangely dated, but it matched my personalised ringtone to the very last note. With more than a little relief, I switched my mobile back to its fully shrill option. I still didn't join in the singing, of course. Still too shy.

Shyness must be quite a common affliction in Bury, though, because for nigh-on three hours we heard barely a bleat from the home supporters, despite them outnumbering us by about three-to-one. Atmosphere-wise, Gigg Lane – a better stadium than Withdean but hardly a design to aspire to, with its breezeblock-and-corrugated-iron functionality – seemed to be facing some stiff competition from the graveyard up the road. I'd say it felt as if we were playing at home, but playing at home is never this passionate. I may not have been singing but I was soaking up a whole new experience. I loved it.

In this unfamiliar setting, among a sea of new faces, with the players in their natty red-and-black change strip (the first time I'd seen them wearing this in the flesh), it almost felt like watching a different team.

After the churn-it-out grimness of our recent home displays, today's performance was radically different too. We could have had six. Well, four.

Bury, mind, were rubbish. Theirs was only one step away, in fact, from the sort of performance you'd expect from a team wearing big red noses, size 30 shoes and revolving bow-ties which squirt water. As it happens, their sponsorship deal meant they wore shirts with 'Birthdays' splashed across the front – promoting the gift-and-gimmick store of that name – so they weren't entirely devoid of titter-inducing garments.

The moment Bobby's second-half goal dropped in – a glorious lob, dipping over the keeper's head, plopping into the corner of the net just in front of us – I knew the journey had been worthwhile. The 12-hour round trip, the £24 fare, the £14 admission, the tenner I'd spent on service station grease – it was all worth it, just for that exquisite moment.

Floating back towards the coach, I bumped into Liz Costa, the supporters' club vice-chairwoman (not to be confused with my mate Liz Fleet). I told her how amazed I'd been by the Bury fans' lack of passion – pretty hypocritical, of course, given that my own noise-making still extends no further than palm-stinging claps and a lot of disjointed yelling. 'Oh, it's always like this, Mike,' she replied. 'Wherever we go.'

Bugger, I thought. One casual remark and I'd drawn attention to myself yet again. If I were a regular away fan, I'd have known all about the Albion's travelling support and how impressively it shaped up against the opposition. Apparently – and at least I'll know this for next time – our away fans are known far and wide for their noise and their passion. It's one of the legacies, I guess, from all the years of grief, and especially from the time when even playing at home meant a 150-mile round trip. It breeds toughness and commitment, does that. Or I assume it does.

Settling into my seat for the long trip back, I found myself – as on the journey up – next to Tim Carder, the supporters' club chairman. We'd hardly exchanged a word on the drive north, but there'd been a good reason for this. Four good reasons, in fact: (1) Tim was asleep for long stretches; (2) I was asleep for even longer ones; (3) On the rare occasions we were both awake, the sodding radio was too loud to make ourselves heard; and (4) I've always assumed he hated me.

'You must hate people like me,' I commented, as Bury reverted to a glistening speck in the distance. Tim looked a bit startled, but I'd decided it was time for some honesty. This had to be a turning point; if I was ever going to move on to a new level of Albion-related commitment I had to start unburdening myself of the guilt. Shedding the sense of self-loathing would be quite nice, too. I had to come clean as to what I really was, what I really wasn't, and what I hoped eventually to be. And Tim was the one who was going to hear my confession, the poor sod.

So I told him the lot. With my Seagulls scarf still draped around my neck – and looking, I now appreciated, stupidly new – I told him I was really an Arsenal fan. Or used to be. 'I'm a bandwagon-jumper,' I told him. And yet, bless the guy, he insisted he still didn't hate me. He accepted that with every football club there would always be a hardcore element – in the Albion's case, he put this hell-or-high-water figure at around 2,000 fans – followed by the wavering element, followed by people who just want to be entertained now and then. And he seemed to accept my argument that, for fans like him who'd dug their heels in and stayed loyal throughout, any success would always taste a whole lot sweeter.

Besides, he insisted, I'd already started doing my bit, with all the stadium stuff. I could have kissed him but he's not my type.

Tim then talked me through the dark days of the mid-'90s, explaining exactly how things had gone so wrong, and who'd been to blame – how the fans had responded, how the likes of Dick and Martin had ridden in to rescue the club from oblivion. It would have bored the arse off 99.9 per cent of the population, but I found it absorbing. I especially enjoyed the bit where he admitted he also quite liked West Ham.

The journey flew by. By the time we edged into Brighton, shortly after eleven, I'd developed an enormous respect for Tim. Better still, I'd got the impression that at least a little of this respect was reciprocated. I'd convinced him, I think, that while I was undoubtedly a bandwagon-jumper, I wouldn't be leaping back off the moment the ride got bumpy. I'd already come too far for that.

Lengthening The Fuse – TUESDAY 4 DECEMBER

CAMBRIDGE UNITED 2 BRIGHTON 1
(LDV VANS TROPHY SOUTHERN SECTION QUARTER-FINAL)

ARSENAL 3 JUVENTUS 1
(UEFA CHAMPIONS LEAGUE, SECOND ROUND, GROUP D)

How difficult can it be to mince a lamb, for God's sake? Had I wanted beef mince, fine; I was staring at beefy options in abundance – regular, extra lean, the faintly ominous one they call 'economy'. There was even a plethora of their Sainsbury's top-of-the-range version, labelled Taste The Difference (although with no indication, I noticed, as to what it was actually supposed to taste different from. Strawberry cheesecake, perhaps? Stonewashed denim?). But lambs appeared to have been granted some kind of amnesty by this branch's butchery department. Which, from my perspective, although maybe not the lambs', was an absolute pain.

If I was going to create my speciality spaghetti for our meal tonight – and you may mock, but it really is very good – then it had to be 500g of lamb mince or nothing. Emily refuses point-blank to touch anything cow-related. She's convinced it'll drive her mad.

Pork mince would have been no problem, had I wanted meat which would turn as tough as sun-baked trainers under the intense heat to which I'd be exposing it. The shelves were groaning with the stuff. Likewise, turkey mince – low in fat, but with the texture of a soggy dishcloth – was in ludicrously plentiful supply. But not a single pack of lamb mince could I locate. And this was the third day running I'd asked.

The point I'm trying to make here (yes, there is one) is that I was angry. And so, given the stupefyingly trivial nature of the complaint, you may conclude that nothing's really changed – that, nearly five months in, this football-based experiment has failed to readjust my perspectives the way I'd hoped. I was still moaning about meaningless minutiae.

You'd be wrong, though. The difference so far may not be radical; my cauldron of fatuous frustrations still bubbles away, and all too often comes to the boil. But these days, almost certainly thanks to the fresh outlook which all this Albion business has given me, I come equipped with something extra. These days I have my built-in Pratometer®.

Beforehand, I just couldn't step back, take a look at myself, and acknowledge the limit beyond which a display of anger or frustration would single me out as a pillock.

In a case such as today's, for example, I wouldn't have moved on to a level of philosophical, chilled-out detachment, still appreciating that my complaint probably wasn't without some justification, but calmly concluding: 'We'll have chicken instead.' I'd have wanted answers. My body tensing, my pulse racing, I'd have collared an assistant – better still a departmental head, best of all the manager himself – and asked why I, The Customer (although actually the store has several), was consistently offered such a ropey selection of basic food items. Despite being a tad squeamish whenever I consider the process by which meat reaches our tables, I might even have offered to drive the manager straight to the nearest lambing farm if he'd felt that this would enable him to rectify the situation.

But thanks to my Pratometer®, I don't do that anymore. Or not nearly so much. When my anger, frustration, pettiness or petulance reaches a certain level, it triggers a small alarm in my head (not a real one, you understand; I think that would scare people), telling me that my point, for what it's worth, has been made.

It also gently reminds me of the consequences should I choose to ignore it. In the case of the supermarket, it reminds me that I used to work in one of these places myself – and that, from what I recall, customers like me can easily become the central topic of the staff's tea-break banter. They'd maybe even give me a nickname – 'Mince Man', perhaps, or 'Meat Boy', or 'Twat' – and sniggeringly update each other, whenever they gathered for their 15-minute breather, as to my latest displays of obsessive pottiness. I'd be a laughing stock, on a par with those customers who mutter, shoplift jam and whiff of wee.

So today I made my point politely and then I shut up. I had bigger, more inspiring things to care about now, I reminded myself. A greater commitment. The fact that it's a commitment to a Second Division football club might strike some observers as equally pitiful, but I knew better.

With greater commitment, however, comes greater vulnerability. The skin becomes thinner; what used to matter little matters a lot. While Arsenal were keeping me chirpy tonight with their surprisingly convincing televised win over the might of Juventus, poxy Cambridge United were about to ensure this chirpiness was horribly short-lived. As the final whistle blew at Highbury, I dashed into the kitchen and clicked on the stereo, anxious for my Albion update. The final whistle had just blown in this one, too – the LDV Vans Trophy quarter-final. The score was 1–1. It was about to go into 30 minutes of extra time.

Or rather it wasn't, because within four minutes Cambridge had done what we'd done to Wycombe in the previous round – namely, netted a golden goal. It was a jammy deflection this time, unlike the splendid strike which had secured the Albion's victory – but apparently, such are the bizarre regulations governing this competition, they all count.

So that was it. We were out. No LDV Vans Trophy for us this year. Ousted at the almost-there-but-not-quite stage they call the quarter-finals. Or southern section quarters, which I guess are more like eighths.

And call me daft, but I felt desperately deflated. 'Bastards!' I grunted, thumping the off-switch.

Back in the lounge, a smiling, wide-screen Arsène Wenger was commenting on his side's impressive win. I sighed and started clearing the plates. Emily had hardly touched her chicken.

Bread And Jam – SATURDAY 8 DECEMBER

BRIGHTON 2 RUSHDEN & DIAMONDS 1
(FA CUP, SECOND ROUND)

It had been five years since I'd last seen Steve and I can't pretend I hadn't missed him. You do when you've known someone for two-and-a-half decades and then allowed that friendship to crumble away. Steve was best man at my wedding. I was best man at his. At both of his, in fact.

To discover him and Laura at my front door this afternoon, just minutes after I'd returned from Withdean, was more than a wee bit surprising. They'd driven down to Brighton, Steve explained, for the Christmas party of one of his customers (Steve has a dull but obscenely well-paid job with some computer firm) and had decided to pop by on the off-chance. Just like that. For the first time since 1996.

'How're you doing?!' he cried.

'Fucking hell fire!' I replied.

The last time Steve and Laura had been in this house, for one of those family get-together weekends we used to make such a habit of, it had been painfully obvious they couldn't wait to leave. You'd have thought Julie and I had just revealed we were suffering from smallpox, or announced we were about to be joined for supper by the Chuckle Brothers. In fact, so awkward had the atmosphere become between us – nothing nasty, just a total lack of common ground – that we'd rented some ropey Tom Cruise video for the evening, rather than risk venturing any further into the increasingly hazardous minefield of conversation. And then, barely 30 minutes into this film, they'd made some politely feeble excuse, packed their bags and sodded off home. A day early.

Steve and I were 36, twice the age we'd been when we'd left school, and for the past 18 years our lives had been heading in dramatically different directions. Steve had always wanted the smart car, the career ladder, the big modern house in Berkshire. And he'd got it. Good for him.

I, on the other hand, had never been too certain what I'd wanted. I'd just felt fairly sure it wasn't that. We'd always known we were different, but it hadn't always mattered. At school, for example, I'd been the one into The Jam, whereas Steve had been happy to admit to owning a copy of Bread's Greatest Hits. School provides you with so much common ground, however, that you can happily ignore such discrepancies. It's once you move on that the equation no longer balances.

Like thousands of old schoolfriends, Steve and I had simply grown apart. It wasn't anyone's fault, and it wasn't a crime. Yet for the best part of two decades, neither of us seemed prepared to acknowledge this, most likely because the friendship had once felt so solid. We'd preferred to continue going through the motions.

The break, when it eventually did happen, was something of a relief, not unlike the feeling you experience when you've put a fatally wounded pet out of its misery. Last Christmas we didn't even send Steve and Laura a card. I did feel bad about this, but not very: theirs to us was barely larger than a gift tag.

But now, ghosting in out of nowhere, they were back. Laura in her country casual finery. Steve in neatly pressed jeans, a light blue shirt and surprisingly shiny shoes for a Saturday afternoon. Me in my shabby green bargain combats and my Bobby Zamora T-shirt. A curious clash of past and present.

As far as Steve's concerned, I've always been an Arsenal fan. That's been my label. Whenever we'd have kickabouts in the park, I'd always be the Gunners. Or at least one of their players. Steve, born in Nottingham, would always be Forest. We'd adopt these same roles whenever we played Subbuteo, as of course we were obliged to do if we wanted to be proper '70s-cliché kids.

The last time we'd met, my allegiance to Arsenal had still been relatively intact. I was no longer especially passionate, and we didn't really talk about football in the way we'd done as kids, but there was never the slightest suggestion that I'd dump them for a different team, or even dare consider the idea. Any more than Steve would have done with Forest.

So I was quite surprised by his reaction this afternoon to my Albion T-shirt. Or rather his total lack of one. Steve didn't even mention it. Not a word. We chatted briefly about their result while I was making us a coffee, but we could just as easily have been analysing Richard Whiteley's performance on yesterday's *Countdown*.

And then Steve asked: 'Are Forest playing today . . ?'

I wondered what else was going through his head as he stood here in our kitchen. Was he sneaking a glance over my shoulder, through the smeary window which looks out over our sorry excuse for a back garden, and observing the three-day accumulation of Barney's turds? Or was his attention focused exclusively on my corpulent form? I must have gained at least two stone since we'd last met. I found myself trying to hold my stomach in.

When the time came for him and Laura to leave, we did what you do in these situations. Made sure we swapped mobile numbers, e-mail addresses etc. Vowed to keep in touch this time. Agreed to fix a date to meet up properly, and then didn't actually fix one.

It had been nice to see Steve again, it really had. Nice to catch up on his news. But there wasn't really much spark between us. I don't see how there ever could be again.

And I don't really think we should look for one. A lot of the questions I'm asking about my life may be middle-age-related, but to try and resuscitate a friendship surely can't be the answer. To inject meaning into your present shouldn't involve having to draw on your past, otherwise it feels like cheating.

That said, I'd like to meet Steve for a drink some time. Just the two of us, exclusively as old mates, without the family factors which add too much confusion and polite, uneasy compromise. And without kidding ourselves that it's anything more than a sociable way for a couple of blokes to spend an evening.

I'm tempted, since he lives in Berkshire, to suggest we get tickets for Albion's away match at Reading on 9 March. That might be fun. The game would give us a neat focal point, the common ground we used to take for granted.

Admittedly, on this afternoon's evidence, it sounds as if Steve's interest in football has long since waned. But maybe I could help him remember how to give a monkey's.

Wouldn't that be ironic?

Great Expectations – MONDAY 10 DECEMBER

My school French teacher, a wiry, whining wimp whose name, for legal reasons, escapes me, once described me as 'phlegmatic'. Since I had no idea what this meant at the time, I wasn't sure whether to take a sweeping bow in front of my classmates, hang my head in shame, or nip and ask the nurse for a dose of Benylin. But since he'd delivered this word with such a pronounced sneer, I got the impression he was probably having a dig.

The moment the class had finished, I dug out my *Collins English Dictionary*, flicked to the words starting with F and sat for several minutes, scratching my head in puzzlement. Then one of those *Dandy*-style light bulbs of inspiration suddenly flashed above my dozy skull and I quickly thumbed onward to the P section. Once there, of course, I soon discovered the elusive definition, and twigged what Mr Name-Deleted had been trying to tell me. He'd been trying to tell me I couldn't be arsed.

He was right, too. I couldn't. When it came to homework, which was what had triggered this outburst, I'd always felt the minimum of effort would suffice. But Mr Name-Deleted's accusation wasn't just the standard moan you'd expect from a world-weary schoolteacher confronted by yet another academic bonehead. This guy was pissed off because, despite my alleged phlegmatism, I kept getting decent marks. My French essays were dull, passionless and utterly devoid of wit, flair, imagination or insight. But by sticking to the most cretinously simplistic writing style – *mon chien a quatre jambes* – they were almost entirely devoid of errors. And since 75 per cent of the marks had to be awarded purely for accuracy – a daft system, ripe for exploitation, but whose fault was that, eh? – I could never see the point of busting a creative gut.

I mention this incident not because I expect you to be impressed or to find it fascinating, but because it was the first time I'd really given serious thought to the colossal power of apathy – not just in relation to school but to the world at large. Before long, I'd drawn to a life-shaping if cynical conclusion. Namely, that when the path of least resistance contains very few obvious pitfalls, it'll always be the most tempting route.

This outlook has shaped much of my thinking, if that's not too generous a word, ever since. And I now tend to work on the assumption – rather arrogantly, I admit – that most normal people, consciously or otherwise, share a similar outlook.

Tonight I joined my Falmer stadium pals for another meeting, where once again we sat around a table in Withdean's hospitality hut – about 20 of us this time – plotting campaign tactics. All well and good, of course, and you certainly couldn't knock our team spirit, but for the entire two-and-a-half hours in which we gabbed away, I was plagued by the same naggingly sceptical question: hadn't any of these fine people ever used the expression 'I can't be arsed'?

From their seemingly insatiable enthusiasm, I concluded that they couldn't have done. And while this indicates a commendably positive attitude on their part, it also worries me. Speaking from first-hand experience, I consider can't-be-arsedness to be one of life's most potent, pervasive forces – one which, when you're out to motivate people, you underestimate at your peril.

What worries me is that these campaigning chums of mine, these people who care so profoundly about Brighton and Hove Albion, are doing just that – failing to appreciate the universal power of apathy.

This tightly knit band of loyal, hardcore supporters loves this football club with an absolute passion. If ever there were a sponsored fund-raising initiative which required Albion fans to lie in front of a speeding juggernaut, or have their tonsils pecked out by geese, in order to raise money for a new set of goalnets, I know who'd be first to volunteer.

Dig out any Albion-related news stories from the last few turbulent years, and you'll see the same names cropping up: Tim Carder, Attila, Liz Costa, Sarah Watts, Paul Samrah. I admire and respect these people enormously. When it comes to consistency, commitment and selfless dedication, they put me to absolute shame.

But.

But I don't think they're normal.

I don't mean this in an insulting sense, other than with reference to the grotesque Isles of Scilly souvenir sweatshirt which Liz chose to wear tonight. I've grown to like these people a lot, and although most of them must now have twigged that I'm a snivelling little bandwagon-jumping git, they've never displayed a hint of resentment towards me.

What I mean is, their attitude towards their club is exceptional. If you'll forgive the sweeping statement – and you've come a bloody long way for a reader who isn't prepared to – the typical football fan is someone who'll bung on their replica shirt, head to the match once a fortnight, cheer, jeer or swear accordingly, then bugger off home. No doubt they'll still chat about the footie in between – at work, perhaps, or down the pub – but they're unlikely to get involved with the day-to-day workings of the club itself. Either because it's never occurred to them to do so, or because it has and it's always sounded as dull as shit.

Admittedly, the campaigning of the mid-to-late '90s suggests that this club has – or at least has had – a higher-than-average ratio of non-typical fans, people who *have* been prepared to go constructively mental on the Albion's behalf if the situation has demanded it. The question is, can those same people still be relied on?

My fellow committee pals seem to take it for granted that they can. Me, I'm not so sure.

The obvious difference is one of urgency. Beforehand, this was a club on its knees, facing imminent elimination from the League and, with it, almost certain extinction. Kind of focuses the mind, that, I'd have thought.

This time, although the likes of Dick and Martin are at pains to point out that the Albion's long-term future will look pretty perilous if this stadium doesn't go ahead, it really doesn't feel that scary. Not only is the team playing well, but I reckon – hush my mouth – that a lot of fans kind of like Withdean. Or at least don't hate it enough to care passionately about moving on. It may be ugly and ramshackle and totally ill-equipped, but there's a friendly buzz about the place. It's become home. Perhaps equally significantly, it's become a home where the Albion tend not to fuck up all that often. Fortress Withdean, people call it. That, in itself, is bound to reduce the incentive, in some supporters' eyes, to pack up and head off to what's still just an architect's drawing.

My hunch is that these last couple of relatively healthy years will have seen a lot of Albion obsessives regaining a sense of proportion in their lives. Sure, they still love their club, but since it seems to be ticking along fairly comfortably-ish, perhaps they've had a chance to step back, to remember they also have families to feed, dogs to walk, shelves to put up, wiring to botch, or whatever.

Well over half our meeting tonight was devoted to a suffocatingly dull discussion about letter-writing. When Albion fans write their next letters of support for this new stadium – and they'll have been asked to put pen to paper at least four times before this whole process is through – then what should we be asking them to say? Which particular arguments ought they to focus on? What sort of wording should they use? How many councillors should they send copies to? Blah blah frigging blah.

I realise it has to be done. But we're bombarding supporters with so many messages that half the poor sods are probably drowning in confusion. I don't mean that to sound patronising; I'm confused myself.

Obviously we can't just cave in to the can't-be-arsed factor, but we should recognise how it shapes people's behaviour. Once we've done that, at least we'll be talking to people in their own language. Don't let's wade in by saying, 'Now, listen, chaps, you're going to have to write four dreary letters, in your own words, to the following sets of people, arguing the case for a new community stadium and taking in as many as possible of the points itemised in our campaign document. *It's very important.*'

Instead, let's say to each person, 'Right, you apathetic bastard. Just do one thing to help us get this stadium, OK? Yep, just the one. Wear the badge, if you like. Or the T-shirt. Or bung one of these stickers in your car. Anything. Take your pick. Whatever you can manage, we'd really appreciate it. And if ever you do fancy going one step further and writing some sort of letter, then any one of these four options would be a huge help. But there's no pressure. I realise you're a very busy man. Or woman. And I'm sorry for calling you a bastard.'

That way, it'd look a whole lot less daunting.

I'm also not convinced about what we're charging for these Falmer T-shirts of ours. In fact, I don't think we should be charging money for them at all; let's give the bloody things away for nothing. Swamp the city with them. It'd show just how many people were behind this campaign. Sod the expense.

But Liz Costa, as campaign treasurer, reckons I've lost the plot on this one. On top of which, she feels they're quite a bargain. Their £7 price tag, she points out, compares very favourably to the £10-plus which fans have to pay for Albion or Skint T-shirts in the Seagulls Shop.

I'm tempted to point out that, while that certainly makes sound financial sense, there's another issue to consider here. Namely, that the Albion/Skint T-shirts are quite stylish and desirable, whereas our Falmer ones are totally grotesque.

But it would be wrong for me to argue nuances of style with Liz. She has years of campaigning experience, she knows her stuff, she instinctively appreciates how best to deploy campaign funds. I respect her judgement 100 per cent.

She's also someone who's prepared to wear an Isles Of Scilly sweatshirt.

For £39 plus VAT, I've just shared an alcohol-fuelled evening with representatives from the likes of Windmill Kitchens, Grate Fireplaces and Nuglas Windows.

Fantastic, I dare say, if I'd wanted to negotiate a special deal on refurbishing my house, or meet the executives responsible for their companies' local radio ads and deliver them a well-earned kicking. Not so fantastic when what I'd really wanted was to see Bobby Zamora dancing to 'Come On Eileen'. To see how he coped with that funny bit in the middle where it speeds up.

It's a shame, because I'd convinced myself that this, the Albion's Christmas dinner, would be a memorable night. I even took a guest – my Albion nut of a mate, Liz Fleet. Julie, I'd decided, would have declined the offer to accompany me, probably with a response which included the expression 'would I bollocks?'. So I hadn't asked her.

The setting was the Grand Hotel on Brighton seafront, most famous for having been radically redesigned by the IRA in 1984. To save us the cab fare, Liz's mum, Maureen, kindly dropped us off outside – Liz in her new sparkly blue top and black trousers, purchased specially for the occasion, and me looking rather dashing, it has to be said, in my navy-blue suit, just back from its annual holiday to the cleaners. It's not often I'm seen in this suit without a patch of silvery dog drool decorating at least one of the trouser legs. This was a special occasion.

Liz was excited about what lay ahead. So was I. Until, that is, I saw the seating plan, pinned outside the entrance to the 800-capacity Empress Suite. I scoured this list for the obvious names – Zamora, Steele, Cullip, Kuipers, Hart, Oatway, Jones – or indeed any first-teamers I might recognise. Then I scoured it again. And how many did I spot? I think you can guess.

I didn't want to let it spoil our evening, so I decided to lower my expectations and settle for less prominent names – fringe players such as Melton, Marney, Ramsay, Wilkinson, Virgo. The sort more likely to sit on the bench, turn out for the reserves or get loaned to some crummy non-league outfit 'to gain first-team experience'.

And did this more modest approach prove rewarding? Did it fuck. Not a single Albion first-team player was present.

To be fair, this was the second sitting. Such had been the demand for tickets that this event, targeted mainly at local businesses, had been spread over two evenings. And with a match coming up this Friday, the players, I realised now, had made their obligatory appearance at Monday's initial do, presumably to allow their livers time to recover.

So we were the B-list.

As far as prominent names were concerned, then, we had to settle for Dean Wilkins (ex-captain, brother of the slightly more famous Ray, and now Albion's youth team coach); John Byrne (who, like Dean, last played for the club in 1996), and former keeper John Keeley (now the goalkeeping coach). And, er . . . that was it, unless you count the obligatory smattering of old blokes who did a fine job for the club in the 1066-67 season, plus a handful of loyal, dedicated backroom staff who, with respect, I don't give a toss about.

Admittedly, Peter Taylor was there, but the last I actually saw of him was around 9.45 p.m., when he waddled up half-heartedly to fish a few raffle tickets out of a blue plastic bucket – none of which, I hardly need add, corresponded to those for which I'd just forked out a fiver. (I'd set my heart on the signed first-team shirt, but I knew I'd already used up a good decade's worth of raffle-winning luck when I landed myself that rug voucher back in Southwick.) This prize draw, from what I could make out, was the only official duty expected of Albion's manager tonight, other than to turn up, eat, smile, and make suitably polite noises as perspiring businessmen clamoured for souvenir piccies on their Kodak disposables. Since he was at the same table as Dick, I thought I'd pootle over and finally get a formal introduction, but the next time I glanced over, Taylor's seat was occupied by a guy who looked 190. It seemed the boss had already buggered off upstairs for an early night.

The biggest disappointment wasn't so much that I didn't get to talk to any current players, but that the event didn't deliver the comedy potential I'd yearned for. I'm past the age where making party small-talk with the likes of Zamora or Steele – even Beckham or Owen – would particularly excite me, since any attempt at conversation would, I'm sure, be strained and embarrassing for all concerned. But I'm not past the age where I'd enjoy standing on the sidelines and poking fun at footballers dancing. If even a smattering of first-teamers had shown up tonight, my theory that all men look prats when they dance – regardless of age, shape, size or athletic prowess – could have been put to its biggest test. 'Told you so!' I'd have been able to yell in Liz's ear.

But just when I was about to write off the entire event as a let-down, who should ride to the rescue but Dick Knight? Just after 10.30 p.m., with a sweaty '80s medley kicking in, the Albion's chairman hit the dancefloor, tie akimbo, to show off his repertoire of moves. I'm thrilled to report he looked absurd.

The big man had rescued my night.

Pick A Card – FRIDAY 21 DECEMBER

BRIGHTON 2 CHESTERFIELD 2
LEAGUE POSITION: 4TH

This afternoon I bumped into Paul Camillin, Albion's press officer, in the Seagulls Shop. We know each other from the campaign team. 'I'm glad I've seen you, Mike,' he said. 'I was wondering if we could meet up after the match tonight. I've got something I'd like you to pass on to Liz, if you wouldn't mind.'

Provided he didn't mean a sexually transmitted disease, I said that'd be fine. It turned out he meant a birthday card.

Paul had been chatting with Liz at Wednesday night's dinner, and at some point Liz must have let it slip that Saturday, tomorrow, is her birthday. Her 33rd. So he'd bought her a card, he told me. A Seagulls card. He planned to get it signed by the Albion players.

I had no idea why he'd done this, but I was impressed. She'd be thrilled, I told him.

So after tonight's game – a nasty, niggly affair – I met Paul at our pre-agreed rendezvous, the mobile souvenir shop, just outside Withdean's South Stand turnstiles.

'Sorry I'm late,' he cried, 'but they wouldn't let me into the dressing-room at first!' He'd had to pop in there, he explained, to retrieve this card, but all hell had been breaking loose when he'd arrived. Not over the particular card he'd chosen (surprisingly, perhaps, considering it featured Santa in an Albion shirt), but in the wake of the match. Not only had Albion's Paul Rogers been sent off for the second time this season (only about ten minutes after trotting on as sub) but Peter Taylor was frothing at the mouth over the wind-up antics of Chesterfield's manager, Nicky Law. Law – or Law-Unto-Himself, as I'm sure he'll now be wittily nicknamed if he isn't already – had not only provoked our players during the game but had continued sounding off outside the dressing-rooms. Things had become so heated, the police had moved in. Golly.

A lot of this hostility, if not all of it, seems to stem from the fact that the Albion pipped Chesterfield to last season's Third Division title. Thanks to various off-the-field wrong-doings at the time, the authorities docked Chesterfield nine points – but since the Albion eventually notched up enough to have won the championship regardless, it seems odd that tonight's visitors chose to focus their anger on us. The fact that these Chesterfield fans were chanting something along the lines of 'we're the real champions' would tend to suggest that there's an alarming shortage of maths teachers in their part of the country.

'Anyway,' said Paul, 'I managed to rescue it. Wanna see?'

At this point he began carefully unsealing the licked-down envelope, trying to do as little damage as possible but failing rather miserably. I told him not to worry, that I'd fix the rips with Pritt stick when I got home.

'To be honest,' he said, 'I just want to make sure none of them has written anything rude. You know what that lot can be like.'

I didn't, but I took his word for it. Then I took the card. 'Thanks,' I said. 'She'll be so pleased.'

Back home, I did a signature count. Thirteen players had signed, including Liz's hero, Gary Hart. Bobby's autograph was there too. Of the 11 other tangled names, I deciphered nine – not thanks to any great skill on my part, but thanks to my recent acquisition of the Albion's latest team photo, which includes reproductions of each player's official scrawl.

Mind you, as tends to be the case with signatures, none of them looks remotely like the name of the player it's supposed to represent. Steve Melton's, for instance, appears to say Cyril Squirrel. Here are some other examples:

Scott Ramsay = Star Bay
Kerry Mayo = Wrighum
Adam Virgo = Cent Vinyl
Matthew Wicks = Math Welch
Dirk Lehmann = Dlllllllllll
Geoff Pitcher = Carlos
Shaun Wilkinson = Swilly Minge-Jelly
Paul Brooker = Pad Brodwin
Michel Kuipers = Niki Wip
Lee Steele = Ice Shits

Robbie Pethick = Royal Pretzel
Richard Carpenter = Piecemeal Crater
Simon Morgan = Sue Muff
Paul Rogers = Pleep

I've no idea what's happened to Nicholas Lyndhurst.

Compliments Of The Season – TUESDAY 25 DECEMBER

On this, the first day of Christmas, my true love gave to me:

- One Albion home shirt, with WARDY and a number eight on the back.
- One Albion away shirt (red and black), with nothing on the back because Julie nipped in and bought it on a different day when she was in a bit of a hurry.
- A grey, hooded Skint sweatshirt.
- A really rather splendid Brighton and Hove Albion watch.

Added to all this, Em bought me the Albion 2002 calendar.
   Consequently, I'm extremely happy.
   Which I think means I'm extremely sad.

Boxing Daze – WEDNESDAY 26 DECEMBER

QPR 0 BRIGHTON 0
LEAGUE POSITION: 3RD

Geographically speaking, I could have gone to this one. Realistically speaking, not a chance. Boxing Day doesn't just mean family commitments and chilled leftovers and what the hell's that yellow stuff you've dolloped on my plate. It also means there are no trains. Other than my nephew's new Harry Potter Hogwarts Express, which I don't imagine stops at Shepherd's Bush.

I consoled myself with Arsenal v Chelsea on *Sky*, where a win would put us – them – back on top. But in the 23rd minute the *Daily Star* rang. I love them to pieces, of course I do, but I could have done without them calling in the middle of flaming Boxing Day. Once we'd exchanged seasonal niceties, it turned out they wanted me to write a review of Christmas Day's telly. No rush or anything. As long as it was with them in the next hour or so.

Fan-bloody-tastic.

By the time I'd e-mailed my completed, spell-checked (and, I hardly need add, witty and incisive) copy, the Arsenal and Albion games – both midday kick-offs – were over. Arsenal had won 2–1 and, as anticipated, overtaken Newcastle at the top of the Premiership.

A 0–0 for the Albion, in the match which obviously mattered most to me, seemed comparatively disappointing. But by the end of the afternoon, I'd cheered up. We were exactly halfway through our season – 23 games played, 23 to come – so third place wasn't bad, was it? What was I saying, third place was bloody great. It wasn't *first* place, admittedly, but it wasn't 21st either, and it could have been. I decided this called for a mid-term celebration.

I went to the back door and reached outside for the last bottle of Cava. There'd been no room for it in the fridge; there wasn't exactly an excessive amount of turkey left in there, but probably just about enough to keep us going for six months in the event of a nuclear holocaust.

'Cheers!' I said, having successfully popped out the cork without having to phone for an ambulance. 'Cheers!' said Julie.

Halfway down the bottle, it occurred to me that I hadn't actually told her what we were celebrating. But then she hadn't asked.

Rude Words – SATURDAY 29 DECEMBER

BLACKPOOL 2 BRIGHTON 2
LEAGUE POSITION: 3RD

While I appreciate that it's neither big nor clever to swear, please indulge me for a moment.

Fuck fuck fuck fuck fuck.

FUCK.

Thank you.

We were seconds away – *seconds* – from ending the year on top of the table. We even saved a penalty in stoppage time, or rather our keeper did. But we just couldn't bloody hold on. *Again.* For the second time in three matches – this happened against Chesterfield too – we've chucked away a two-goal lead. Hold on, I can feel another fuck coming on.

Fuck.

My reaction to Blackpool's 94th-minute equaliser – ninety-flaming-fourth, note – was almost on a par with some of my England-related tantrums. Obviously I didn't kick a skirting board this time because I now appreciate that this is stupid and petulant. Instead, I picked up a video (tape, not machine), with a view to cracking it against the wall. Luckily, I checked the label first, noticed it was episode three of the latest *Cold Feet* series, which we've not got round to watching yet, and thought better of it. But I was still very angry, I really was. So instead I shouted, 'Cunts!'

It's not a word I use often. Julie hates it. But she and Em were out, so I thought I'd treat myself.

A Good Lot Of Fat – TUESDAY 1 JANUARY

No match today after all. Apparently, Withdean is like an ice rink. Personally, I'd have thought this would have made for quite an entertaining game ('Oh, I say, a magnificent triple salchow there from Zamora – and doesn't he look a picture in that sequinned catsuit?') but I guess it wouldn't have done the players a whole lot of good.

In one sense, then, I'm quite hacked off. You psyche yourself up for a fixture for days, go through all those nerdy hypothetical calculations about what a win would mean in terms of league position etc., and then – whoomph! (or whatever noise it is that rotten weather makes) – you're left with a big fat nothing where your regular fix of football should be. A hollow feeling. On top of which, from a drearily practical perspective, I'd rather we had the points than the games in hand.

But in another sense, more of a selfish one, I'm relieved today's match was called off. Not just because I'm suffering from one of those colds which make you feel as if a satsuma has been rammed up each nostril, but because it allows me a timely opportunity to do a wee bit of chin-stroking, mid-season reflection. Not so much about the football, but about the effect it's been having on me. As I write this, I may even decide to gaze wistfully from my window and make curious, contemplative humming sounds.

The central question still stands – namely, is this whole exercise actually working? Has jumping on the Albion's bandwagon helped me rekindle that passion I was wittering on about?

In a word, yes. In five words, of course it bloody has. If anything, it's been *over*-kindled. I could probably do with an ice-cold shower, or a dose of bromide in my tea, or whatever equivalent treatment they recommend for a football fixation.

Just look at me, for God's sake. Every day of the week now I'm dressed in one or other of my Albion T-shirts. If I can't find a clean one, I'll wash one specially – which, believe me, is alarmingly out of character. If I can't find one to wash specially, I'll wear one which I hope hasn't started to pong too much. I get tetchy if I can't drink my coffee, tea or Lemsip out of my Albion mug (its blue-and-white stripes are already beginning to fade from over-exposure to dishwasher detergent). And then there's the Seagulls watch. My old one was a natty little Casio model I'd grown very attached to, with day and date functions, multiple alarms, illuminated fascia and – a huge deal, this – a voice-memo facility which I'd convinced myself I couldn't live without. This Seagulls one just tells the time, and suddenly that's enough.

Obviously, I haven't a clue how this season will end for the Albion – play-offs? Automatic promotion? Another title? Mathematically, I think we could probably still get ourselves relegated if we put out minds to it – but there's no doubt I'm on target from a personal point of view. I'm getting excited about stuff which doesn't really matter. I'm rediscovering a passion for the relatively pointless. I think that's what I set out to do.

But in another sense I've fucked this whole exercise up. Racing off in my blinkered, self-obsessed manner, I've left behind something rather important. Namely, my family.

Now, please don't panic. I promise these pages aren't about to turn to treacle as I ramble on about My Lovely Wife And Daughter and how woefully I've neglected them these last few months. It's just that I think I misjudged what I wanted from all this.

Put simply, I want them to feel a part of it too, even if only to a minor extent. I want this to be about more than just Mike and his strange new obsession. Otherwise it's not nearly as much fun at it ought to be.

Not that I've got much hope of getting Em on board. Football to Em is about Becks and Man United and England and that's about it. Her Saturdays aren't about fixture lists. They're about shopping centres and

Clearasil boys and swapping text messages with mates standing three feet away. I suppose that's how it should be.

So what about Julie? Will she be more open to persuasion? I'd like to think so, but I'm not convinced. She's way too kind ever to admit this, but I think all this Albion business has unnerved and unsettled her. Not so much the fact that it's brought out the tosser in me – the T-shirts, the mug, the watch, the ringtone etc. – but that, after 15 years of marriage, a part of me which she'd come to take for granted, as predictable as the way I curl up next to her in bed, doesn't seem to be there any more, and that something else, something a bit odd, has taken its place. As if she'd come home one evening and discovered I'd had a nose job.

From the day we met – and we're talking about more than 17 years ago now – Julie has gone along with the football thing. Not that she was a football-hater before I showed up – her dad wouldn't have allowed it – but her deeper interest really grew as our relationship did. And since this was back in the days when I was still heading up to Highbury fairly regularly, football came to mean the Arsenal. She went to several games with me, stood on the North Bank, even in the most ridiculous weather, contracted laryngitis after a grim goalless draw with QPR, and progressed from a loving tolerance to a genuine interest. But always – and this is the point – with the Arsenal at the centre of it all: the star names, the huge crowds, the top-notch opposition, the Highbury magic. On the few occasions when it wasn't Highbury, it was Wembley, and England. Even starrier names, even huger crowds, even toppier-notchier opposition. Frankly, she's been spoilt.

When I jokingly suggested, some months back, that she ought to come to Withdean some time, she almost shuddered. I thought it was a bit of an over-reaction, to be honest, but I could half-see her point. She'd been though all this once before, all those years ago, gradually learning who she was meant to care about, football-wise, and why. And eventually, through time, patience, hard work, commitment and – dare I say it – love, it actually worked. The rewards, when they came, were big and colourful, tinged with glamour. It was the best of the best, or thereabouts. In more recent years, as my own active interest in football has waned, it's as if Julie has felt able, with some relief, to ease off too, still enjoying the game but largely coming to think of it, as I've done, as something we just watch on TV. So why should I want her to chuck the whole arrangement up in the air again – to waste even one afternoon on a parochial bunch of Second Division nobodies (as she'd see it), hacking away in the mud at some glorified municipal park?

In short, I shouldn't. I just do.

We've always been close, even at times when we've not been getting on as well as we'd want to. I've never liked heading off to 'do my own thing', leaving 'the wife' out of it, buggering off for, say, a thrice-weekly skinful. To be honest with you, I don't even like pubs very much. Since Andy's been working up north, renovating some dump of a house, I've barely set foot in one.

I know it's corny and clichéd, and I really am so fucking sorry, but the simple fact is that we're great mates, Julie and I. So if I've discovered something new and fun, then I want Julie to enjoy it with me, to share at least some of the experience. In the case of the Albion, I'd just like her to come to one game. That way, at least she might begin to understand.

Tonight, at what I felt was a cunningly opportune moment – i.e. when she felt sufficiently recovered from her New Year's Eve hangover to have uncorked a new bottle of wine – I casually asked if she'd reconsider. She casually told me to bog off. Work being the way it was, she reminded me, her weekends were more precious than ever.

I was going to have to do some lateral thinking.

But that was OK, because moments after she'd rejected this invitation of mine – all right, thrown it back in my face – the inspiration suddenly hit me. I'd spotted something which I reckoned I could use as a bargaining tool. Something about which we both had strong feelings.

I'd caught sight of my belly.

'Tell you what,' I suggested tentatively. 'How about a deal? What if, as a sort of New Year's resolution, I were to lose half a stone?' I jabbed at the wobbly protuberance beneath my Zamora T-shirt. 'And, in return, you agreed to come and watch the Albion?'

Julie hesitated. I sensed I was onto something. If I could just persuade her to come to one match with me, pretend that's all I was really asking, the rest, I felt sure, would fall happily into place. She'd get the bug. She might, for old time's sake, even get laryngitis.

'I'm sorry,' she eventually sighed. 'I'm just not prepared to give up my Saturdays. Especially not for that lot.'

'No, no, not Satur*days*!' I quickly reminded her. 'Satur*day*. Just the one away game.'

Note how I'd sneakily slipped in that last little detail. Because, of course, that was the other hurdle I was going to have to overcome, persuasion-wise: Julie couldn't join me at Withdean even if she wanted to. There weren't any spare seats, at least not in the bit where I sat.

'*Away* game? You've got to be joking. Ten lousy hours on a coach to God-knows-where and back. You need your head examined.'

I was getting desperate here.

'A stone, then. If I lose a stone, will you come to an away game? Honestly, you'd really enjoy it.'

I had a feeling I'd overdone it with that last bit.

'A stone and a half.'

'A stone and a bloody *half*!???'

'Take it or leave it. Lose a stone and a half in the next three months and you're on. Just the one game, though. I'm not making a habit of this.'

So I've checked the fixture list and I've found us the perfect match. Julie will make her Albion début at Colchester on 30 March.

Hang on a minute. '*Will*', did I say? Shouldn't that be 'she *might*', or at least 'she will, *so long as I've stuck to my side of my bargain*?' Nope. Because I'm not going to. The fact is, I'm never going to lose a stone and a half by the end of March, and Julie knows it. We both do. But she'll still end up coming to the game.

So what's been going on, you're probably wondering? All that negotiating, all that bargaining, what the hell was all *that* for? Well, it's a bit hard to explain, really. But I'll try.

Julie and I have absolutely no will-power. Neither of us do. Not a scrap. And the point is, this is one of our greatest bonds, one of the qualities which has kept our marriage strong. Diets, exercise regimes, healthy new habits – we're never talking more than a week, tops. But we like to *pretend* we've got it. And then we humour each other. One of us, every so often, will vow to quit this, or take up that, and the other one will go along with it, effectively saying, 'Fine. Good idea,' and knowing full well that it's never going to happen. When, within a matter of days, the quitter, or taker-upper, has done the decent thing and fucked up, the other one of us will say nothing but feel quietly comforted. Common sense, equilibrium has been restored. We feel closer for it.

So in the case of the stone-and-a-half thing, it's almost more important that I break my promise – at least, once I've briefly gone through the motions, made some sort of token weight-loss gesture – than I keep it. Seriously. I'm sure that's what Julie expects of me, just as I'd hope she'd do likewise after promising to go vegan. I'll be breaking a small, short-term deal, but only so as to stick to our big, long-term one. It'll confirm that, despite what she may have begun thinking recently, I'm still essentially the Mike she married. It'll mean I've not gone *doubly* weird on her. And then she'll be a lot more relaxed about coming to the match.

OK, so you may think we're a bit strange. Granted, it's probably not an understanding which would work for every marriage. But it works for us. Trust me.

Oh, and by the way, I've quit smoking again. It was making me feel sick and pongy. I'm not sure how I'm going to break that one to her.

The Boy Done Pud – TUESDAY 8 JANUARY

Who'd have thought it? Not merely that I'd head down the replica-shirt-wearing route, given the sniffy nonsense I was spouting a few months back, but that when I unwrapped my Wardy-inscribed Albion shirt on Christmas day, the first match for which I'd be wearing it would be one in which I was playing.

Yes, *playing*.

Me.

Me playing football.

With the boys in blue and white, would you believe?

It must be a good ten years since I last played football, other than the odd brief, wheezy kickabout with Em (or my nephew Ollie, since Em's ingrowing toenail has effectively put an end to her not-very-promising-in-any-case career). But last night, at the end of another crushingly dull but no doubt still desperately important stadium committee meeting, I got chatting once again with Albion's press officer, Paul Camillin, this time about getting fit. Or in my case, at least going through the motions. And after about ten minutes of not very enthusiastic natter about going for runs and all that tedious, soul-destroying rubbish, Paul came out with nine words which were music to my ears: 'Why don't you come and play football with us?'

For a split second – well, OK, more like the tiniest minuscule fraction of a split nanosecond – I found myself thinking he meant with the Albion. Not actually playing *for* them, obviously, but at least *with* them. At training or something. Knocking in a few corners to test Michel Kuipers, sending a couple of soaring, inch-perfect passes into the path of Bobby Z. Running into space to receive a neat little flick from Lee Steele. Competing with Paul Watson to see who can fire the most lethal 25-yard free kick. Weaving rings around . . . sorry, I'm over-egging this a bit now, aren't I?

But then I twigged that he didn't mean the Albion at all. What he meant, stupid me, was that I could play with him and a bunch of other Albion *fans*. If I was up for it, that is. Which I was.

'We play up at Bluggle-Splodge-Doodle-Flop every Tuesday night,' he explained, 'as long as there's not an Albion match that night.' Paul didn't actually say 'Bluggle-Splodge-Doodle-Flop', as you may have guessed, but since I didn't catch the name of wherever he did say, he may as well have done.

In fact, the setting turned out to be on the outskirts of Portslade, a place just up the road – more Hove than Brighton – which is a wee bit like you'd imagine Slough would look if time had stood still since the day Maggie Thatcher took office. Since this would be my first game, and since I obviously didn't know how to get there, Paul and I rendezvoused, or however the hell you spell it, at a petrol station down the road, so that he could lead the way. I wore my Albion shirt beneath the grey Skint hooded sweatshirt – finished off rather fetchingly, I felt, with a pair of figure-squeezing tracksuit-bottoms which I'd picked up for a tenner a few hours earlier. I was looking forward to this.

Until we arrived.

'The standard's really hopeless,' Paul had promised, so I'd conjured up a fairly unthreatening image of a dozen-or-so wobble-bellies lumbering around a five-a-side pitch. Instead, there were masses of blokes dashing about on floodlit, full-sized Astroturf.

Shit.

What's worse, they were shouting. Those urgently gruff, no-messing shouts you hear whenever blokes are playing football and taking it even half-seriously. 'Man on!' 'Space!' 'Time!' Even in the days when I did play the odd game, this was something I struggled to cope with. It made me laugh. It still does. And I know I'm not supposed to. Whenever I hear a player shouting: 'Time!' there's a huge, puerile part of me which still wants to yell back, 'Quarter past three!'

On top of which, there was the nickname business. One of the guys there tonight, I soon sussed from the shouting, was called Pitbull. Now, I had a real problem with this. Not that Pitbull was attempting to live up to his nickname; he wasn't violent or intimidating or sinking his fangs into opponents' faces. It was simply the fact that he had a nickname full-stop. Had he been called, say, Poodle – or, I dunno, Pork Scratching – I'd have felt just as unnerved. Nicknames, I'm afraid, are yet another of my problem zones. I've never felt comfortable using them – no matter how firmly established a particular nickname may be, no matter how close the friend. I have one pal, for example, called John Barton, who is known to absolutely everyone – mates, work colleagues, even his own partner – simply as Barton. He even refers to himself by that name. And what do *I* call him? I call him John. It's almost more baffling, this problem, than my discomfort with dancing, or joining in with football chants. I can only imagine that I find it too presumptuously pally – as if somehow I shouldn't consider myself sufficiently close to this person to permit myself to call him (or her) by anything other than their regular name.

Anyway, there it was – big pitch, floodlights, loads of blokes, nicknames, shouting. Please sir, can I be excused?

'You wearing stripes under that?' shouted the guy guarding the nearest goal. 'Yep,' I replied, as nonchalantly as I could manage.

'Right,' he went. 'Just join in with us lot.'

Strangely enough, it turned out that Paul and I had brought the numbers to exactly 22 – and I was the 11th bloke to show up in an Albion shirt. Despite all my other misgivings, I felt childishly proud.

The pitch was really two pitches, divided by a thin white line, with the combined playing surfaces surrounded by a high wire fence to reduce the risk of the ball ending up in Kent. I immediately took up position on the left.

God alone knows why, mind you; I'm no more left-footed than I am three-legged. But there seemed an awful lot of space down that side, so it struck me as a good place to hover if I wanted a few touches.

But *did* I want them? Might I not have been wiser to let this lot get on with it while I maintained a low profile? After all, what the fuck would I do if the ball actually did come my way? In all the excitement about actually playing football again, I'd hardly given this not-insignificant detail a moment's thought. All I could remember, now that I was out there, was that I wasn't actually any *good* at football. Not even vaguely. I never had been.

I'd always longed to be, same as any fan. But until the age of about 17, I was overweight and desperately out of shape. (Now that I think about it, I've probably spent less than a third of my life being the weight I'm supposed to be.) Even so, I can vividly remember, probably up until a couple of years before that, seriously believing I might still become a professional footballer. Never mind my total lack of fitness, that I had absolutely no talent and – best of all, this – the fact that I was a speccy kid at a Home Counties grammar school where we didn't even sodding well *play* football – somehow I still convinced myself there was a genuine chance I could make the grade. In truth, there'd have been more chance of Bob Wilson joining Boney M.

So did I really want that ball to come my way tonight? For the first ten-or-so minutes, it made precious little difference whether I did or not; it didn't roll within a mile of me, not even when I made an effort to lumber into what I imagined was a superb position – acres of space, loads of room to run, easy to reach with a cretinously simple pass.

Obviously, in one sense, this was a sound strategy on my team mates' part. Even in the twenty-first century, the average football team, no matter what their level, will fall back on the old-fashioned 'don't pass it to that bloke who's shit' philosophy. But the point is, they didn't *know* I was shit. They couldn't have done. Not yet. They'd never even met me, let alone seen me play; I'd only been on the pitch a matter of minutes. Until such time as I made contact with the ball, they couldn't possibly know how jaw-droppingly hopeless I was. That said, I suppose there were clues: my weight, for one. Plus the fact I'd kept my specs on.

When the ball eventually did reach me, I quickly confirmed what most of them had probably already guessed. I set off diagonally towards the goal, spotted a team mate in a good central position, and tapped a little pass in his direction. I say 'in his direction' because it goes without saying that it never reached him. It was another ten minutes before anyone passed to me again.

By this time, however, I'd discovered something which had raised my spirits a little: I'd discovered that nobody else was much good either. Sure, they were loads better than I was – it would have been hard not to be – but not to the point where I stuck out like the sorest of appendages. Once I'd twigged this, my body language must have changed for the better because I suddenly began getting more of the ball. I don't think I'll ever forget the moment, roughly 35 minutes into the game, when Pitbull roared, 'Unlucky, Wardy – good effort!' I'd never heard a line like that as a kid. The lines I'd heard as a kid had nearly always included the word 'spastic'.

Three-quarters of the way through, however, my lack of fitness began to tell. The only way I'd last the full hour was if I slowed to a virtual standstill. Not that this mattered, provided I chose the right parts of the pitch to stand in. What I'd do, I figured, was concentrate on the 'memorable one-touch' approach; in other words, if the ball came my way, I'd try some smartarse flick or back-heel which would, in theory, lay it off to a team mate in an impressive manner, while consuming little or no energy. Amazingly, this worked, too. Twice, in fact – once with a back-heel near the corner flag (not that there was actually a flag there, you understand), the other time with a delicious outside-of-the-foot volley which delivered the ball straight in to the path of a team mate. Neither move got us anywhere, needless to say, but they fulfilled the only two criteria which mattered by now: (1) I didn't miss the ball altogether and look an arsehole; and (2) I didn't give it straight to an opponent and, erm, look an arsehole.

As we moved into the last ten minutes, I decided to make my presence felt in defence. Big mistake. As I lunged for a loose ball, I suddenly felt a strange pinging sensation in the lower half of my right leg. At the risk of confusing you with complex medical terminology, I'd buggered my calf. I could barely walk, let alone unleash a netbuster.

When the floodlights eventually dimmed – indicating that, thank God, our time was up – we trudged off, gathered the various belongings we'd dumped behind each goal, handed £2 each to the bloke who'd hired the pitch, and trundled away. Limped, in my case.

'Coming for a drink?' asked Paul, oblivious to my agony, motioning towards a bar where most of the lads were now headed. 'Er, no, thanks,' I replied. 'I need to get back.' In truth, I was a bit concerned that whatever I drank would undo any good I'd just done myself. More significantly I was worried that I'd find myself in a situation which I dread when I'm drinking in male company: heading to the loo at the same time as another bloke, then finding myself completely incapable of weeing at an adjacent urinal. Indeed, I could almost visualise how this nightmare would unfold. 'Wardy can't wee!' my new footballing chums would cry, possibly with a view to turning this into an official North Stand chant. Believe me, I have nothing but envy and admiration for blokes who can happily stand and urinate in the company of others, spraying the stuff around as if they're tackling a minor house blaze. Me, I just seize up; the only solution I've found is to shut myself in a private cubicle, where somehow I'm able to relax enough to start the flow.

Back home, I couldn't wait to tell Julie all about my reintroduction to football. I figured she'd be especially keen to hear about that beautiful side-of-foot volley. But – can you believe this? – she hadn't waited up. She hadn't just gone to bed either; she was snoring like a warthog. You'd almost imagine she didn't care.

I consoled myself with hobbling into the bathroom and stepping on to the scales.

Not bad. Not bad at all. I'd gained two pounds.

Meanwhile . . . SATURDAY 12 JANUARY

WIGAN ATHLETIC 3 BRIGHTON 0
LEAGUE POSITION: 4TH

Oops.

'Don't suppose I'll be needing this after all,' muttered Paul S, sadly, laying his dusty yellow loudhailer on the table beside him. The rest of us could have tried to argue with the bloke, but we wouldn't have sounded very convincing.

Poor sod. He deserved better than this. I felt as if we ought to be rallying round our campaign chairman, showering him with comforting clichés. 'It's not so bad.' 'Things could be worse.' Maybe even, in a desperate attempt to lighten the mood, 'Falmer wasn't built in a day.' But none of us seemed up to the task. It was 10.15 a.m. on a miserable, misty Sunday, and the dominant mood in Withdean's hospitality hut was one of thinly veiled despair. The only emotion threatening to match it was one of pure embarrassment.

We'd speculated as to how many Albion fans might show up this morning, for this Falmer Petition Day. A reminder had gone in the programme, another on the club's website, yet another had been broadcast over the PA at the last match. Volunteers should gather here at ten, it said, to pick up a heap of petition forms and set off to one of several carefully targeted points around the county. Paul had it planned with precision, the way you'd expect. All we'd wondered was how *many* volunteers we'd need to cater for. Would we have enough forms, badges, stickers and information packs for them all? Paul had talked about 150 people showing up.

It turned out he was almost spot-on, give or take 140.

'I don't suppose yesterday helped,' I suggested, referring to the Albion's performance at Wigan. 'Quite,' he replied, with surprising force and a rare hint of bitterness, as if the same thought had already occurred to him and he was contemplating legal action.

We waited, twiddled thumbs, shuffled papers for no obvious reason, hoped perhaps it was just Sunday morning sloth, and that maybe a few people would roll up late. A few did. By 11, at least another dozen had appeared. It was still a depressing response.

Once the late arrivals had been issued with instructions and sent on their way, the rest of us – myself, Paul S, Liz Costa-Too-Mucha, Tim Carder, Adrian Ground-Tour – sat in a semi-stunned, mildly despondent stupor.

We'd all go off and do our bit fairly shortly, but for a few minutes it felt as if the collective stuffing had been knocked out of us. We just needed to talk.

The subject turned inevitably to the team. Yesterday was the fourth match on the trot without a win – the last three having been draws. The league position is still pretty good, especially if we win the games in hand, and yet I've this horrible feeling – I'm sure I'm not alone in this – that this is where our season turns sour. Christmas, postponements, New Year, more postponements, all seem to have disrupted what had been a fantastic momentum, and with it the collective sense of confidence. It still amounts to only one league defeat under Peter Taylor, but the mood just doesn't feel right anymore.

I wasn't looking forward to my signature-collecting stint – the idea of approaching strangers, especially over an issue where some of them might decide to argue back quite aggressively, filled me with horror – but I was glad to leave the hut in the end. It was getting me down.

My destination was Asda at Brighton Marina. We'd already been given written permission from the manager to station somebody at the entrance – provided we didn't 'intimidate' his customers – but I pocketed his letter just in case I was challenged. Not that I need have worried. A lot of the Asda staff were really keen to sign. One or two of them even pinned our badge to their uniforms. I bet that went down a storm with the boss.

The customers were slightly trickier. My line of approach – polite, measured and reasonable, I reckoned – was, 'Excuse me, would you like to support the community stadium campaign?' So when the first three all looked at me as if I'd said, 'Excuse me, would you like to perform fellatio on my dog?' I began to get a bad feeling.

So that's when I rang for Julie.

Yes, I know what you're thinking: Julie doesn't give a stuff about the Albion. And you're right, she doesn't. But it was Sunday morning, she was bored and lonely, and so she agreed to come and give me some moral support. Once she'd finished her toast.

At first her presence was more of a hindrance than a help, purely because I spent the time chatting to her, rather than approaching passers-by. But then, astonishingly, she volunteered to take over. And it turned out she was a natural.

Gradually we – *she* – filled the first sheet. Then a second. Then a third. Pretty soon we'd stopped counting. Being a sales person, Julie is used to approaching strangers, and will laugh dismissively – and a wee bit madly, to be honest – in the face of rejection. I, on the other hand, had been growing more depressed and despondent with every refusal.

Even with Julie taking charge, mind you, one or two people seemed to derive enormous pleasure from snottily dismissing us – not, I suspect, because they had a strong opinion either way, but because it looked as if this was their instinctive response to anyone with a clipboard who happened to approach them in the street. It did occur to me that I do the same thing myself, but obviously that's for very different reasons. In my case, I'm aware that anyone with a clipboard who approaches me in the street is intending to snatch me away to their sinister subterranean commune where I'll be forced me to disown my entire family, thrash myself hourly with rusty barbed wire and change my name to Thworb. Either that or they're going to try and flog me a subscription to *Reader's Digest.*

Not surprisingly, one or two people assumed we were after money. One customer fumbled in his trouser pocket, scooped out a clammy fistful of coins and tried to shove them into my hand. He seemed so disappointed when I told him we only needed his signature that I wondered if maybe I should have accepted his contribution in any case; I could have nipped in and bought us some chops.

At no stage, of course, did I dismiss any potential signatory purely on the basis of their appearance. Unless they looked too posh, that is. Or too old. Or too old-fashioned. Or too much like a member of the Christian Union.

Of those who looked as if they'd sign, the huge majority did. One group of lads surprised me by refusing, and quite aggressively, but I decided not to read too much into this. In expecting them to write their own names, I'd probably just been a tad over-ambitious.

We packed up and headed home just after four, satisfied that we'd had a fairly productive few hours. It had turned out that there were plenty of people in favour of the stadium after all. There just hadn't been many who'd fancied giving up their Sunday to stand around in the cold, collecting signatures. Perhaps it was because Arsenal were on the telly.

Whatever, I felt kind of smug.

'So did you enjoy that?' I asked Julie as we climbed back into the car. 'Actually, yeah,' she admitted. 'I did.'

We were getting there.

Fit For Nothing – MONDAY 14 JANUARY

I have a stock excuse which I like to trot out whenever the subject turns to fitness regimes – or, more specifically, to my refusal ever to commit myself to one, long-term. I point out that it's a waste of time if you don't enjoy it. I've heard experts arguing much the same thing on GMTV, so how much more scientifically plausible do you need me to be?

Over the past decade, I've been a member of three different health clubs. I've also been a walking cliché: the lump of lard who never shows up. These places must love idiots like me, customers who continue to fork out their monthly direct debit, experiencing an odd blend of guilt and gullibility whenever they spot it on their bank statement, but who never show up to spill so much as a pipette-full of sweat on the Stepmaster. I bet there's even an official name for our sort; these clubs probably build us into their business forecasts. If we passive members quietly joined forces and agreed to turn up all at once, there'd be chaos. Maybe we should try it one day, just for a laugh.

But we never would, and they know it. It's two years since I last set foot inside the actual gym section of my health club (it's probably a bit daft to keep calling it 'my', but then I'm still helping to fund the bloody place). I'd done an interview for the *Daily Star* with a guy called Chris Moon – an ex-army officer who'd lost half a leg in a landmine accident, but who'd since returned to running thanks to a high-tech artificial limb. This bloke was such an inspiration that by the end of the interview he'd somehow persuaded me that, like him, I could run the next London Marathon. Even more impressively, he'd kept a straight face when he'd said this. He'd told me I could easily shed the surplus blubber, that I'd have no difficulty building up my fitness, and that I'd feel a zillion times better into the bargain. The very next day, I was up on the running machine – taking it gently at first, as Chris had advised, but already feeling I'd turned a significant corner.

I kept this up for, ooh, about six weeks: nipping to the gym every other day, building up my speeds, my times, my distances. On the days in between, I'd swim. In just over a month, I lost about half a stone. Chris had been right. I did feel better. I felt fantastic. Instinctively, I also found I wanted to drink less alcohol, and to eat less crap.

But all the time there was The Voice. A nagging, sceptical voice, telling me to take a glance around that gym. The moment I gave in and did what The Voice told me to do, I was in trouble. I looked at my fellow gym-users and realised they nearly all fell into one of two categories: they were either sad, purple-faced wobble-bellies, pounding away in what you knew would ultimately be a fruitless (possibly even dangerous) quest to regain shape ('That's how sad *you* look,' said The Voice, sounding strangely like David Baddiel). Or they were serious fitness freaks, all thickly-gelled hair, sticky-out veins, and glazed, mildly manic expressions. It was hard to admire or respect either type. Sure, there was probably a middle ground – a relatively sane bunch of people simply keeping in trim – but I managed to avoid spotting any examples. So it was easy to convince myself they didn't exist.

Even so, I'd have probably stuck with it if I'd thought any of these people were having fun. But if one thing seemed to unite the loons and the lard-arses, it was the misery etched on their faces. The back-snapping, lung-scorching, soul-destroying agony of the whole process. In their fight for fitness, these people seemed to be making themselves utterly miserable. Maybe some got a kick out of that, but I didn't want to be one of them.

So that fitness regime was doomed. It only took a couple of unexpected work commitments, followed by some minor family gathering, to knock me off track. Once the routine was broken, that was it. The momentum was gone. Within a fortnight, I was back to square one. Within a couple of months I looked like a pig again. Chris and I lost touch. I decided to give the Marathon a miss, just so as not to trouble St John Ambulance.

Which brings me back to my point: that if you hate it, or have the potential to hate it, then this kind of regime will never work. Sooner or later you'll think, 'Fuck this for a game of soldiers,' and tumble back into old habits.

So here's the fundamental philosophy behind the Ward Fitness Alternative: only do stuff you enjoy. It may seem a tad lacking in ambition, but one of the bonuses of middle-age is that you know quite a lot about yourself. Or you should. So it's fairly easy to step back, examine your life, and be honest about how much of it you're ever likely to change.

When it comes to enjoyable exercise machines, there's only one and I'm afraid it's in Cyprus. I came across this piece of equipment a couple of years back, hidden away in the basement of our holiday hotel, in the establishment's musty excuse for a health club. I liked using this machine because it felt like a game. Unlike the humourless efforts I'd come across before, this one had its own little TV screen on which two computer-simulated boats were competing, one of them powered entirely by my own efforts. In other words, I could concentrate on the contest rather than on the exercise. I was hopeless at it, obviously, but it was fun. By the end of the fortnight I was definitely a bit less hopeless than I'd been at the start, when I'd consistently allowed the other boat to win by such a convincing margin that its cartoon occupants had had time to clamber out, get showered and sink a round of virtual reality lagers.

Jogging is a pursuit which I'd particularly advise against. Obviously there's nothing wrong with running in itself; it's handy if you're late for a train, for example, or being chased by people with knives. But to run when it's not necessary is a mistake. Never forget: joggers get the piss ripped out of them. I should know; I'm one of the people who do it.

Competitive sports, then, would seem the best answer. They distract you from the physical discomfort and let you focus on the challenge itself. Unfortunately, I'm useless at them. The Tuesday-night footie was a reminder of that. I used to be reasonable at badminton, but that was about it. Tennis I've never fancied, on the grounds that tennis clubs are packed with the sort of people who join tennis clubs. Golf seems to attract an unhealthy proportion of Mike Baldwins (and I can't believe it helps your fitness much anyway). Cricket requires teamwork, strategic thinking and physical co-ordination — and since I gather the ability to play cricket kind of helps, too, that's four reasons for me to rule it out. And basketball? I'm not American and I'm not an 11 ft freak, so fuck off.

I could go on. I frequently do. But for now I think I've achieved my objective. I've written off my latest fitness regime before it's even begun.

I believe that's some kind of record.

Part-timers — TUESDAY 15 JANUARY

BRIGHTON 0 PRESTON NORTH END 2
(FA CUP THIRD ROUND)

'I've won! I've fucking won!'

It was half-time, and the bloke behind me was jabbing the number on his crumpled Withdean Wager ticket, yelling to the mate beside him. 'Five hundred fucking quid!'

I allowed myself a smile. Or more of a smirk, really. For the last 45 minutes I'd had to listen to this guy slagging off just about every Albion player on the pitch. 'You're a fucking waste of money, Zamora!' he'd yelled, after Bobby's 19th-minute penalty, which would have pulled us level, had been slapped to safety by Preston's keeper.

(The Albion, I should point out, paid £100,000 for Bobby Zamora. Thanks to his virtual goal-a-game record, he's now valued at around £5 million. I'm no genius when it comes to arithmetic, but at a rough calculation, to within 10 per cent either way, I'd say that made the bloke behind me a wanker.)

OK, we were poor tonight – and after the disappointment of Wigan, and the bad mood which followed, we could have done with some cheering up. But what really hacked me off about this gobby wassock was that he clearly wasn't a regular. He hadn't earned the *right* to slag off the team. To slag off *my* team.

Gobby and his mate had obviously taken advantage of the fact that, this being a cup tie where season ticket allocations don't count, the seats behind had been going spare.

I know what you're thinking: what right have I, Bandwagon Boy, to come over all protective? I don't know, really. It just gets to you that way.

Obviously I wasn't going to turn round and give Gobby a mouthful. It never achieves anything, and besides, he might have decided to try out some amateur dentistry on me. I just hoped the team would answer his criticism on the pitch. Or that fate would, by some other means, put the little runt in his place.

Being half-time, when standing up and stretching your legs is obviously standard behaviour, it wasn't too hard for me to sneak a casual glance at this guy's ticket. And sure enough, the four-figure number matched the one just announced over the PA.

'I've fucking won 500 quid!' he was still yelling, just in case we hadn't heard him the fifth time.

But I'd seen all I'd needed to see. I was happy now. I sat down, settled back, pulled out my plastic bottle of warm Diet Pepsi and allowed myself a celebratory swig.

Smug? Oh, very. But I guess that's one of the perks of becoming a regular fan. Regular enough, at least, to know that there's such a thing as the Seagulls Lottery, and that it bears absolutely no relation to the Withdean Wager.

And that, when winning numbers are read out over Withdean's ropey PA system, you really do need to pay close attention. Otherwise you just might get the two competitions mixed up. And wouldn't that be terrible, if you were clutching what you assumed was a winning number?

Thank you, God. I owe you one.

BRIGHTON 4 CAMBRIDGE UNITED 3
LEAGUE POSITION: 4TH

I marched to the ground as quickly as I could. I tackled the journey home at an equally brisk pace. I wasn't in a hurry, or being chased; I just thought it might do me some good. The sooner I tell Julie what she already knows – that this weight-loss thing just isn't going to happen – the sooner I can stop all this nonsense.

Mind you, if watching a game burns up calories in itself – up from your seat whenever the action demands it, down again the moment it fizzles out – then today's match provided the ultimate workout. One–nil up, only to concede an equaliser two minutes later. Two–one up, then making the same twattish error within five minutes. Three–two – and then guess what happens six minutes after that? The only reason it didn't end 4–4, I'm convinced, is that the seventh goal, Bobby's winner, came too close to the final whistle. Another couple of minutes and I'm sure the pattern would have repeated itself. By the end, we were laughing as much as cheering. Lousy football, top entertainment. Absolutely draining, mentally and physically. Seven goals. Two penalties. One sending-off. Three bookings. One hat-trick. And, most crucially, three precious points. I thought it was rather a pity they didn't bring on a troupe of dolphins to perform the can-can at half-time, but I guess you can't have everything.

Half an hour before the end, I'd been thinking this could be it. This match – seemingly a walkover before kick-off, against the second lowest team in the division – could be our season's turning-point. If we lost, or if we just didn't win (and we'd not won for five bloody matches), then everything could, to use a specialist football expression, turn to poo. Confidence would crumble, team spirit would evaporate, the crowd would turn nasty. 'Taylor out. Taylor out. Taylor out.' Was this how the final weeks of this campaign were going to pan out? Was my fair-weather fandom about to face its toughest challenge? It was spitting with rain and I felt deeply pissed off.

So my roar when Bobby headed in his 88th-minute winner – completing his hat-trick – was largely one of relief. A simple enough goal, but 12 weeks from now it could make all the difference in the world.

All the difference in *my* world.

Communication Breakdown – MONDAY 21 JANUARY

CHESTERFIELD 1 BRIGHTON 2
LEAGUE POSITION: 2ND

Stomp stomp stomp stomp stomp. Click. Stomp stomp stomp stomp stomp.

Any idea what that's the sound of? Have another listen:

Stomp stomp stomp stomp stomp. Click. Stomp stomp stomp stomp stomp.

Give up? Thought you might.

It's the sound of me applying my latest method of keeping up with an Albion away match. Stomp stomp stomp stomp stomp. Click. Stomp stomp stomp stomp stomp.

You'd imagine bog-standard Teletext would be the simplest, most convenient way of checking a match score, short of actually tuning in to the radio commentary. Not for me it isn't. Not because my TV isn't sufficiently sophisticated, but because, as far as I can make out, its sophistication is so acute that it considers handling such a dreary, old-fashioned analogue service to be somehow beneath it. In short, my telly is a snob. Try as I might – and, believe me, I've pressed every button, every combination of buttons, every sequence of buttons, every permutation of buttons, on every sodding remote control in the house – but since I've had digital telly I've found it impossible to pick up the plain, creaky old version of Teletext which served me so well for so long. I dare say it's hiding in there somewhere, but I'm buggered if I can find it.

In theory, I shouldn't need to. The nature of my job – writing about TV programmes – means I've been rigged up to receive digital television in its slickest, swishiest form. And since digital TV services are forever banging on about their latest clever-cloggy interactive gimmickry, I ought to have shed any dependence on the old-fashioned, clunking Teletext yonks ago. By now I should be a dab hand with the super-whizzy digital alternatives.

But I'm not. I hate them. I hate them all. Not one of them seems capable of providing me with simple, quick, effortlessly accessible information, the way the old service did. Beforehand I could just jab the appropriate button on my remote, key in the page number and – bingo! – there was the score. I could even superimpose it on top of whatever programme we happened to be watching at the time. OK, you sometimes had to wait a few seconds for the page to spin round to the one you were specifically looking for – and poor reception could sometimes turn the words on the screen into gibberish (Ars al hav b aten iverpoo ith a ast-minut nalty at Anfie) – but by and large it was stress-free.

These days the standard old text button on my basic remote just gives me a black screen. Great. Thanks a bundle. I'm only amazed it doesn't flash up a message saying, 'Fuck off, Grandad.'

Admittedly, my other, more 'sophisticated' remotes offer me something rather different. They offer me a plain blue screen instead, usually with some stupid white symbol spinning away in the corner, accompanied by the infuriating words, 'Loading, please wait.' Again, this only tells half the story. A more accurate message would be, 'If I were you, I'd go and make yourself a cup of tea, mate. I'm so painfully slow, we could be here till bloody Easter.'

When the menu eventually does flash up, it gives me the option to move into the sports section. Followed by the option to move into the football section. Followed by Nationwide Division Two. Followed by 'latest scores', Followed by 'oops, sorry, dear viewer, I appear to have seized up altogether, but, hey, don't worry – all you need to do is unplug me, wait a couple of minutes, switch me back on again and start this whole process from scratch. I'm a heap of bollocks, really, aren't I?'

As an alternative, I've tried subscribing to one of those services which sends the scores as text messages to your mobile. Unfortunately, the one I chose was about as effective as signing a deal with an arthritic carrier pigeon. Some days it just didn't bother. Other times it was alerting me so late that the players were already tucked up in bed. What the pigging hell use was that? Other than maybe to a footie fan halfway up Everest, where perhaps a delay in receiving Albion score flashes might be of less significance than, say, fighting off yetis.

Anyway, sorry – back to where we came in. Stomp stomp click etc.

It's the sound – and maybe you've guessed this while I've been ranting – of me running up the stairs, clicking on the BBC sports website and getting the latest Albion score via its Division Two page. And then running back downstairs again. It's a major innovation, this service, because it doesn't just palm you off with the score itself. God, no. It actually treats you to move-by-move detail on every game, updated every two minutes. So for a match such as tonight's, for example, this might read something like:

12:51 Cross by Paul Brooker (Brighton), diving header by Lee Steele (Brighton), narrowly wide.

14:31 Desperate clearance off the line by Paul Watson (Brighton). It's a crap game, this, by the way. Be grateful you didn't pay to come and watch it.

Or words to that effect.

Anyway, like a coward, I followed Albion's progress tonight almost exclusively via this method. Stomp stomp click, 1–0 up (Bobby Z). Yessss! Stomp stomp click, 2–0 up (Bobby again). We're back!! This went on until there were only about five minutes left. Then, feeling pretty chilled about the scoreline with so little time remaining, I stomp-stomped down to the kitchen and turned on the radio commentary. It was safe now. I could relax and just savour the victory.

Except it wasn't 2–0 at all. It was 2–1. Had been for ages. Whoever's job it was to update that web page had obviously popped to the BBC canteen for a fucking doughnut.

We held on, but that was hardly the point. Yet another score service had let me down. It turned out that what they'd done, as I found out when I looked at the page more closely after the game, was mention Chesterfield's goal in the downpage text but forget to update the score at the top. I expect they were planning to get round to it.

Still, no harm done. I suppose. What matters is, we're back on track. Next stop: Brentford on Thursday, live, in front of the ITV cameras. That'll be great, because it'll mean Julie can sit and watch it with me. She can drool in anticipation of watching the Albion in the flesh. OK, so she hasn't officially agreed to do that yet; I've neither shed the blubber we talked about, nor got around to the bit where I officially own up that I'm never going to. Believe me, it's vital to pick the right moment to make these announcements. That's how we do it. Until then, we'll remain in a kind of limbo.

Mind you, once she sees for herself just how good the Albion can be, I reckon she'll forget all about it.

BRENTFORD 4 BRIGHTON 0
LEAGUE POSITION: 2ND

Well, thanks a bundle, lads. That was just plain embarrassing. There I was, perched on the sofa in my tight, shiny Wardy shirt, excitedly telling Julie and Em what a feast of football they could look forward to, when all along what I should have said was, 'I'd go upstairs and watch *Friends* if I were you. We're about to be mullah'd.'

As it happens, Em didn't need any such prompting and did precisely that within minutes of the kick-off. We were so sluggish, so shapeless, so uncoordinated, so Not Man United – that she'd probably have been just as tempted by a repeat of *Gardener's World* from 1976. Julie hung on, bless her, but only so as to keep me company.

'It's, er . . . not very good, is it?' she whispered, after the third had flown in. But neither her gently cautious tone nor her relatively sensitive choice of words could disguise what she was really thinking. Julie was clearly stunned by our pure awfulness. She had every right to be. It wasn't as if Brentford were great, but they did at least look as though they'd quite like to win. Most of the Albion players looked as though their minds were on anything but the match. It was as if they'd suddenly realised they'd programmed the wrong video channel before setting out, and that, rather then being able to go home and watch themselves later, they'd be returning to a tape full of fat Japanese blokes in giant nappies.

Still, maybe it was my fault. I'd had a bad day, and bad days rarely turn into good ones. Once the pattern sets in, you're stuck with it. All you can do is grit your teeth and remember not to step into traffic.

What had hacked me off the most was that, just before lunchtime, I'd realised I'd forgotten my godson's birthday. Not only had I felt as guilty as hell about this, but it had also meant a frantic dash into town to find him a prezzie.

If you want to put a specific time on it, then, I'd say I officially wrote off the Albion's chances against Brentford at 12.45 p.m. this afternoon, when I found myself in Argos, urgently trying to choose between an Action Man shark-hunter kit or a set of Thunderbirds Are Go-Ing To Be Frigging Expensive.

My day, I knew then, was jinxed. And the jinx was bound to transfer itself to the team tonight because . . . well, because that's what jinxes do. They don't just affect you, they affect everything which touches your world. Jinxes are little shits, really.

I'm almost tempted to send Peter Taylor a message to this effect, assuring him he needn't blame himself, nor the players, nor bother with a post-match inquest. 'It was my fault, not yours,' I could say. 'So relax, there's no crisis.'

I'm just afraid he might take me seriously.

Sour Notes – THURSDAY 31 JANUARY

BRIGHTON 1 CARDIFF CITY 0
LEAGUE POSITION: 2ND

Along with the zillion-and-one other things which I've not quite got around to doing this season, I've still not attempted to sing. At an Albion game, I mean. I've warbled to Travis at the traffic lights, but I don't think that counts.

I have, however, come up with a couple of impressively plausible excuses.

Perhaps the most significant is that I attend these games alone. Well, obviously I'm joined by about 6,869 others, other than for midweek ties in the Tonka Truck Trophy, but the point is I don't sit with friends. And this immediately presents me with a massive psychological barrier. Belting out footie chants with a handful of mates seems perfectly OK – perhaps not the kind of behaviour everyone's inclined towards, but certainly not the kind which would be considered especially odd. (Not unless you were doing it in, say, Furniture Village.) The fact is, if you're singing with a bunch of your mates, you're effectively performing for each other almost as much as you are for the team. It's a communal experience. A bonding thing. Unity. Solidarity. And no doubt several other puffed-up words ending in a Y. At least, that's how it looks from the outside. Singing by yourself, on the other hand, I've always considered to be the behaviour of a mental person, like muttering to yourself about cauliflowers or Prince Edward.

Also, let's be honest, most football songs are silly. Take, for example,

'We're by far the greatest team, the world has ever seen.' I'm sorry to strike a disloyal note here, but in the case of Brighton and Hove Albion, love them as I do, I'm reasonably certain this isn't true. If that song has ever been sung with even a hint of validity, I doubt it would have been in English. Historically speaking, a rendition in Portuguese, sometime during Brazil's 4–1 trouncing of Italy in the 1970 World Cup final, would probably have struck the most convincing chord. As far as the current Albion side are concerned (or Bright'n-Ove Alb-Yurn Eff See, as it has to be to fit the tune) a more realistic lyric – one with which I might feel a tad more inclined to join in – would be, 'We're not at all bad when we pull our fingers out, but there are weeks when we're such shite that me and my mates sneak out ten minutes before half-time so we can be first in the queue for the hot dogs.' Admittedly, you might struggle to get this to scan.

The Albion do, of course, have their very own song, 'Sussex By The Sea'. It's fairly safe to say that, unlike 'You'll Never Walk Alone', this one probably won't be hijacked by rival supporters, if only because of the restriction imposed by its geographical focus. 'Good old Sussex by the sea' would sound a wee bit silly coming from the mouths of, say, Colchester fans. (Although I suppose, if they felt the tune was strong enough to merit pilfering, they could sneakily change the Sussex bit to Essex. Good old Essex . . . erm . . . up a tree, perhaps?) But in all honesty – and I appreciate it's bordering on sacrilege to say this – I find the song mildly naff. For one thing, the version which crackles across the PA before kick-off sounds as if it dates from the earliest days of recorded sound. I've got a vision of some cobwebby old soul in the control box, hunched over a dust-caked 78 and a wind-up gramophone. Obviously I'm in a minority here because it's one of the crowd's favourite chants during play, but I still find it funny to hear football fans coming out with, 'And we're going up to win the cup for Sussex by the Sea,' with its archaic, rosette-and-rattle, Brylcreemy feel, sandwiched between, 'When the ball hits the net / Like a fu-cking rock-et / That's Zamoraaaa.'

Of the other favourites, I'm afraid I'd also struggle to inject any real venom into, 'We hate Pal-iss and we hate Pal-iss / We hate Pal-iss and we hate Pal-iss / We hate Pal-iss and we hate Pal-iss / We are the Pal-iss . . . ha-ters.' Partly because I really couldn't give a toss one way or the other about Crystal Pal-iss (I reckon that would actually make a more powerfully patronising lyric), and partly because it's one of those football chants where, in order to lend it the authentic tone and resonance, you need to adopt a voice which makes you sound mildly brain-damaged, even if you normally speak like Stephen Fry. (Which I don't, by the way.) Whenever I hear chants like these, I can't help wondering whether, somewhere across the far side of Withdean, Des Lynam is joining in. I suppose I'd be kind of impressed if he were.

Bang up to date, we have 'Stand Up If You Want Falmer' – sung to the tune of the Village People's 'Go West'. Now, in one sense this is fantastic; it means I can respond to a chant without actually having to sing. Its only weakness is, we're not really meant to stand up during matches. We do, of course, when something interesting happens, but technically I think it's against the licensing regulations, or whatever it is we agreed to when we started playing here. So, ironically, this one might actually harm the very cause it's meant to be promoting. The obvious compromise would be to re-word the song as '*Hands* Up If You Want Falmer' – creating a similar effect, but without the risk. But then I guess it might look as if we were staging a Nazi rally.

Until tonight, I must admit, I hadn't heard anyone at Withdean singing 'Always Shit On The English Side Of The Fence'. But then I'd never met the Cardiff fans before. I'd heard they liked a song, these blokes, and this one, to the tune of Monty Python's 'Always Look On The Bright Side Of Life', seemed to be their favourite. Since they'd also trotted out the traditional anti-Brighton taunt of 'Does Your Boyfriend Know You're Here?', the only surprise was that nobody from our side had picked up on the Pythonesque theme and responded with 'The Lumberjack Song'. I don't know, I'm new to these things so maybe I was misjudging the mood, but I couldn't help feeling that several thousand blokes chanting, 'I put on women's clothing / And hang around in bars' would have quietened the visitors down a wee bit.

Instead, the response from the people around me was actually quite unsettling. This was genuine, steaming anger, on a level I'd not witnessed at Withdean before. Almost everyone was on their feet. Most were barking something raw and shapelessly abusive. One bloke in the row in front of me looked as if he was about to have some kind of seizure, his face turning Phil Mitchell-beetroot as he jabbed the air repeatedly with a succession of short, jerky V-signs. 'Faaaak off!!!' he roared. 'Faaaak off, you faaakin' Welsh caahhnts!'

A bunch to my left preferred to treat the faaakin' Welsh caahhnts to something slightly more tuneful – although I stress the word 'slightly'. Their choice was a nationalistic, knuckleheaded anthem about St George – apparently very popular with travelling England fans and traditionally accompanied by the rhythmic application of café furniture to continental heads.

Even when Bobby did what Bobby does and knocked in tonight's only goal, the Albion fans' reaction was tailored to the occasion. 'One–nil to the Inger-lurrnd,' they chanted. This one didn't strike me as particularly scary; just stupid and sad, as if one of our players scoring didn't count, other than in presenting the cretin contingent with an excuse to gloat about some entirely unrelated issue.

And yet perhaps most alarming of all was that, despite my discomfort, despite the fact that I loathed and despised all this nationalistic crap and the hostile, hateful undercurrent, I couldn't deny that the atmosphere this evening was electric. There are times when a match at Withdean will throb with all the passion of a WI coffee morning – it's obvious I'm not the only one with an aversion to singing – but tonight it was pulsating.

I'm not sure what conclusion I should be drawing from this.

It's probably best not to think about it.

The Rover's Return – TUESDAY 5 FEBRUARY

BRIGHTON 1 TRANMERE ROVERS 0
LEAGUE POSITION: 2ND

'Hey! Lost a bit of weight, have you, Mike?' cried Andy.

'No,' I replied.

'Didn't think so,' cried Andy.

'Fuck off,' I replied.

My, but it was good to have him back.

Given that affectionate greeting, I assumed Andy intended to launch straight into a string of jibes about my transparently disastrous fitness campaign. In fact, I half-hoped he would, if the alternative was an evening of his hilarious house-renovation anecdotes. I wasn't sure I could face a night of wacky wiring stories.

But then I remembered he knew nothing about it. We've never been the sort of mates who keep in contact on an intimate, ring-us-with-your-daily-gossip basis, Andy and I. Ours is more of a let's-meet-for-a-drink-every-few-weeks-and-take-the-piss-out-of-each-other relationship. I like it that way. Low maintenance. Low expectations. Lowbrow. No doubt any detailed analysis of our pub banter, for want of a less cringe-making expression, would reveal it to be disturbingly shallow, but I've always found it rather comforting.

So I decided to own up in any case. To my fitness failure, I mean. To the fact that I'd begun a regime and abandoned it about ten minutes later. And to how Julie would react when I admitted this.

'Blimey,' exclaimed Andy, in that downbeat way which doesn't quite merit an exclamation mark. 'So you've actually lost no weight at all?'

'Nope. Not an ounce. At least, not intentionally.'

'God. That's quite an achievement.'

'Thank you.'

'And let me get this right: that means Julie won't be coming to this away match with you?'

'No.'

'What – no, she won't be coming? Or no, it doesn't mean that?'

'No, it doesn't mean that.'

'But I thought . . .'

So I explained it all over again. I still don't think Andy understood, but at least he drew the conclusion I'd expected.

'You two are weird,' he declared.

'Thank you once again. I shall pass on your compliments.'

After topping up our glasses (Andy had switched to bitter, I noticed, but I didn't want to ask him why and suffer some beer-bore explanation), I returned to find him flicking through my match programme.

'Still going to every game, then?'

'Every home game, yeah. And Bury away, of course.'

'Of course. And I bet you're feeling pretty pleased with yourself, aren't you?'

'Am I?'

'I mean, considering how well they're doing. How much do you stand to collect?'

'Sorry? How do you mean?'

'How much money? If they go up.'

'What – from betting? Oh, for God's sake, you know that's not what this is about.' I hadn't meant to sound so pompous. It just came out that way.

'Yeah, yeah, of course it's not,' he conceded. 'So how much?'

I sighed. 'About 50 quid, I think.'

Andy had a smirk and a slurp. 'So anyway,' he went on, 'do you reckon the experiment's working? Your can-I-learn-to-love-another-team thing. I mean the Arse are doing pretty well in the Premiership.'

'It's working fine, thanks. But I'll tell you what – it doesn't half fucking drain you.'

'What, financially? All those tasteful Seagulls mugs and T-shirts?'

'No, you twat, I mean emotionally. It's like the strain of watching England at a World Cup, only stretched out for nearly nine months.'

'Diddums.'

'No, I'm not moaning. I'm just saying. If you've never really supported a team before in the proper sense, all season long, match after match . . .'

'Which you haven't.'

'. . . which I haven't, then you don't appreciate how much it can sap your strength.'

'Sap being the operative word in your case, you saddo.'

'Yeah, but that's the other thing. Compared to a lot of fans, I'm not that committed at all. Up against them, I'm a hopeless part-timer. Don't forget, I've still only been to one away match. There are Albion fans who trek to every game, home and away. They live and breathe the club.'

'God. So is that the next stage, then? The full 42 games a season?'

'Forty-six.'

'Forty-six. Whatever. Is that what's next?'

'I don't know. But it's a lot more appealing than it used to be, put it that way.'

'Uh-huh. And what happens when they turn shit? Still going to fork out 30-odd quid to travel to some meaningless mid-week, mid-season, mid-table, middle-of-fucking-nowhere match? Still going to hack up the motorway in the pissing rain for four hours to witness yet another clogging 0–0?'

I let out another sigh. I was sighing quite a lot this evening. Perhaps I'd subconsciously been saving up several weeks' worth of sighs, especially for Andy.

'So,' I said. 'I see you've switched to bitter.'

Owning Up – THURSDAY 7 FEBRUARY

It was a mere formality by this stage, of course, but tonight I finally confirmed to Julie that I wasn't going to meet my fitness target. And, yep, bang on cue, she agreed to come to the Colchester game in any case. To join me on the official supporters' coach on 30 March, just as we'd talked about, so that she could savour the full, exhilarating experience of an Albion awayday. Obviously she didn't agree to it in an instant-leap-up-and-down-with-excitement-oh-gosh-I-can't-wait sense, because that's not how our game works. That would be silly. She agreed in the way you're meant to agree, in a tell-you-what-seeing-as-you've-caught-me-in-a-good-mood sense.

But I already knew I had. It was all part of my strategy. (And, come on, Julie will do the same to me, the next time it's her turn.) I'd waited until the very right second of the very right minute of the very right hour of the very right day of the – well, you get the general idea – before making my official announcement. I'd caught her in the right *sort* of good mood. It was perfect timing. Pure instinct. I felt suitably smug.

'But I'm only doing it because I love you,' she added.

Oh. OK, then.

City Limits – SATURDAY 9 FEBRUARY

OLDHAM ATHLETIC 2 BRIGHTON 0
LEAGUE POSITION: 2ND

Another of *those* days. Days when I instinctively know, moments after waking – before I've fed the dog and remembered we're out of coffee but after the bit where I've worked out whether or not it's the weekend yet – that everything is going to be shit. I don't know, it's just a vibe thing. It tells me what the future holds, at least between now and bedtime. On days like this, on *those* days, I could almost reinvent myself as Mystic Mike. Think how much money I'd make, sitting in a tent with a hanky on my head, telling a string of punters that their days, too, are going to be shit.

Admittedly, as the season edges closer to its conclusion and each match takes on a scarier significance, the pessimistic side of my nature is taking a firmer grip. Every game now is A Worry. One of the most startling factors of Division Two football is the laughable inconsistency of just about every team. Take a typical set of Premiership fixtures and, allowing for maybe a couple of freak results each time, you can pretty much predict their outcome. Not a chance in Division Two. Especially not with us. One week we'll be buzzing around the pitch, knocking passes together with pin-point accuracy, running into space, all on the same wavelength, crafting chance upon chance – and usually against one of the better sides, too – the next, we'll be scrambling around like a bunch of hungover Sunday league bloaters.

So what I'm saying is, I knew we were going to blow it today. I just knew.

The scene with Nikki was the sign. Nikki and Fergus, two very dear friends of ours, had travelled down from London to see us for the day, so Julie had suggested we all nip into town for a spot of lunch. 'Or into the *city*, as we now are!' I'd quipped, in what I'd hoped would sound suitably self-mocking.

Nikki had instantly seized on this silly, throwaway remark. 'A city?!' she'd exclaimed. 'What on earth qualifies Brighton to be a city? It's a nice little seaside town, but it's hardly a city. *London's* a city.'

And that was all it had taken. She'd broken the golden rule. If someone's being self-mocking, you're not allowed to join in, are you? Because *you're* not being self-mocking if you do that. You're the third party, so what you're doing is taking the piss. It's like it's OK to say something rude about your own parents, that's up to you, but if a third party joins in, you think, 'How *dare* you be rude about my parents. Fuck off.'

Now, it was obvious what I should do if I wanted to be adult about this. I should sneak out into the street and drag my door-key down her paintwork. Failing that, I should have just ignored her. First, because she was clearly trying to wind me up, and second because, to be honest, I don't really give a stuff what we're called. Town, city, metropolis, conurbation, fishcake, it's all the same to me. But somehow she'd touched a nerve, and I couldn't hold back.

I shan't bore you with the details of how I replied, partly because I was so wound-up that the words are now a blur, but also because I suspect, on reflection, that I sounded a bit of a wanker. What's more significant is the lasting impact of this seemingly trivial incident. An hour later, although I'd long since shut my trap by this point, I was still running it through in my head. She was wrong, wasn't she? Of course she was. She was wrong. Definitely. How dare she?

Stupidly, I'd let it put me in a foul mood. Not only was I cross, but I was cross about how cross it had made me. I was doubly cross. She'd doubly-crossed me.

And I knew that this horribleness, this grey cartoon raincloud hovering exclusively above my head, would remain stubbornly in place for the rest of the day. Which, this being a Saturday, meant a big problem.

I tried to act as if the match simply wasn't happening. I wandered around the town – oops – with the others, until well after four. If I could just pretend there was no fixture this afternoon, almost hypnotise myself into believing this was a Sunday or the middle of July or something, then maybe the bad vibes wouldn't be transmitted up to Oldham. That's what I was really afraid of: that somehow a row between a couple of mates on the south coast could have a direct impact on 22 professional footballers running around on a patch of grass in Lancashire. That transferable jinx nonsense again.

It was 4.35 p.m. by the time we got back to the car. Plenty of the match still left. Should I stick on BBC Southern Counties, I wondered, to catch the last chunk of commentary? Best not, I decided. Not if there's even the slightest chance that the jinx theory might have some scientific validity. Leave the radio off for once, just to be on the safe side.

Fat chance. The moment we were out of the multi-storey and I knew we'd get a signal, on it went.

Idiot.

Idiot. Idiot. Idiot. We were 1–0 down. And it was obvious who was to blame. We'd have been 4–0 up if I hadn't switched on.

Still, all was not yet lost. Nothing to stop us pulling one back in the last few minutes. Course not.

Idiot.

Two–fucking–nil now. A 'great' Oldham goal, apparently. I'm so fucking pleased for them.

THUMP!!!

I punched the off-switch. I didn't want to hear another word. What a crappy, crappy, horrible, crappy day it had been. All your fault, Nikki. Plus a bit of mine.

And it's now turned out to be crappier still. A *lot* crappier, in a so-crappy-it-could-wreck-our-whole-season kind of way. Just after I'd thumped the off-switch, Bobby, I've now found out, got himself sent off. By all accounts, he deserved it, too: there was no give-us-a-break-ref or lets-go-to-appeal about this. Our top man, our talisman – the one who *scores* – is going to have to serve a three-match suspension. In a moment of frustration, he'd kicked out at an opponent. Honestly, some people can be so petulant.

Making Hay – MONDAY 11 FEBRUARY

BRIGHTON 3 READING 1
LEAGUE POSITION: 2ND

A dream result. More to the point, a dream performance. Bugger.

I mean, I'm not complaining. *Obviously* I'm not complaining. It's just frustrating, that's all. Why can't we stop messing about and play like this every week? It'd make life a whole lot easier.

Reading are top of the table, probably favourites for the title, and yet tonight was like weaving round lamp-posts. If we can beat this lot, our closest rivals, so convincingly, then we ought to have knocked at least 48 past the likes of Cambridge. Up against Division Two's relegation fodder we ought to have become football's equivalent of the Harlem Globetrotters, playing tricks, pulling stunts, taking the all-round piss. We shouldn't have been doing back-flips just to celebrate goals; we should have been using them as a means of actually propelling the ball into the net.

Yet it never quite seems to work out that way. So I guess it's the old motivation thing. Human nature. You'll do it if you *need* to. You won't if you don't. A bit like me and shaving, in a way. I can look quite smart when I've shaved, when I've *needed* to shave. But most days I don't need to shave, so I don't shave. By Fridays I'm often approached in the street and asked when we'll next be touring. Me and the rest of ZZ Top.

Of course the other problem tonight is the shadow. The huge, ominous one, lurking just around the corner. One more game after this, and then we're going to have to get by without Bobby for three whole matches.

The cynics are dismissing us as a one-man team, but that doesn't really bother me. What bothers me is that the non-cynics are doing the same.

Skye Won – SATURDAY 16 FEBRUARY

BRIGHTON 1 HUDDERSFIELD 0
LEAGUE POSITION: 2ND

At times in this diary, I think I may have sounded a wee bit, what's the word, unappreciative, where Julie is concerned. I've certainly not gone to enormous lengths to stress how close or loving our relationship is. Not because 15 years of marriage have stripped us of intimacy, tenderness or affection, but because I see little point in making you vomit.

If you insist on conclusive proof of our marriage's enduring strength, however, how about this? Today, for the first time this season, I missed an Albion home match. Yes, the ultimate sacrifice. Aren't I just the big man?

Weeks ago, I'd promised we'd go away together for Valentine's weekend, or the closest we could get to it, calendar-wise. And, no, of *course* it wouldn't be a problem if the Albion were playing at home. So even after I'd sobered up and slapped myself, there was no getting out of this one; I was morally obliged to stick to my promise. This wasn't one of those will-power-won't-power deals of ours, where the real deal is a completely different one, hidden beneath the surface, pretty much meaning the opposite of the deal on top. This was just a simple, straightforward *deal*. The sort of deal even Andy would understand.

Still, what was the problem? I mean, really. It was hardly the end of the world. Plenty more fixtures in the season. I'd just have to treat this one as if it were a regular away game, as if they were really playing, say, at Wigan, rather than Withdean. Keep up via radio, Teletext, whatever. Shouldn't be a problem.

Shouldn't.

Skye is an extraordinary island, which is precisely why we wanted to cash in a few hundred Air Miles and fly up here for a closer look. Actually, flying up here was out of the question, due to its lack of anywhere for a 747 to land without killing everyone on board. But Inverness Airport is only about a three-hour drive away, and with Julie at the wheel of the hire car we were able to cut that down to 11 minutes.

With its bleak, rugged, melancholic beauty, Skye looks like the backdrop for an early Echo and the Bunnymen video. I could happily up sticks and move here, but only if I were allowed to up them again and leave by teatime. To all intents and purposes, it's another planet. Greetings, Earthling.

We knew about its remoteness before we got here, of course. That was part of the attraction. There's not a lot of point in booking a weekend in a place like this and then moaning that it lacks the amenities of downtown Manhattan.

What I hadn't anticipated was the communication problem. I don't mean with the islanders, I mean with Earth. My mobile can't pick up a signal here, not that I really expected it to, but I'd hoped at least the car radio would work. Well, OK, the car radio does work, but not on medium wave, which is what we'd need to pick up Five Live. For that matter, even Radio Two's FM reception is pretty iffy. Halfway through his show this morning, Jonathan Ross suddenly lapsed, alarmingly, into alien gibberish, as if, mid-sentence and live on air, the poor sod had suffered a stroke, or some supernatural entity had taken temporary control of his body, as happened to Whoopi Goldberg in *Ghost*. The truth was more mundane, of course, as the truth usually is. Glimpsing at the stereo's display panel, I realised it had simply retuned itself to the local Gaelic station, Radio Phlegm, which had muscled in with a stronger signal. I believe it was a show about sheep dip.

The TV in our bedroom does have Teletext, and it's even the non-digital version. But unfortunately this set turns out to be one of the earlier models, powered by peat, and so once again the reception is dismal. If you really want to find anything out on Teletext you have to play the guess-the-missing-letters game. And then, after about half an hour, you realise that even this is a waste of time because the whole thing is geared towards Scotland, and you're about as likely to find English Nationwide Division Two as you are to find the Turkish Topless Bowls League.

I switched to the live rugby on *Grandstand* – Italy versus Scotland, both sets of players putting in a sterling performance considering they were having to play in Technicolored snow – and tried squinting at the teasingly tiny, transitory score flashes in the top right-hand corner of the screen. But by the time I could decipher each pair of names through the fuzz, it would flick to the next match, just to wind me up.

It was well gone five before I managed to find out about the Albion. And here's the funny thing: I needn't have got myself into such a silly old state after all. It turned out the Scottish football round-up included a rundown of all the English scores as well, in a special segment entitled something like The Results Which People Actually Give A Fuck About. We'd won, that's what mattered – the goal coming not from Bobby, for once, but from Junior Lewis, on loan from Leicester. Senior Lewis would be very proud of him.

'Happy now?' inquired Julie, looking up from the Jilly Cooper she'd only read five times before. 'Yes, thanks,' I replied. 'Sorry if I've been a bit distracted.' Julie had been wonderfully patient for the past two hours; it was time for me to pay her some attention now.

We put on our jackets and went out to stare at some rocks.

Reading Matter – MONDAY 18 FEBRUARY

I really don't think holidays are worth it sometimes. Not even a teensy-weensy mini-break. Honestly, I pop away for five minutes – OK, 48 hours in this case – and what do I return to? Disaster.

Usually it's a credit card bill the thickness of the Yellow Pages, or a nice letter from the tax people, asking for the sort of money I'll have no problem raising provided I'm prepared to sell a superflous body part. Today it was the news that my plan for a reunion with Steve, my old school mate, is going to have to be scrapped. Maybe that's not strictly a 'disaster' by the United Nations definition, but we're easily looking at a seven-out-of-ten on the bitter-blow scale.

What's happened is, the tickets for the away game at Reading – the focus for Steve and I getting together again without having to drag our families into the arrangement – have all sold out. The lot. Whoosh. Just like that. It turns out that the details of how to get hold of them were announced at Saturday's match – typical, the first one I've missed all season – and the tickets themselves went on sale this morning, while Julie and I were still tucking into our hilarious airline lunches. By early afternoon, I've discovered, they were all sold out. Every last one. It's a choker.

But here's the stupid thing: my immediate reaction to this news was that this sell-out couldn't possibly apply to me. I was a special case, surely. They'd have held a few back. They were bound to have done – in the same way that a fully-booked restaurant can always manage to find a spare table when a top celebrity swans in, or Shane Ritchie.

Yep, it's come to that. A few hours spent gathering petition signatures, a few afternoons co-manning our campaign table, a few meetings in the hospitality hut – during most of which I've contributed about as much as my dog would have done – and I've managed to convince myself that I merit special treatment. Never mind the fact that, on a league table of effort put into this stadium campaign, I'd be thrashing around in the quagmire of relegation, Cambridge United-style. I've actually convinced myself that I deserve privileges which are out of the reach of regular Albion fans.

I am officially up my own arse.

The fact is, there are no more tickets full-stop. Not even a special consignment set aside for self-important twats. Even if Reading do release a few extra, these will go to people who've already applied for – and missed out on – the first batch. I won't stand a chance.

I've just texted Steve to break the bad news to him. It's not really my favourite means of communication, this – a bt 2 wnky if U ask me – but on this occasion it's saved us from an embarrassing conversation. One of us would have felt obliged, I'm sure, to suggest a Plan B, and I know what Plan B would have been. A full family get-together, just like the old days. A disaster in the making.

Alert the UN.

Curl Power – FRIDAY 22 FEBRUARY

So at half past ten on what, until that point, had been an aggressively average Friday morning, I was suddenly having a conversation about curling. The sport, that is. I really hadn't expected to hear from Steve again, and obviously my immediate reaction had been to panic, fearing that he was about to come out with that Plan B thing. If he had done, then, hell, I was just going to have to be honest with the bloke: thanks all the same, mate, but, enjoyable-experience-wise, I think I'd rather gargle with Head & Shoulders.

In fact, he wanted to talk about the Reading match. Specifically, he wanted to talk about an alternative means of us getting to see it. That and, like I say, about curling.

For no obvious reason, Steve asked whether I'd happened to stay up last night to see our British women (Scottish women, to be strictly accurate; there wasn't any noticeable English input) win the Winter Olympic curling gold medal. The bizarre thing is, I had. God knows why; I know nothing about curling, care even less, and in TV terms I find the Winter Olympics about as gripping as *My Favourite Hymns*. Yet somehow I'd channel-hopped to the final dramatic stages of this peculiar event. And they *were* dramatic. Honestly. Sleep had to be put on hold until well gone midnight.

Steve – equally ignorant and indifferent, he pointed out – had done likewise. We laughed at the sheer unlikeliness of all this, of how we'd both been absorbed by the sight of these no-nonsense women on ice, wielding stones and brooms. We agreed that, unlikely or not, there was just something about it – possibly the fact that a British Winter Olympic gold medal is only marginally more common than a pole-vaulting dachshund – which had kept us on the edge of our seats until the early hours. I'd actually watched it in bed, but I allowed myself this smidgen of poetic licence.

'Did you notice the captain?' I added.

Steve had. Well, obviously he had. He's not blind.

'Don't you reckon she looked like Gordon Strachan?!' I went on.

Steve hesitated just that fraction too long. 'Er, yeah. Yeah, I suppose so.'

I knew then that I'd lost him again. A fleeting re-meeting of minds, and then the moment had passed. For 30 seconds or so, maybe even a minute, we'd found ourselves back on the same wavelength, as if this was a Friday morning at school and it was no great surprise that we'd both been watching the same channel the night before because we'd had precious little choice in those days. And then, like a freakish radio signal, like picking up Radio Wales as you pull into a Little Chef just outside Southend, the reception had faded again. It was pointless to try and re-tune.

I had to face the truth, however distressing: Steve didn't really think the British women's curling captain looked like Gordon Strachan. Not at all. He was humouring me.

Even so, it's good news about the Reading game. It turns out that some business acquaintance of his – customer, client, colleague, I never know how these things work – can get us some seats after all. Free ones. They'll have to be among the Reading fans, but fair enough; it's that or nothing. What matters is, it means I'll be there. Steve and I can have our reunion after all, and I'll get to see one of the Albion's biggest games of the season.

I'll just have to keep my mouth shut when we score. And if it strikes me that any of the Reading players bears an uncanny resemblance to a Scottish sportsperson of the opposite gender, perhaps I'll keep that observation to myself.

Desperate Measures – SATURDAY 23 FEBRUARY

BRIGHTON 0 WREXHAM 0
LEAGUE POSITION: 2ND

How easily recognisable is your average Division Two footballer? More to the point, how observant is the typical Division Two referee? In our case, for instance, would he be able to tell a Paul Watson from a Paul Rogers, without having pored over their profiles in advance? Similarly, would he know a Daniel Webb from a Danny Cullip, or, for that matter, a Danny from Hear'Say? I bet he wouldn't.

What I'm driving at here is, would a relatively inexperienced match official necessarily know what Bobby Zamora looked like?

I only ask, because I'm thinking we should cheat. On the evidence of this afternoon's woeful display – Wrexham are wrubbish, but you'd never have guessed – I'm thinking maybe we should find a way to sneak Bobby back into the starting line-up, despite the fact that, strictly speaking, he's still got two matches of his ban to sit out. If his team mates wanted to show they could get by without him, that they weren't really a one-man team and shut your bloody faces for saying so, then they had their chance today and they screwed it up.

So let's think this one through: adjusting Bobby's kit would be simple enough. He could run out wearing the shirt assigned to one of the little-known reserve players, provided they had it in his size. Failing that, the Seagulls Shop would, I'm sure, be happy to sort out a nice new one for him – think of a number, pluck a name out of thin air (ideally, something low-key and innocuous, such as Smith or Jones, rather than anything which might draw attention to him, such as Beckham or Pele or Hitler) and, that should just about do it. Borrow some fake facial hair from the fancy-dress shop in town – both to be on the safe side and to add a nice comedy twist – and, well, Bobby's your uncle.

Absurd? Possibly. But if you notice the big deal which some refs like to make about checking a player's number before they book him, you can see that the suggestion has a certain twisted logic to it. If an official really hasn't a clue who half these players are – and provided the crowd promised to keep quiet and not spoil the prank – then I'm sure it'd be worth a try some time.

Except, of course, 'some time' isn't good enough. It's now that we urgently need him, to restore some confidence, shape and purpose to the team. To give the other players direction and co-ordination. To pick up those heads and sew them back on the relevant chickens.

That's assuming I've not blinded myself to the real problem here, the true cause of all our troubles. What worries me is that it might actually be nothing to do with Bobby's absence. It could be my shirt that's to blame. This afternoon was the first time I'd worn my blue-and-white Wardy top to an actual match, so it wasn't the most auspicious of débuts; if you then take into account what's happened on the other three occasions I've worn this thing, you'll notice a rather worrying pattern emerging:

1. Saturday 29 December: Alone at home, listening to the Blackpool away match. I didn't tell you this at the time, but just before we'd conceded that 94th-minute equaliser, I'd dashed to the wardrobe, grabbed this shirt from its hanger and tugged it over my head, leaving myself neatly kitted up and poised to savour our imminent away triumph. On reflection, I should have done something altogether less ridiculous, such as try on Julie's Wonderbra.

2. Tuesday 8 January: Kickabout with Albion fans at Bluggle-Splodge-Doodle-Flop. I wasn't keeping track of the score that night,

but we did concede more goals than the other lot. Technically, I think that's called losing.

3. Thursday 24 January: The televised 4–0 tonking at Brentford. Fucking hell fire.

See my point? And with another televised away match coming up next Friday, this time at Stoke, I have to ask myself how long I can persist with this bloody thing. I feel like an over-loyal manager who's stubbornly sticking with his golden-boy striker even after the lad's reported for pre-season training with his right leg missing.

Maybe it's time to get ruthless.

Are You Bobby In Disguise? – TUESDAY 26 FEBRUARY

BOURNEMOUTH 1 BRIGHTON 1
LEAGUE POSITION: 2ND

A spectacular goal from Brooker, by all accounts.

Or at least that was the name on the shirt.

Camera Shy – FRIDAY 1 MARCH

STOKE CITY 3 BRIGHTON 1
LEAGUE POSITION: 2ND

On his old Channel 4 show, *Big Night Out*, Vic Reeves used to have a regular character – Les, I think his name was – with a morbid fear of chives.

The running gag was that this guy, a happy-go-lucky bald geek in a lab coat, would shuffle on stage, wander over to Vic's desk – then suddenly reel back in horror as Vic whipped out a clump of the offending plant. It made absolutely no sense, of course, and that's why you laughed. That and because, as is the whole idea of a running gag, you knew it was going to happen.

The Albion players do a Les whenever they spot TV cameras. For reasons nobody has been able to establish, they go completely to pieces. The confidence drains from them like water from a gashed paddling pool. Likewise, any vestige of mutual understanding. The Albion react to the sight of a lens in much the same way that nineteenth-century simpletons once did, as if convinced it carries some dark, despicable strength-sapping curse. 'Them there new-fangled magic picture devices, they do devour your very soul.'

It's the same for every Albion player. Show him a TV camera and he immediately loses any hint of skill or co-ordination. He becomes Mr Blobby.

Consequently, I've just spent 90 minutes kicking the sofa, give or take a minute here and there for trips for the loo. Running jokes don't usually have this effect on me, not unless they feature an appearance by Anne Robinson, but it's becoming remarkably easy to lose your sense of humour, watching this lot.

Tonight wasn't quite another Brentford – we did at least make a game of it – but it may as well have been. Dropping the Wardy shirt made not a blind bit of difference. However well we performed in odd spells, we were effectively doomed from the moment ITV Sport decided to televise this match. The jinx lives on.

Maybe it wouldn't have been so bad if their coverage hadn't annoyed the hell out of me. In terms of pre-match research, I got the impression they'd flicked through a copy of *Shoot!* about ten minutes before going on air, spotted a microscopic mention of Bobby's ban, and decided, fuck it, nobody's watching, that'll do.

By mid-way though the first half, I was wishing I'd kept a Zamora count, totting up how many times the commentator referred to our absent leading scorer and the extent to which we relied upon him. This guy's only other observation of any note was to imply that Kuipers was a liability. Clueless prat.

But, hey, perhaps I was in a sensitive mood. The 23 quid's worth of dog-sick takeaway probably hadn't helped.

Nor had Julie. She'd come into the room and settled down on the sofa beside me, not so much to watch the match but, from what I could make out, to underline the fact that she didn't want to. On the floor beside her was a heap of cookbooks to which she gave her undivided attention for the whole game, regardless of what was happening on screen. If her plan was to irritate me, to make a grand, dramatic gesture of her indifference, then fucking well done because it worked. It reminded me of cinema-goers who make a big melodramatic deal of hiding their heads in their hands when the scary scenes come on, as if eyelids haven't yet been invented.

Anyway, on a positive note – amazingly, there is one – Bobby's back next week. Thank Christ. Since he's been out, we've managed two draws and a defeat.

If I were him, I'd be feeling a bit smug.

Business As Usual – TUESDAY 5 MARCH

BRIGHTON 4 WYCOMBE WANDERERS 0
LEAGUE POSITION: 2ND

So he's back and, waddya know, we win 4–0. In one night we pick up more points, manage twice as many goals, as we achieved in the whole time he was suspended. So a great result and an unsettling implication.

Still, no point in being nit-picky. Enjoy the moment. And just pray that, fingers crossed, the silly sod doesn't pick up another suspension, or get crocked, or fall off the pier and dash his brains out on a passing paddle steamer.

Besides, it's not often I've been able to relax and enjoy – I mean really *enjoy* – the closing minutes of an Albion match. So in that sense tonight was a treat.

And with Reading only drawing tonight – second time on the trot – the damage from our last three matches isn't looking so bad. Five points behind, a game in hand – and we play them at their place on Saturday.

I hope Steve's remembered the tickets.

Away And A Stranger – SATURDAY 9 MARCH

READING 0 BRIGHTON 0
LEAGUE POSITION: 2ND

Neither of us was going to say so, but we didn't need to. In less than three hours, it had become embarrassingly obvious: we had no future as mates, Steve and I. We hardly needed further confirmation.

But we got it anyway. With 6 minutes and 23 seconds of normal time remaining – according to Reading's eff-off electronic scoreboard – Steve turned to me and asked The Question. He obviously assumed it was a perfectly reasonable one.

'Shall we shoot off early,' he suggested, 'and miss the traffic?'

Well, that was it, wasn't it? Never mind bitter religious divides or furiously conflicting political perspectives; can there honestly be a gulf any wider than the one between those who stay until the bitter end of a football match and those who think it's fine to bugger off early?

I should have just smiled and said no, but I couldn't hold back. We were in the 84th minute of our biggest game of the season – *the* biggest game of the season, top of the table, first versus second – and one goal now could change everything. *Everything.* This was nerve-wracking, knuckle-gnawing stuff. We could be on the brink of a life-shaping moment here.

And Steve wanted to miss the traffic.

'Bloody hell!' I snapped. 'I cannot believe you've just asked me that.' (I even said 'cannot', rather than 'can't'. That's how much I couldn't believe it.) 'Don't tell me you've become one of them.'

Steve looked quite hurt. 'One of what?' he said.

'One of those people who walk out before the end of a match. Jesus. What the hell makes people *do* that?'

Steve smiled nervously and swivelled back round for the dying minutes. Like me, I think he'd sensed it wasn't just a game of football that was reaching its natural conclusion here. An hour earlier, he'd asked me how long they allow for half-time at matches these days. Steve used to want to play the game professionally.

To be honest, I twigged that this reunion would be a one-off the moment I reached Albaruma. Albaruma is the name which Steve and Laura have given their new house, about 25 minutes from Reading's ground. It's the same name they gave to their old house, a couple of miles up the road, which I last visited six years ago; apparently they liked it so much they decided to take it with them when they moved. The name, I mean, not the house. They did once tell me what it means, but I've forgotten.

Albaruma (*Alba-roomier*, I waggishly dubbed this one as soon as I arrived, having clocked that it was about double the size of their last place) had its own electric gates. So had the place next door, I noticed, to an identical design. As I pulled up outside, Steve was pottering on his enormous driveway, an England rugby shirt tucked into his jeans, this sporty ensemble topped off with a Damon Hill baseball cap. I prayed he wasn't planning to accompany me to the match in this get-up, but God must have been on the other line.

Steve prodded a remote on his key-ring and the gates began to ease open. 'I'm impressed,' I told him, once I'd decided which time zone to park in. I figured he'd rather hear me saying this than, 'What the fucking hell have you got those for, you daft sod?'

It was already gone two, so there was only really time for a quick coffee before we headed off to the match. Steve made me a Nescafe, then left me in the kitchen while he went off to dig out the complimentary tickets. I calculated that you could probably fit our own kitchen twice into this one, along with most of Wolverhampton.

Josh, Steve's ten-year-old, was going to be joining us for the game. This wasn't quite the arrangement I had in mind, but I couldn't really say anything. It was Josh's second trip to a Reading match, I was told, but his first outside a hospitality box. As we clambered in to Steve's dusty Jag, Josh seemed a lot more excited than his dad.

'So you've lost a bit of interest in football?' I casually asked Steve, as we edged away from Leafyland. 'I've lost interest in most things,' Steve replied, flatly. Since I couldn't imagine how the heck I was meant to respond to this, I was relieved when he chose to qualify his remark. 'Except for golf and skiing,' he added.

By the time we'd parked, ridden, and found our three pre-booked spots in the East Stand, there were only five minutes until kick-off. The place was packed. 'Great seats, aren't they?' commented Steve, as we shuffled down the row. 'Actually, no,' I thought. 'They're way too far forward. This is one of those horrible dugout-type views. We're virtually at ankle-level.'

'They're brilliant,' I told him. 'Thanks.'

The mass of travelling fans, a few yards to our left, were already making a fantastically uplifting racket. 'And we're – go – ing – up – to – win – the – cup – forrr – Sussiiiix – byyy – the – seeeea . . .' It was just as I remembered from the Bury game, only this time there must have been three times the number. No wonder I couldn't get a ticket in the right end.

'Alby – yurrrrn – Alby – yurrrrn – Alby – yurrrrn.'

I felt a stab of jealousy. I wished I was over there with them, not sitting here, forced into an agonising, anonymous silence, locked out of the party. What the hell was I playing at? I even convinced myself that, given the opportunity, I'd have been joining in with the chants. 'Zamor-ah! Zamora-ah! Zamor-ah!' I'd have been going.

Possibly.

Instead, I had to bottle up my emotions as the Reading fans sprang to their feet all around me, spitting abuse at their guests. 'Town full of faggots, you're just a town full of faggots.' The repertoire was a bit over-familiar (yes, pop-pickers, that's 'Does Your Boyfriend Know You're Here?' – a non-mover for the 38th week) but they looked ever so pleased with themselves, bless 'em. Realising what I should already have been acutely aware of – namely, that I was a lone away supporter surrounded by about 20,000 home fans, and that some of these people, as is statistically inevitable, weren't very nice – I quickly switched my mobile to silent. My mother would never have forgiven herself if she'd decided to give me a quick call, triggered its giveaway ringtone and prompted these people to pummel her youngest son into paté. At the same time, I realised it might also be advisable to remove my watch – the one with 'Brighton and Hove Albion: The Seagulls' splashed across its fascia – on the off-chance that someone amongst this lot might be able to read.

The longer the game went on, the wiser these decisions began to look. I'm sure I'd simply caught them on an off-day, or found myself in with a particularly dire set of supporters, but what staggered me is that these Reading fans seemed to display only a passing interest in their own side, preferring instead to spew out a relentless stream of anti-Albion abuse. When Bobby pulled up on the far side with some sort of leg injury, the guy on my left immediately turned to his girlfriend, cackled, and announced gloatingly, 'That's him out for the rest of the season! He's done his hamstring! Hahahahahahahahahaha!!!!'

To her credit, the girlfriend flashed him a look which said, 'Oh dear. I appear to be dating a wanker.'

The daft thing is, I hadn't expected to feel this frustrated. Obviously I knew I'd need to button my lip, just as I'd have to button my jacket to hide my Seagulls T-shirt. But I hadn't imagined this would all be so hard. And the harder it became, the more I began to contemplate the unthinkable: that, sod it, I'd turn and have a go at these cretins. This would, of course, have been about as advisable as jay-walking across the M25, and yet that almost didn't seem sufficient deterrent. As for what I'd do if we actually scored, I seriously thought about standing up, ripping open my jacket and gleefully flashing the Albion logo beneath it. In the end, perhaps wisely, I abandoned both these plans. Pride is one thing, but I hate it when people dance on your head.

So when we did score, all I did was sit stock-still and grab Steve's knee. That, and emit a strangely constrained squealing sound, as if in urgent need of a laxative. We were already three minutes into stoppage time at the end of the match, so this scrappy close-range shot from Gary Hart – 'oh Gary Hart, Gary Gary Gary Hart' etc. – had surely sealed a priceless victory for us. The home side couldn't possibly pull one back. There wouldn't be time.

Three points had rarely felt so special or so richly deserved.

Except we hadn't got them. The referee – a Mr F.N. Fuckwit, I believe, from South Fuckwitland – had awarded Reading a free-kick instead. During the goalmouth scramble, Junior Lewis had apparently breathed on their keeper. I almost wished I'd taken Steve up on that stupid idea of his.

Almost.

After the game, as we sat in solid traffic facing roughly towards where he lived, I told Steve what I'd thought of the Reading fans. I think he assumed he was agreeing with me when he said he found them disgusting. 'If I'd known they'd use language like that,' he declared, 'I'd never have brought Josh.'

He went on to tell me how he mostly goes to rugby internationals these days. 'It's such a great atmosphere,' he explained. 'You even find people setting up barbecues in the car park. The crowd is so different, you wouldn't believe it.'

Oh, I think I would.

Back at Albaruma, Arsenal's FA Cup quarter-final was underway, live on BBC1. I'd already asked if I could stop overnight so that we could watch this game together as well, and Steve had sounded genuinely keen on the idea. Beers and televised footie, just like it used to be. Besides, he'd appreciate the significance of this fixture far more than the Albion's. He was bound to.

Ten minutes into the second half, he had another question for me. 'Is this the FA Cup?' he said.

Later, while Steve was out in the kitchen fetching more cans, I took a casual glance through his and Laura's CD collection. At the bottom of one pile, I spotted the name Chicago. Steve had never particularly struck me as a West End musical kind of bloke, but it could have been worse. I pulled out the case, just for a casual glance, wondering if maybe Claire Sweeney was on this version of the soundtrack, or whether it dated from Denise Van Outen's time in the cast. And then the chilling truth hit me: this wasn't Chicago the *musical*, this was Chicago the *band* – the criminally insipid '70s feather-cut droners. In a blind panic, I quickly shoved this foul abomination back into the pile, before Steve could wander back in, find me clutching the bloody thing and ask if I'd like to hear a snatch of 'If You Leave Me Now'.

The rest of the evening went Perfectly Pleasantly, possibly helped by the fact that at least Arsenal had managed a win. Over dinner, the conversation flowed smoothly enough, although the fact that they'd also invited a neighbour to join us suggested that maybe they hadn't expected it to.

Anyway, the salmon really was delicious. Laura had gone to a lot of trouble.

Admittedly, I could have done without the bit where she stood up and showed me her new belly button stud. 'Please don't,' I'd pleaded. 'It's nothing personal. It's just that if you lift your shirt and show me this thing, I've got absolutely no idea how I'm meant to respond.' But she went ahead and showed me it anyway. 'It didn't hurt a bit,' she insisted.

'Oh,' I said. 'Good.'

The wedding video, I suppose, was inevitable. But I didn't really mind them digging it out. It's 11 years since Steve and Laura got married, and I was fairly sure I'd never watched this thing. Odd, considering I'd been Steve's best man. Had I been a wee bit more sober tonight, I think I'd have found it quite poignant, given the emotional distance between us now. Or maybe I'd have needed to be more drunk. Either way, Steve looked a lot less grey. And I looked a lot less fat.

Just after midnight we all turned in – almost as if 12 a.m. had been a diplomatically acceptable target we'd all silently set ourselves. In the end we'd coped quite well, possibly because we had so much catching up to do. Steve and Laura are genuinely decent people, but in six years the gap between us – not just in our relative levels of affluence but in our tastes, perspectives and everyday priorities – had become a chasm. This was never going to work. I thanked them for a lovely day, headed to the spare room and, as I closed the door behind me, wondered if I'd ever share an evening with these people again.

I was going to have to leave early in the morning, I reminded them. 'Mothers' Day obligations!' I quipped, feebly.

It was that or say I wanted to miss the traffic.

Tickety-Boo – TUESDAY 12 MARCH

BRIGHTON 2 NORTHAMPTON 0
LEAGUE POSITION: 2ND

'Fuck me, you look drenched.'

'Yes, that's because I *am* drenched, Andy. And before you ask, yes, it was worth it.'

'You won?'

'2–0.'

'Against mighty Northampton Town?'

'Indeed, you sarcastic bastard. On top of which, guess who only managed a draw tonight?'

'Dunno. Scunthorpe United? Accrington Stanley? Bexhill Brownies?'

'Brentford.'

'Brentford, eh? Ooooh.'

'Who happen to be our closest rivals, other than Reading.'

'Right. So things are looking pretty good?'

'Not half, you might say.'

'Well, yes, I suppose I might say that, if I wanted to sound like Alan 'Fluff' Freeman. So go on, then, how many games have you got left?'

'Just seven now – four of them at home. And we're only two points behind Reading.'

'Who are top?'

'Who are top, the jammy shits.'

'Jammy?'

'Oh, don't start me.'

Bury The Dead? – SATURDAY 16 MARCH

BRIGHTON 2 BURY 1
LEAGUE POSITION: 2ND

I now have my name on a seat at Gigg Lane, the home of Bury Football Club. Or I will do, any day soon. Not because I deserve such recognition, but because I've paid them ten quid to stick it there.

I feel vaguely hypocritical about this, considering I was less than flattering about the team, the ground and the fans when I went up there to watch the Albion run rings around them back in December. But now it turns out that Bury are on the verge of going out of business, and suddenly I feel a huge, no doubt irrational, and almost certainly patronising, soft spot for them. This buy-a-seat-for-a-tenner scheme of theirs – or at least have-your-name-on-a-seat, since I doubt they've got the slightest intention of posting mine to me – is one means by which they're desperately trying to raise funds. The man who gratefully accepted my Visa details over the phone told me I was the third Brighton fan who'd rung that morning. I went a bit watery-eyed when he told me this. Apparently they plan to flog the bricks next.

Since my trip to Gigg Lane was my very first Albion away match, that December day has since taken on a slightly weird retrospective glow. It's rather like I feel when I think back to summer holidays as a kid, conveniently glossing over the tedium and the tumbling into nettles and the endless bloody reruns of *Robinson* fucking *Crusoe*.

So it felt odd having Bury at Withdean this afternoon. The cliché will tell you there's no room for sentiment in football, but I'm not sure it was designed for days like this.

Would the compassion spill onto the pitch? It was certainly there in buckets before kick-off, including several plastic ones into which home fans were chucking their loose change. I guess if anyone knows how Bury are feeling, it's Brighton and Hove Albion fans. Proper ones, I mean.

And the Bury players didn't forget their manners. As the teams ran out, the visiting side unfurled a huge banner to express their gratitude. 'Thank You,' it declared. 'You're welcome,' I whispered, slightly wankily.

Attila had penned a special poem for them too. Honestly, the guy positively oozes verse. Some of the visiting fans may have been a bit baffled by his contribution – 'Who *is* this bloke? He's written us a *what*?' – but I'm sure they appreciated the sentiment. They certainly clapped.

Forty-five minutes later, they didn't seem quite so favourably disposed towards anyone in an Albion shirt. A Junior Lewis shot had struck the post, pinged off their keeper's back and rolled into the net, comedy-style, putting us 1–0 up. By half-time we'd notched up another, this time thanks to a Bobby penalty. And by now it had turned a bit ugly.

Bury, players and fans alike, were convinced Bobby had dived, and they weren't exactly chuffed about it. In fact, they were so decidedly unchuffed that the defender responsible for the alleged trip treated our top scorer (this goal had moved Bobby's tally on to 30 for the season) to a rather too obvious thwack. Two–nil down, and now they'd have to complete the match with only ten very pissed-off men. I half-expected them to emerge for the second half with a freshly printed banner, reading, 'Shove Your Patronising Charity Up Your Arses.'

Thanks to a relentless icy drizzle, plus a quagmire of a pitch, the rest of the game felt strangely '70s. If you were old enough, you could almost have imagined Billy Bremner out there. Or Charlie George. Or Ron 'Chopper' Harris. Mostly dressed in a sludgy brown.

Performance-wise, it was your typical second-half game against ten men – i.e. a ridiculous, illogical struggle. As if to underline the point, Bury pulled one back. It was blatantly offside, but I guess they deserve a bit of luck.

Yet a-flaming-gain, then, we faced an anxious last few minutes. Only at the final whistle did my blood pressure drop back to a medically acceptable level. But we'd done it, thank God.

And now, still in second place, we've got just six games left to play: three at home, three away.

What's significant tonight – although I'm not sure how my doctor would feel about this – is that I realise I cannot let go. Not now. I'm going to have to attend all those remaining away matches too. What choice do I have?

Julie *will* be pleased.

Our Worst Nightmare – SATURDAY 23 MARCH

BRIGHTON 2 NOTTS COUNTY 2
LEAGUE POSITION: 2ND

You'd think he'd been hit by a sniper, the way he fell. These weren't the drearily familiar tumble-and-roll histrionics of the thespian footballer; this was a man hitting the ground and seriously hurting himself, the way you do when you've just bounced off some bloke from Notts County.

I say 'bounced off' because the referee considered the whole thing to have been an accident. He must have done; he didn't even give a free kick.

Not that Bobby would have been in any position to take one. By the time play had resumed, with one of those drop balls which aren't really drop balls any more, he was being nursed gingerly along the athletics track in front of us, obviously in agony, the front of his Albion shirt gathered up and fashioned into a makeshift sling. They were taking our top scorer straight to the medical room, where, once the door had been closed behind him, he'd presumably allow himself to burst into tears like a great big girl. Seriously, Bobby was hurt, and clearly not in a way he'd shake off by the morning. Suddenly, out of nowhere, we were in profound poo.

It seemed only fitting, then, that a match we'd begun with such confidence and flair – 2–0 up and cruising – finished two-apiece.

But the fact that we threw away yet another two points ('Now remember, lads, as soon as you go 2–0 ahead I want you to start giving the ball to our visitors. Show some manners') seems a pifflingly minor irritation tonight, up against the deep, long-term worry. It turns out that Bobby has injured his shoulder/collar-bone area in some complicated way which I don't really understand, and we're going to have to get by without him for 'at least two weeks'. The 'at least' bit particularly worries me.

So that's it. The one thing we prayed wouldn't happen has gone and happened, and it's hard to avoid the conclusion that our season is now effectively over. No, I mean *really*, this time. Without Bobby, we're not as hopeless as some people have implied (yes, OK, me included), but we're not very special either. We've seen the evidence. I can't remember when I last felt this miserable.

Funny, but I hear reports about injuries all season long – other players, other teams, other leagues – and they just wash over me, like a weather forecast or a stock market report or an Oasis-split rumour. If I react at all, it's usually just to assume someone else will be slotted in to fill the gap, and that life will plod along much as before. What's the big deal? One player, after all, is less than ten per cent of a football team. However good he is, surely his absence can't make *that* much difference. Not unless, I don't know, they try replacing him with a penguin or something.

During what seemed an interminable trudge home, the significance of today's date suddenly occurred to me. It's eight months to the day since I took the plunge and bought my Albion season ticket. On Monday, 23 July, 2001, I didn't even know what Bobby Zamora looked like, let alone gave a stuff about his stupid collar-bone.

It seems like a lifetime ago.

Love Hurts – SATURDAY 30 MARCH

COLCHESTER UNITED 1 BRIGHTON 4
LEAGUE POSITION: 2ND

Julie was not happy. We'd woken to Brighton brightness and dressed accordingly: me in a crumpled Zamora T-shirt which I'd chosen specially from the yet-to-be-ironed pile, Julie in a flimsy pink vest-top. Each of us had slipped a thin denim jacket on top – Julie's blue, my own a fading black – but more for the fact that these had pockets than as any form of serious protection. And now, a two-and-a-half-hour coach ride later, here we were in a grimly grey Essex, gently shivering, listening to the raindrops persistently pinging on the corrugated roof above our heads. I'd bought us each a coffee from the tiny bar at the end of the terrace.

The logo on the plastic cup said it was 'Really Smooth'. It Really Wasn't.

Still, just the 85 minutes till kick-off.

'Look,' I sighed, 'if you're really that unhappy, let's just go home.'

I had no idea what I meant by this; how I proposed to get us straight back to Brighton without it involving a cripplingly expensive cab ride or holding our coach driver at gunpoint. But I did know I'd made the most enormous mistake: Julie wasn't just bored or indifferent about joining me here this afternoon. She was seething. I hadn't anticipated this at all.

Stupidly, I'd assumed she'd enter into the spirit of the occasion. I'd imagined she'd see it as a bit of a laugh, finding out what the hell it was I'd been getting so worked up about all this season. After all, it wasn't as if we'd never stood on a terrace together before. We'd done it loads of times, on the North Bank at Highbury, back in the mid-'80s.

But then this, as she was quick to remind me, wasn't Highbury. It wasn't even Lowbury. It was, with respect to our hosts, a shit hole. I'd nipped to the loo a few moments earlier, down a small flight of steps at the back of the terrace, and considered myself profoundly fortunate to have made it back alive. These were The Toilets From Hell: filthy, foul, fetid. I prayed that Julie's bladder would hold out until we got home, because a trip to the ladies' equivalent would have finished her off. The graffiti of hate seemed to occupy every square inch of the men's cubicle door – there was only the one WC, plus a tiny tin urinal which could scarcely accommodate two abreast – so the scribblers had turned their attention to a chunk of wonky plywood nailed above the cistern, presumably housing some pipes or the resident rat. Mostly the words were cretinous, futile declarations of loathing, penned by pinheads, invariably aimed at the home side and – as is usually the case, for some bizarre reason – signed off with the date of inscription. Some, I noticed, went back as far as 1998. Nobody had made any effort even to slap a thin layer of paint over them. The loo roll was coated in grime. I thanked God I only needed a wee.

And yet I could really only take so much of Julie's moaning. 'You cheated,' she insisted, as if all of a sudden our rules had changed and the weight-loss deal really *had* been a weight-loss deal and I'd dragged her here under wholly false pretences. But bollocks, she didn't *have* to come, did she? Not really. I'd forked out 11 quid for her ticket, but big deal. If she objected that strongly, if she hated the idea *that* much, then I'd never have forced the issue, for God's sake. I'd honestly assumed she didn't mind. I'd assumed wrong.

I edged to the front of terrace, taking up a position directly behind the goal. I figured that once the action began, the chance for Julie to experience things this close up – to sniff the sweat, to feel the ball fizz across the goalmouth, to hear the ripple as it smacked the net – might gradually draw her into the drama of the occasion. Ten minutes later, she edged forward to join me. The rain was easing off.

As the players trotted out in dribs and drabs, still in their warm-up gear, the sun finally emerged. There wasn't the clear blue sky we'd left behind in Sussex, but the greyness had at least peeled back sufficiently to allow us some warmth. Kuipers headed for the goal immediately in front of us and began his stretching routine, with Albion goalkeeping coach John Keeley pinging balls at him from every angle. Julie pointed out that Keeley had nice legs. It was an uncharacteristically girly remark, but a vast improvement on sulky silence so I wasn't going to complain. She seemed disappointed when I explained that Keeley wouldn't be playing.

Gradually the pitch began to fill with players from both sides, subs included – jogging, bending, gearing up. I hoped this might help my cause still further. Fifty minutes spent staring at an empty playing field, from a terrace still barely half full, hadn't been the greatest mood-setter, particularly for someone who didn't want to be here in the first place. The arrival of some actual footballers seemed to remind Julie that something was about to happen. I hadn't brought her all this way just to gaze at some grass.

Red and black balloons, dished out to us on the coach by Liz Costa, were being puffed up and released onto the pitch. A female steward in sinister shades was stomping around with a garden fork, seemingly desperate to burst as many as she could in as short a time as possible, as if this was It's A Knockout and her side had just gambled the joker on her performance. Kuipers rescued a few for us and handed them back for later re-deployment. 'All right, boys?' he cried to a couple of lads to our right, pausing to scribble his autograph on their programme. Julie seemed impressed by that bit. 'I don't suppose you get that at Old Trafford,' she admitted. I hadn't even prompted her.

The Albion singing was getting louder, almost deafening, by the time the teams retired to the dressing-rooms. 'We are Brigh–ton, we are Brigh–ton, super Brigh–ton, from the South.' The home fans were virtually silent. For me at least, this was beginning to feel like Bury again. Or Reading. What it was beginning to feel like for Julie, I didn't dare ask, but I had a hunch she was being won round.

The toss meant that the Albion would spend the first 45 minutes attacking the far goal, or at least trying to. Which was fine, because that's how I like it. Save the fun bit till last.

'The ball doesn't spend a lot of time on the ground, does it?' Julie observed, barely ten minutes into the game. She had a point. Even by Division Two standards it wasn't looking pretty.

Half an hour later, I didn't care. We were already 3–0 up. Richard Carpenter had scored from a free-kick, Wayne Gray – on loan from Wimbledon to help plug the Zamora gap – had slotted in the second on his début, and for the third, from a Brooker cross, there'd been some sort of pinball deflection which we couldn't really see but certainly didn't object to.

Delirium had ensued.

'Three–nil to the one-man team!' sang the Albion supporters. From the seats to the left of the Albion dugout, Bobby glanced across and gave us a wave, wisely opting to use the arm which wasn't in a sling.

Half-time brought Julie's first proper smile. 'I'm not hating it so much now,' she admitted, and I believed her. I really couldn't have asked for anything more from the Albion players. They'd been a huge help. All it really needed now was for them to knock in a few down our end.

Unfortunately, Peter Taylor saw things differently. In fact, I got the impression that he didn't give the tiniest shit about Julie, or about the positive impact a few second-half Albion goals would have on her mood. Instead, he seemed more focused on the team not fucking up yet again – of not chucking away yet another decent lead – and appeared to have issued half-time instructions to that effect. I suppose I couldn't really blame him, but it scuppered my plan for Julie to enjoy a feast of close-up Albion action in the final stages. In fact, the fourth goal was, once again, scored at the far end, as Colchester pulled one back with about five minutes left. It wasn't a disaster, just an anti-climax. I could sense Julie's mood beginning to turn again. The sun had gone in.

And then we got the comedy free-kick.

About two minutes into stoppage time, Colchester's keeper picked up what was adjudged to be a back pass, barely ten yards in front of us – one of those rare situations when the attacking team can win a free-kick in the penalty area without it amounting to an actual penalty. It would be indirect, of course, so assuming we planned to try and score from it (and it doesn't always do to assume, believe me), then at least one other player would have to touch it before it found the net, even if he didn't mean to.

'These are always a farce,' I reminded Julie, as the entire Colchester team – plus several of their relatives by the look of it – crammed into the goal mouth. 'It'll cannon straight into the wall. It always does.' It would have been daft to raise her hopes, after all. Daniel Webb, our No. 30, was on the line too, muscling in amongst the Colchester players, just for nuisance value. As Richard Carpenter prepared to line up his shot, pretty much from the corner of the six-yard box, Webb turned to the Albion fans and grinned. For a moment, I could have sworn he was grinning specifically at Julie. Maybe he was. She was certainly grinning back.

Carpenter took a couple of paces back, ready to take what would surely be the last kick of the game. This would be perfect, I thought to myself. And yet too much to hope for, sadly. I mean, let's be realistic, he's never going to . . .

WHOOSH!!! Bang into the roof of the net. We even felt the ripple. And since the ref reckoned it had taken the necessary ricochet en route, it actually counted. So it seemed only right to go mental with joy. Julie included.

'Well,' I remarked, as our coach pulled to a halt outside Hove Station almost exactly three hours later. 'Not so hideous after all, was it?'

'It was OK,' Julie admitted, with a half-smile.

I toyed with the idea of suggesting a next time. Of making the most of her good mood. Of seizing the moment and attempting to convert her to the Albion full time. But I thought better of it.

It had ended up a fabulous day, for God's sake. Why push my luck?

No Kidding – MONDAY 1 APRIL

BRIGHTON 2 BRISTOL CITY 1
LEAGUE POSITION: 1ST

A misty Monday lunchtime, and nobody seems in the mood for a game of football. Least of all the Albion team. Easter Monday has fallen on April Fools' Day (or is it the other way round?) and while some of the players display hints of over-indulgence – slow, sluggish, sloppy, sleepy – others appear to be waiting for a premature final whistle, for the referee to unmask himself as Jeremy Beadle and for this fixture to be rearranged for sometime sensible. Maybe on a day when the sea mist has melted and Bobby's back.

But when 40 minutes have ticked by and that still hasn't happened, they seem to twig that it probably isn't going to, and that, consequently, they ought to start making a serious effort to win this game. Paul Watson whips in one of his trademark crosses from the right, and somehow it ends up in the net. Junior Lewis is thought to have got 'the faintest of flicks', meaning he probably hasn't touched it at all. Nobody really cares much either way.

It's in. We're 1–0 up. They all count, as we used to say at Highbury.

And today they all desperately need to, because things are getting horribly tight. Horribly tight and horribly tense. Four games to play, this one included, and still it's anybody's guess as to how our season is going to finish. Mathematically, we could still take the title. Or the runners-up slot. Or a play-off place. Or bugger-all. A slip or a trip, and months of hard work – of hard-fought victories and our fair share of flukes – will count for nothing. Maybe I'm doing the players a disservice, then. Maybe all we're really witnessing here is 11 stripy blokes, plus subs, experiencing a collective attack of the jitters.

But then the visitors must be feeling the same, perhaps even more so. City's most realistic hope is a play-off spot, so they're hardly likely to make things cushy for us. They prove this very point, the fuckers, by playing better than we do and equalising seven minutes into the second half.

And that seems to be that. The South Stand almost shifts on its foundations as thousands of Albion fans slump back in their seats – dejected, deflated. It just isn't going to happen, is it? One goal was hard enough to come by, for God's sake. Please don't say we've got to score another. It's not fair. Brooker has hobbled off to be replaced by Steele, and loan signing Wayne Gray, doing his best but today about as effective as a hat-stand, has been swapped for another newcomer, Phil Hadland. It really makes stuff-all difference. Only Kuipers is keeping us in the game, flinging himself around like Mr Flingy. Other than that, we're looking clueless. I knew I shouldn't have worn my sodding Wardy shirt.

In fact, Steele's arrival – once the signal for celebration, for genuine hope, for a meaty chorus of 'There's Only One Lee Steele' – has been greeted with a deafeningly silent indifference. The bloke's early-season sharpness, and the respect it commanded, seems to have eluded him some while back. With this match, and perhaps our chance of promotion, in its death throes, a bloke in the row in front yells, 'Useless wankers!'. I expect he thinks that'll help.

'The referee has signalled there'll be three minutes' stoppage time,' declares the announcer, glumly. You can almost sense him wanting to add, 'For all the fucking good it'll do us.'

Either way, it's obviously three minutes too long for hundreds of Albion fans, who are already making their way to the exit. As ever, I watch incredulously as they shuffle out. I'm pissed off myself – like you wouldn't believe – but I still can't understand what makes people do that. There's a difference between *being* pissed off and actually pissing off. I mean, you never know, something might happen.

Something like a cross being fired over by Gary Hart in the 91st minute, meeting the close-cropped head of Lee Steele and landing up – oh fucking hell he's done it!!!! – in the Bristol City net.

I go as mad as I've gone all season. Madder. No one gives me funny looks because they're too busy going mad themselves. The lads behind have grabbed the bloke beside me and pulled him over the back of his seat. His legs are in the air like a flailing bluebottle. But it's OK, he's laughing.

The final whistle sounds and the announcer seems perkier than he did three minutes ago. Odd, that. He can barely wait to tell us what this victory means, even though we already know. 'And that puts the Albion three points clear at the top of the league!' he cries.

He's right. It does. For now. Our early kick-off has given us a two-hour headstart over Reading and Brentford, and we've taken full advantage of it. Let's enjoy it while we can.

Back home, I realise I need to calm down. I certainly don't want to listen out for the Reading and Brentford scoreflashes. My heart couldn't take it. For want of anything better to do – Julie's out buying clothes with a pal, Em's at Churchill Square with her mates – I scribble down a list of groceries we need. A strange post-match reaction, but it focuses the mind. I wonder how I'll react if they're out of lamb mince.

Shortly before 5 p.m. I'm back in the car and heading home. The seat is laden down with shopping, including one or two items we actually needed. The giant pack of Diet Cokes has toppled to the floor. The sharp-edged plastic packaging from one of Em's Crunch Corners (special offer: 3 for 99p) has left a gash in its carrier. I'll have to watch that.

Oh, for fuck's sake, stick the radio on.

'And in the Second Division, it's finished up as . . . Bury 2 . . .'

Blimey.

'Brentford 0.'

Oh. My. GOD!

'And leaders Reading . . .'

Uh-huh.

'Have been held at home by . . . '

Yeaaaaaaaaaaaaaaaaaaaaaaaaaaaaaaaaaaaaaahhhhhhhhhhhhhhhhhh!!!

For the next three miles, I drive without due care and attention.

'Meanwhile, in the Third Division, it's a sad day for . . . .'

Yeah, yeah, whatever. Click.

So it's not an April Fool, then. We really are back on top tonight. Two points clear of Reading, five ahead of Brentford. Three matches left. It really has been a pretty good day.

I could curse myself for saying this, but it's hard to avoid the feeling we're in for some even better ones.

Don't Tempt Fate – TUESDAY 2 APRIL

Dick and Martin joined us late tonight, as they often have to. Apparently they'd been to some footie chairmen's meeting in London. Bet that was a laugh a minute.

I noticed Dick was sniffing a lot, but it looked more like hayfever than a cold. I sympathised; my own eyes were itching too. Tonight was the first night we'd been able to hold a meeting with the door wedged open, letting a fragrant but pollen-packed breeze waft through the hospitality hut. There were red wine stains on the tablecloth, presumably from yesterday. They'd take some shifting, those.

Tonight's was a relatively low turnout, just 14 people, but then there's a limit to what the average stadium campaigner can really do for the moment. For now, until whenever the council planners meet to give their verdict on this whole thing, it's mostly about dotting Is, crossing Ts and sticking tails on Qs. It's the tireless die-hards doing most of that stuff, allowing the ones like me to focus on the task of feeling useless. Tim's been busy working on the petition, now a teetering tower of sheets. He reckons we'll have more than 60,000 signatures by the time it's handed over, which is a bit brilliant. That's getting on for three times the number the place is going to hold when it's built.

Sorry, *if* it's built. Doesn't do to get complacent.

Which brings us to the other thing: Whens versus ifs. Wills versus mights. Optimists versus realists. Try as we might to focus on the official reason for us being here this evening, it was hard to steer the subject away from what was uppermost in our minds.

Dick seemed irritated by the 'when' faction – probably amounting to about half a dozen of those around the table. The ones already talking about life next season in the First Division. The ones who already wanted to plan the party, order the champagne, stock up on the Cheesy Wotsits.

'Don't tempt fate,' he kept repeating, mantra-like. 'Don't tempt fate.' Our poor bugger of a chairman was obviously as nervous as hell, and I was with him 100 per cent. So was Sarah, the supporters' club secretary.

'Yesterday was like Hereford,' she remarked. What Sarah clearly meant was that the tension at the Bristol City game had been as horrible as the day five years ago when the Albion nearly fell out of the League. Obviously I could only take her word for that; I'd had to buy floor tiles that afternoon. All I knew for certain was that yesterday was hell.

But then, of course, we'd ended up in heaven, or at least somewhere on the ring road, so I could half-understand how the optimists – the 'whens' – were feeling tonight. The calculators have been out and the maths have been done and the facts are compellingly indisputable.

Regardless of what happens elsewhere, five points from our last three games will see us promoted. Win the lot and we're champions, simple as that, for the second year running. Do you realise, the last lower-league team to achieve two titles on the trot was Wolverhampton Wanderers, back in 1989? I realise it, because Adrian told us this evening, and that's good enough for me. While he was at it, I should really have asked him to recite the names of every member of that doubly triumphant Wolves squad and then tell us each player's favourite Kajagoogoo track. I just didn't think.

Perhaps more important is that we could be up in less than 96 hours. If we win at Peterborough on Saturday, and if Brentford and Huddersfield draw, and if nobody comes back and says we have to replay last August's Blackpool match because they had the sun in their eyes and it just wasn't fair, then we've done it. We're there. Brighton and Hove Albion will be a Division One football club. When they read out the results on a Saturday afternoon, there'll be weeks when our name will be first up after the Premiership. Maybe even straight after Arsenal, if the fixtures pan out that way. Kind of weird.

And also kind of weird to think that I hadn't originally planned to go to any away games. What a bloody lightweight. The way things are shaping up, I could have missed out on the biggest party of all.

Miracles And Mouthfuls – SATURDAY 6 APRIL

PETERBOROUGH UNITED 0 BRIGHTON 1
LEAGUE POSITION: 1ST

If there's such a thing as a text message from heaven – and I appreciate it's fairly unlikely – then surely this had to be it. The clock was showing just gone 2.15 p.m., and the five of us – myself, Paul C, and three mates of his

I'd only just met – were sat on the steps opposite Peterborough's Burger King. I'd plumped for the Chicken Flamer myself, partly because at 'only 301 calories' (clever of them to have measured it right down to that 'one', I felt) it was the most I felt I should add to the service-station full-English I'd shovelled into my face two hours earlier, and partly because it had struck me, as I waited in the queue, that 'Flamer' was an anagram of Falmer. Perhaps it was a sign. Or perhaps I was being a prat.

I was certainly in the mood for signs. We all were. Hard facts seemed an even better option, though, so Paul prodded the button on his mobile to pick up this pre-match Albion text alert. They may cost him 25p apiece, these updates, but the news this one delivered was priceless. 'Yessss!' he cried – and held up the handset for the rest of us to read. 'I knew it!'

I shielded my eyes and squinted at the screen. 'Oh, fucking yesss!' I concurred, articulately, when I saw what it said. In expressing my excitement, I'd managed to spray Paul with a good 20 calories' worth of semi-chewed bun and diet mayo, but he didn't seem to mind.

'Zamora to start against Peterborough,' announced the message.

This was more than we could have dreamed of. The assumption had been that we'd be Bobby-less for at least another week – maybe longer, maybe for the rest of the season – but now he was ready to play in less than 45 minutes. We decided to finish our burgers en route to the ground.

'Talk about a miracle!' I remarked to Paul as we stood impatiently at a pelican crossing. He just smiled. 'It bloody is, though, isn't it?' I added. And I meant it. This was, after all, the same Bobby Zamora who'd been sat wearing a sling at Colchester last weekend, looking more than mildly sorry for himself. The one who'd turned up on Sky's Soccer AM in the same invalid attire just hours earlier. Bobby the long-term crock.

Paul was still saying nothing. Just grinning. I began to wonder what he'd meant back there when he'd cried, 'I knew it!' Being an Albion employee himself, did the sneaky bugger know something the rest of us didn't? Was that why he'd sounded so relaxed when I'd rung him a couple of days earlier, while my own nerves were red-raw by that stage? Had this Zamora injury thing been an elaborate piece of kidology, blown out of proportion to catch our rivals off their guard? If so, top marks to Taylor. It could prove a managerial masterstroke. If not, top marks to the doctors. I wondered if they could heal lepers too.

By the time we'd clicked through the turnstiles, squeezed through the thousands of roaring Albion fans packed onto Moy's Terrace, pondered over who the hell Moy was, then edged into a decent spot behind the goal – same as I had with Julie last week – I'd hoped to have forced an honest reply out of Paul. But I'd hoped in vain; he wasn't letting on. Still, I had to respect his loyalty and professionalism. The git.

Anyway, who cared? All that mattered was, the man was back. I thought about ringing Julie to tell her the great news, but then I remembered that Julie wouldn't give a fuck.

An hour later, I was almost envying her indifference. Bobby's dramatic return wasn't proving so dramatic after all, other than in the sense that it was going dramatically wrong. Within two minutes we'd been awarded a penalty down the far end, which he'd eagerly stepped up to take. But he'd fluffed it, delivered it about as effectively as Diana Ross would have done, and you could feel the confidence starting to slip. His and ours. It had slipped even further a few minutes later when he'd been clean through – or looked it from where we were standing – and thumped the shot against the keeper's body.

'He's fucking useless!' a bloke behind us had decided.

Added to which, Brentford had already knocked in three without reply against Huddersfield, in don't-fuck-with-us fashion. So there was no way we'd be promoted this afternoon. Not now. All we could do was focus on winning. This, in itself, would be easier said than done.

I spotted a couple of other familiar faces on the terrace and, while we waited for the teams to reappear, shuffled over for a chat. Bill and Jan Swallow, from the stadium campaign team, looked as jittery as hell. Likewise, Paul Samrah. Paul was sporting that familiar old-geezerish cloth cap of his, the sort you rarely see on people who still have their own teeth. I half-wished I was wearing one as well. The sun was blinding.

Which was more than could be said for the Albion's play as the second-half began. The wind wasn't helping, but the problem seemed mainly down to nerves. Just like last week, we weren't seeing much second-half action down our end. If anyone was going to score, it looked increasingly likely to be Peterborough. Optimism had given way to mass anxiety.

Then, in the 64th minute, the ball bounced over to Bobby yet again, this time on the edge of the six-yard box. He still had a defender to deal with, plus the seemingly charmed Peterborough keeper, but maybe this would be third time lucky. Please, God.

'Oh, OK,' sighed God. 'If you insist.'

Bobby swivelled, unleashed a close-range shot and – whoomph – it smacked straight into the net. He'd finally done it. The boy was back. Four thousand Albion fans were dancing. I counted each one.

The relief was enormous, or as enormous as it can be with 25 minutes still left. Sorry, 26. Bill must have looked at his watch every 15 seconds from then on. Paul S was right at the front, leaning against the wall, conducting the Albion fans through countless choruses of 'Sussex By The Sea'. I'm sure these wild, shapeless gesticulations of his were just a way of trying to deal with his own nerves; I don't think he really believed he was helping in any musical sense. At least I hope not, or I might need to have a quiet word.

When the referee finally remembered where he'd put his whistle and decided he may as well blow it and finish the game, Paul leaned back, raised his arms to the sun and just roared. I think it was the first time I'd seen an accountant do that in public. 'We're up!' he cried. 'We're UP!!'

'No, we're not,' I very nearly replied, but I didn't want to spoil his moment, or anyone else's. Amid all the hugs and handshakes, how could I be the one to suggest we put our celebrations on hold, until the sums made it a certainty? This was an afternoon when logic made no sense.

The fact is, we're tantalisingly close. We need two points from our last two games – the first is at home next Saturday to Swindon, the other at Port Vale a week later – to guarantee going up. *Then* we can celebrate.

Unless, that is, Reading do us a huge favour – and themselves an hilarious disservice – by fucking up at Tranmere tomorrow.

If that happens, if they fail to win, we'll be a First Division club within 24 hours.

You'll tell me if I'm boring you with all this, won't you?

Sunday Best – SUNDAY 7 APRIL

Halfway down the Droveway I squealed. Then I bashed the steering wheel. Not in anger, but in minor celebration. It probably wasn't the wisest thing to do while driving, but it was that or pull my shirt over my head.

Odd, though, to think it wasn't an Albion goal I was celebrating. Nor even an Arsenal one. The team which, to my hazardously expressed joy, had just gone 1–0 up was Tranmere Rovers. Their match against Reading was nearing half-time, and I was heading to The Eclipse, a pub in Hove, to hear the rest. To listen in the company of friends. I could have stayed at home, of course, but then again I couldn't. Word had spread that Albion fans were descending on the pub to hear the commentary, just in case something happened. Just in case Reading, light-years ahead of us not so long back, screwed up yet again by failing to win. If they did, we'd be promoted. Today. None of us wanted to celebrate that on our own. If it were to happen, that is.

If.

Liz Costa was already there when I walked in – of course she was – supping a pint and looking desperately tense. She came over and tugged at a clump of her hair. 'Have I got any black ones left, Mike?' she asked. Sarah looked just as anxious but was getting by on Diet Coke. Adrian Ground-Tour was kitted out, for once, in entirely neutral colours. 'Is that deliberate?' I asked him. He confirmed that it was, that whenever he was holding out for a result involving two neutral teams, he refused to wear anything Albion-related. I nodded, appreciating some vague kind of logic in his superstition.

'Got any others?' I asked.

'What, superstitions? Yeah, loads,' he admitted. 'You should see my underpants.'

I felt I probably shouldn't. Especially right now.

Rendering the occasion mildly surreal, the commentary we were listening to was biased entirely against the Albion. Southern Counties were taking it from their Berkshire counterpart, so everything was delivered from a Reading-are-Gods point of view. Meanwhile, there was us lot, sat in a pub in Sussex, cheering a team from Merseyside. Added to which, the unfamiliar names meant it was all we could do to work out which side had the ball – a point perfectly illustrated just three minutes after the break when, blimey, another goal went in. No roar, no groan, just a tense, confused silence. We knew someone had scored, but for which bloody team? God, this was a nightmare. We all sat rigidly, speechless, not daring to believe what we desperately wanted to believe, waiting for some clue in the commentary.

'And that leaves Reading with an absolute mountain to . . . '

The pub went potty. So did the people inside it. This was unbelievable. Surely Reading, with the title still a possibility, weren't just going to roll over and die. Not against the team in tenth.

Correct. Two minutes later, the fuckers had pulled one back.

Still, never mind, we were still on target. They'd need two more goals, and they only had . . . how long . . ? Oh, shit – another 40 minutes.

With 18 of those minutes remaining they did exactly what we'd feared. Tranmere, our adopted team for the day, our brave boys ('Come on, you . . . whatever-the-fuck-it-is-you-call-yourselves') had chucked away a two-goal lead. We knew exactly how they felt. Were they, in fact, Brighton and Hove Albion in disguise? Stranger things have happened, after all.

Actually, no they haven't. That's bollocks. Sorry.

So here we were, for the millionth time this season, forced to sweat it out for the last quarter-or-so of a match. The place was getting busier, louder, more beery by the minute. We could barely hear what we'd come to listen to, as blue-and-white shirts kept crackling though the door. Some people were clearly anxious not to miss out on the chance of a party. Others were just clearly anxious. I'd have bought myself a beer, but it would have taken me 20 minutes to reach the bar. And now there were only five minutes left. To the die-hards this must have felt like a strangely poetic symmetry, preparing to celebrate promotion in a pub in Hove, barely half a mile from what used to be the Goldstone. Four minutes, three minutes, two minutes, one minute. It was almost impossible to hear the commentary. 'Shhhhhh!' went Liz, which usually does the trick.

There couldn't be much stoppage time, surely. There'd been no sendings-off, no notable injuries. It might even be just one minute. No, that's daft. It's hardly ever just one. Two, probably. Yeah, two. Three at a pinch.

'And the fourth official has indicated there'll be four minutes' injury time.'

The groan was almost louder than the roar which had greeted the second goal. *Four minutes?*! Four bloody minutes?!! How the fuck did he work that one out? Tell you what, mate – why not use a more elaborate illuminated sign, one which can display actual words. 'Carry on till Reading get a winner' you could make it say. Or just, 'Fuck off, Albion' if you wanted to save on light bulbs.

We were quite nervous.

John, a bloke I'd stood with at the campaign table countless times during the season – most memorably, don't ask me why, at that LDV tie with the wafer-thin match programme – had his hands clasped in front of his face. So did Liz. They looked as if they were praying. I think that's because they were.

Sixty seconds. Surely it couldn't be much longer than that now. Adrian made it 90. This was torture. Yet again.

But then those 90 seconds were up and he *still* hadn't blown the final whistle. Come on! We still weren't promoted. It could all still go wrong. *Come on!* Mathematically, we could still be in Division Two next season. It would only take a fluke, a jammy mis-kick, a freak own goal.

Fucking come ON!

And then, hang on a second, he'd blown it. He'd actually blown it. The referee had blown the final whistle. The game was over.

We'd done it.

We were really up.

I cried my eyes out.

Liz hugged Sarah. I hugged Adrian. Then I hugged Liz. Then Liz hugged

John. We exhausted all the hugging permutations and then we started all over again. This was the moment. This was *the* moment. This was perfect.

The singing began. 'Albee – yurrrn! Albee – yurn! Albee – yurn!' And deep within this jubilant chorus I detected an unfamiliar voice. Strained, a bit off-key, but obviously not the tiniest bit self-conscious about it. I listened more closely. Yep, thought so: it was me. 'Sea-guuuulls! Sea-guuuulls!' Not even just mouthing the words, like I used to do for 'There Is A Green Hill Far Away' in the school choir, but singing at the top of my voice. Chanting, too. 'We. Are. Going up, I said we are going UP!' Because we were, weren't we? And today, if only for these brief, blissful hours, Bright'n-Ove Alb-Yurn Eff See *were* by far the greatest team the world had ever seen. What was so silly about that?

Adrian confirmed as much when Southern Counties' roving reporter shoved a microphone his way. He was focused, articulate, passionate, just as Liz had been moments earlier when asked for her own reaction. Ditto Sarah. Then the reporter made a big mistake: he came to me. And for reasons I doubt I'll ever fathom, I answered him in Martian.

'Urrrrrghhhhhhhhm,' I went. 'Shbrrrrrrrrrrrrgggg giaduwhf-apaof.'

Sarah managed to get hold of Micky Adams on her mobile. I had no idea she even had his number, but he must have been delighted that she did. With his Leicester side relegated yesterday, I'm sure he was thrilled to hear that he'd be sniffing a Withdean Portakabin again next season.

And then I stepped outside to call Julie. She was on her way back from her mum's. Em was in the car too. 'Come and join us,' I suggested. So they did. Julie didn't hesitate. Nor did Em. As they arrived, Julie took one look at the scenes of celebration, spilling onto the street now, and started blubbing, as if suddenly it all made sense. Even Em seemed to appreciate the significance of what she was witnessing. 'Can I have a Brighton shirt?' she whispered to me. I smiled, and remarked on her audacity. 'With Glory-seeker on the back?' she added.

She was teasing, but she had a point. For all my tears, my willing acceptance of hugs from all these people, for all my Albion T-shirts and fading mugs and bubbly car stickers, I was ultimately still the Bandwagon Boy. I was savouring the moment, but it was *their* moment. I was happy because *they* were happy – Liz, Sarah, Adrian, the Pauls, the whole bunch of them. Maybe one day I'd qualify for a moment of my own, but this wasn't it. It couldn't be.

Before we left, I joined in with a chorus of 'Brighton Till I Die'. But only because I figured that might be a start.

BRIGHTON 0 SWINDON TOWN 0

Suddenly we were spoilt for choice: Champions 2002 flags; Champions 2002 banners; Champions 2002 scarves. Unfamiliar faces lined the road up to Withdean, urging us to snap up their unofficial wares. Some of these souvenirs didn't look too shoddy, but I preferred to wait for the official ones. I've become a bit of a creep that way.

I also preferred to wait until we'd actually won the title. It was only two o'clock, and we wouldn't be champions of anything for at least another three hours. If then. These blokes, whoever the hell they were, had taken a whopping great gamble, hoping their prematurely manufactured mementos would allow them to cash in. A small, cruel, sniggering part of me – a deeply hypocritical one, of course – wanted their shameless exploitation to backfire.

A far bigger part of me wanted it not to, of course. It wanted this, our last home game, to be the one where we took the title. As, I assumed, did the thousands of others heading for Withdean. Except for the ones wearing red.

Swindon had clearly come to poop our party, and I suppose you couldn't blame them for that. There can't be much else to do when you're stuck in 14th spot and the soppy rules still oblige you to play out your two remaining fixtures, rather than, say, bugger off to Benidorm for a fortnight. And while I assumed Swindon's travelling fans would be reasonably laid-back about the Albion winning the Division Two championship, I had a hunch they'd rather it didn't happen at their expense.

The maths had become fairly simple now. A win this afternoon would make us champions. A defeat would be a crushing anti-climax, obliging us to try again next Saturday at Port Vale. Three points from either game would clinch it, but we really wanted the ultimate end-of-term celebration to be here at home. Either way, the team had promised us a post-match lap of honour, but the sun was beginning to break through the slate-grey cloud and we desperately wanted to be dazzled by the glint of comically oversized silverware. We all knew the Division Two championship trophy was somewhere here in the stadium – presumably under armed guard in the hospitality hut, or locked in someone's boot – because this was the only match where it could legitimately be handed over this afternoon. We didn't want it packed away in polystyrene for another week. Worse, we didn't want it escaping our grasp altogether.

Of course, there was a third possibility: we could witness a tedious, frustrating, seemingly inadequate draw, and then discover we'd won the title in any case. But this would need equally inept performances from Reading and Brentford. Before kick-off, it had seemed such a ridiculously unlikely combination of events that most of us had suggested it only as a joke. Two hours later, you couldn't hear many people laughing. It's difficult to laugh when you're praying. It's a bit rude, too, I'd have thought.

Our own match had fizzled out grim and goalless, thanks to the sterling efforts of Swindon's 93-man defence, but then news had filtered through that Brentford's game at QPR had also finished in stalemate. So maybe we could do it after all. I wasn't sure how the good Lord traditionally dealt with requests for rival football teams to fuck up, but we were about to find out. Reading were being held at 2–2 by Peterborough. Barry Fry's side had very kindly equalised with seven minutes left. So if Reading failed to come up with another goal, the Albion would be Division Two champions here and now. All we could do was wait and hope.

So we waited, and we hoped.

Then, in the absence of any further news, we waited and hoped some more.

And then some more.

And then came the roar. It began in the North Stand, just near the press box, but within a microsecond it had swept around the rest of the ground like a Mexican wave. A Mexican *sound* wave, ha ha. It could only mean one thing: Reading's game *had* ended in a draw. We'd done it! We were champions!

Ooops, sorry – no, we weren't.

Attila came on the PA and warned us not to start celebrating. 'That result has *not been confirmed*,' he pointed out, with the instinctive caution of a bloke hardened by years of Albion-related hell.

What he actually meant was, it hadn't yet flashed up on the Teletext screen beside him, at least not in complete words. Shit. We thought it was all over etc.

So we waited and hoped some more, having got this down to a fine art by now. And then some more. God, how much longer is that bloody match going to . . .

'We have that missing result now,' announced Attila at last. Something in our poet-in-residence's tone suggested he couldn't wait to read this one out, perhaps because – fingers crossed – it would kind of rhyme. 'The final score,' he declared, 'is Reading 2 . . . '

The stadium shook. The party began. Our cake had its icing.

Within seconds, the Withdean pitch had turned from green and brown (mostly the latter, by now) to blue and white, peppered with odd bits of yellow and orange as stewards struggled to keep it clear. 'The players won't come back unless you return to your seats,' a cross voice announced. Eventually just about everyone did, barracked by us goody-two-shoes types who'd heeded the request. The rest were persuaded back as far as the running track.

I finally believed it was real when the podium went up. The sign said Nationwide Division Two Champions and it was standing there in the middle of the pitch. In the middle of *our* pitch. So it must mean us. Blimey.

Oh fuck, I'd started crying again.

I turned to the bloke on my right, my neighbour all season, and grinned like a goon. He didn't look the sort to appreciate a hug, so instead I held out my hand. He looked at it, then looked up at me for an uncomfortable second or five, as if I'd gone slightly mad or sneakily sold him a time-share while he wasn't paying attention. Then he smiled and shook it. We'd sat through a lot together, me and him.

Walking home, amid the euphoric honking of horns and the shoving of unofficial flags out of car windows, a strange, rather melancholy thought occurred to me: since I'd applied to move seats next season, I might never see that guy again. It felt odd, after so many nerve-rackingly emotional hours in his company.

I wonder what his name was.

End Of The Road – SATURDAY 20 APRIL

PORT VALE 0 BRIGHTON 1

I felt privileged, getting my hands on the cup. Admittedly, it was only a plastic one, and of the picnic variety, but it was nice to be a part of this end-of-season celebration. Quite moving, in fact. I took a sip, as the other Albion fans were doing from theirs, and sniffed the air. It smelt of diesel.

Over on a patch of grass, a bunch of younger supporters were having a kick-about. One of them nearly got the ball stuck up a tree.

We weren't exactly celebrating in style – we were celebrating in the car park at Warwick services – but it turned out that Liz Costa had boarded the coach with ample supplies of fizz and orange juice, determined we'd make our final halfway-home stop-off a bit special. Obviously I'd shuddered a little at first when she'd promised us Buck's Fizz, so I was relieved when she started unloading Cava and orange Tetra-Paks.

The Bournemouth fans, on the other hand, weren't so impressed. It was unfortunate that their coach – I think it was just the one in their case, rather than the God-knows-how-many vehicles which were ferrying victorious Albion fans back from Port Vale – had stopped here too. The Cherries had just lost to Wrubbishy Wrexham, which meant they were in a bad mood. They'd also just been relegated to Division Three, which meant they were in a worse one. The cherries weren't cheery.

So not only were they less than thrilled to see Albion fans arriving in vast numbers and popping open celebratory bubbly; they also failed to appreciate the impromptu chants dedicated specially to them. 'We'll Never Play You Again' proved particularly unpopular. 'Going Down! Going Down! Going Down!' didn't go down too well either.

One Bournemouth fan, a lanky, balding guy, looked so upset, his face had turned the colour of his shirt. Or maybe it looked like that the whole time. I decided to wander over and offer him a few philosophical words of consolation. I think he thought I was trying to be funny. 'I'll fucking kick your fucking head in, you cunt!' he spat. I had a feeling he probably fucking wouldn't, if only because of the ratios here, but I decided not to put this hunch to the test.

The actual match, truth be told, had been a feast of mediocrity, disrupted only by Paul Watson's spectacular winning free-kick in the 73rd minute. Peter Taylor had blown what I felt had been a priceless opportunity by insisting on fielding more or less a full-strength side. His priority, he'd declared, was to finish on 90 points.

Personally, I thought he was being a killjoy. I couldn't have given a toss how many points we finished on. We were already champions, so why not experiment a little? I didn't mean in the yawny sense of allowing less established players a run-out. I meant in the sense of taking the piss. Why hadn't he sent the team out in snorkels and flippers? What was the bloke trying to prove?

For the travelling fans, easily matching the home support in terms of numbers – and runaway winners, needless to say, on sheer volume – today was the day to blow the dust off the Greatest Hits package, chant-wise. I hadn't heard half these songs, but it was obvious they were tributes to long-departed players and managers. In fact, one of the blokes they were singing about was over there on the touchline: Brian 'Nobby' Horton was doing his best to look as if all that mattered to him these days was being boss of Port Vale.

The song which to me sounded the most affectionate was, I assumed, one of the oldest, dedicated to legendary Albion striker Peter Ward, who joined the club in May 1975 and scored nine million goals. 'Walking in a Wardy Wonderland!' sang the fans, just as they – or in a lot of cases probably their dads – must have sung at the Goldstone a quarter of a century back.

I smiled. Had the name slapped across the back of my own shirt, I wondered, helped trigger this blissful memory?

Had it bollocks. I was in Row Z.

Don't Rain On My Parade – SATURDAY 27 APRIL

Julie has purple knees. I don't mean on a permanent basis, but after spending two hours collecting petition signatures. And before you start getting strange ideas, they're purple because she's so cold. She's been semi-frozen since half past eleven.

Once again, the watery spring sunshine deceived her. As we got ready to head out to the Albion's victory parade – the traditional open-top bus ride along the seafront, followed by a balcony appearance at the council offices – Julie figured shorts would be a good idea. But shorts weren't a good idea, and she knows that now. Shorts were a very bad idea. Purple flesh with goose bumps. Nice.

Still, I was extremely moved by her gesture, I really was. It hadn't been my idea. I hadn't even hinted at it. I hadn't dared. But when I'd happened to mention that, with around 20,000 very upbeat people expected either to line the route or swarm beneath the balcony, the stadium campaign team planned to take full advantage, petition-filling wise, Julie had immediately volunteered herself. I had no idea why, but I wasn't going to stop her. It meant I could concentrate on taking some pictures.

So what we did was split up. Julie headed into the crowd, wearing my XXXL 'Have You Signed Yet?' campaign T-shirt, and armed with the clipboard which I'd so lovingly customised for her – if you must know, I'd taped a pro-Stadium sticker to the front, pinned a Falmer badge alongside it, and made sure the pen, like the clipboard itself, was exactly the right shade of blue – while I went and stood with my Fuji, ready to grab a few decent shots of the players with the trophy. In the end what I actually grabbed was a few lousy ones: mostly the sort you get on holiday when you ask a passing stranger if he'd kindly take a snap of you and your family, and then discover, when you collect the prints from Boots a fortnight later, that what he's actually done is photograph your flip-flops.

What disappointed me even more, though, was that the batteries in my camera had drained before I could get a shot of Freddie Mercury. It wasn't the *real* Freddie Mercury, you understand, or I'd have been alerting the *Daily Star* newsdesk; it was the Albion's assistant manager, Bob Booker, who'd emerged onto the council's balcony in the full get-up and begun miming to 'We Are The Champions'.

Someone behind the scenes must have pushed the wrong button at first, though, because 'We Will Rock You' had briefly kicked in, triggering quite a petulant response from Freddie-Bob. (I suspect he hadn't bothered learning the lyrics to the entire Queen back-catalogue and was afraid the limitations of his act were about to be exposed.) Anyway, other than his teeth, which seemed to made of paper, it was an impressive impression. There was no way the bloke could have perfected those gestures without spending hours in front of his bedroom mirror.

By one o'clock the celebrations were effectively over. Dick had delivered his speech, peppered with plenty of hints about needing a new stadium. The fans had sung the songs of praise and booed the council leader accordingly. The players had passed the trophy up and down the line several dozen times, and then up and down several dozen more, and then stood grinning at the crowd for another half-hour or so, wearing happy but what-exactly-are-we-meant-to-do-now expressions. And then it was 'thank you and see you next season'. I felt a bit empty, to be honest.

Amazingly, Julie had managed to find me in the crowd. She showed me all the petition forms she'd managed to fill. I was so proud of her. 'That's brilliant,' I said, and I meant it. 'It must make the hypothermia feel almost worthwhile. I take it you'd like to go home now.'

'No rush,' she replied, and dashed off to thrust a form at a passing policeman.

Déjà Vu – MONDAY 29 APRIL

I spotted it on a board outside a newsagent as I was driving Em home from school. It would have been hard to miss. 'ALBION BOSS QUITS,' it announced, in fat black type – one of those headlines which conveys a piece of news so shocking that it needs no superfluous wording. Rather like 'QUEEN ABDICATES' or 'WORLD ENDS' or 'GERI HALLIWELL STOPS BEING PAIN IN ARSE'.

Except I'm not shocked. Not really. And here's the slightly alarming thing: nor do I feel that upset. If you wanted to see me upset, you should have seen me five minutes earlier in the journey, when Destiny's Child came on Southern FM, singing the old Bee Gees hit 'Emotion', showing off their aren't-we-so-bloody-clever vocal skills by splitting each existing note into 38 warbly new ones. Just sing the frigging song, all right? Or better still, don't, because it's shit. I hate the Bee Gees, too, by the way.

Blimey, what's happening to me? When Micky quit, back in October, when I didn't even think the Albion meant that much to me, I was choked. When Peter Taylor took up the post a week later, I was moved to tears. Surely this latest announcement demanded yet another emotional outburst?

Maybe that's just it. Maybe I've exhausted my repertoire. Maybe those two responses, plus all the ups and downs of the season itself, have left me emotionally drained. Burnt out. Maybe, now that the football bit is over and the title's ours, I'm back to where I started. Maybe I'll be banging on about cyclists next, or Lisa's EastEnder eyebrows, or how Sainsbury's never stock enough lamb mince. (Which they still don't, incidentally, unless you get there after 11 a.m., when apparently the daily deliveries come in.)

But I don't think so. I think my reaction – and this is going to sound a bit over-the-top, so bear with me – reflects how much my life has moved on since then, in the sense of what this football club now means to me. When Taylor arrived, I guess I was still thinking along traditional lines; still subscribing to the big-is-best-and-small-is-frankly-a-bit-embarrassing school of thought. Back then, I hadn't much confidence in the Albion in their own right, so a 'big-name' manager was, the way I saw it, giving them a kind of credibility boost.

I now appreciate that this was stupid, patronising bollocks. The club has a spirit and strength which can easily survive the departure of another manager. I understand that now. Another year, another boss? Ho-hum.

Taylor has come out with several excuses as to why he's leaving, the least feeble being that he doesn't reckon his budget will be good enough next season. The most pathetic is that he reckons he's frustrated by delays over the new stadium. Now, unless I've lost track of something here – and, admittedly, I'm speaking as someone who struggles with the plot of *Emmerdale* – then nothing has changed on that front since the day he arrived. So I've a suspicion that, alongside his famous Norman Wisdom impression, Peter Taylor has also now learned to talk out of his arse. In which case, what a shame he didn't unveil this new novelty act on Saturday, up on the victory balcony, maybe as a kind of support act to Freddie-Bob. He'd have brought the house down.

Anyway, he's gone and that's it. Job done, I grant you (although a part of me is still convinced that Freddie-Bob was the Albion's key motivator this season) and if you're determined to bugger off, then, hey, you may as well bugger off on a high.

It's hardly the end of an era, though. Just the end of a chapter.

'You're not crying, Dad,' observed Em, as we pulled up at the lights. And she was right. I wasn't.

But was she puzzled, I wondered? Or just relieved?

I don't think she was either. I think she was taking the piss.

Glory, Glory – WEDNESDAY 8 MAY

MANCHESTER UNITED 0 ARSENAL 1

'So . . .' sighed Andy.

'So?' mumbled me.

'So,' he repeated. 'Been a complete waste of time, really, hasn't it?'

You see, stupid, naïve idiot that I am, I'd expected Andy, at some point this evening, to say well done. About the Albion, I mean. Congratulations, he could have said. You backed a winner there, mate. Nice one. Whatever.

But from the moment he'd shown up on my doorstep, cradling a Thresher's carrier, the game already seven minutes old, I'd sensed that he'd been rehearsing a different script. I don't know, he'd just had that look on his face. *That* look. If you knew the bloke, you'd know the look I meant: a bit too pleased with himself. Julie would have wanted to slap him, but she was up at her sister's and it probably wouldn't quite have merited the 48-mile detour. Em, meanwhile, seemed to have resigned herself to the fact that United were about to finish their season trophyless, with Arsenal needing only a draw from this match tonight to secure the Double, and had quietly slunk off to a mate's.

I'd been a bit surprised, given that Andy had arrived wearing *that* look, that he'd then held back for the whole of the first half. He'd barely said a word, other than to mumble about minor details of the match itself and how he hoped, watching this as a neutral, that Old Trafford was about to erupt into anarchy. But now I understood his game plan: he'd wanted beer inside him first. Plus – and this was the key thing – he'd wanted my undivided attention. He knew this little speech of his, the end-of-season analysis which he'd so lovingly prepared for me, would be wasted if I kept leaping to my feet every time Freddie Ljungberg steamed in on the United goal. He'd have to pick a moment when I'd be fully receptive.

So half-time had come – 0–0 – and I'd reached for the remote. A single jab of the mute button and Richard Keys had lost his voice. May as well get this over with.

'Sorry?' I replied. 'What's been "a complete waste of time, really"?'

'Your season,' he said, clearing his throat in that ominous fashion which suggests he has plenty of pre-rehearsed pronouncements to get through. 'Your experiment. Your *passion project.*'

'Oh, right,' I said. 'And how have you worked that one out, oh wise one? We've won the bloody championship, for God's sake. By a six-point margin.'

'Quite,' he said.

'Sorry?

'I mean quite, that's my point. It's been too easy, hasn't it? You've hardly broken sweat. It's proved bugger-all.'

Actually, I knew what Andy meant. The same thought had already occurred to me. But I wasn't going to let him know that, the smug bastard. Not yet, anyway. For the moment, I knew I had to respond with an equally persuasive, rational line of argument.

'Bollocks,' I said.

Andy gave a derisive snort and ploughed on. 'Think about it,' he said. 'Your original idea was to learn how to care again, right? To get excited about stuff.'

'And, what, you're telling me that hasn't happened? You should have seen me the day we won the title.'

'But that's just it. Anyone would have got worked up about that. The point is, you've never been tested. It's easy to tell yourself the Albion matter to you now because they haven't really struggled all season, have they? They've delivered the goods. But what if they'd spent nine months playing shit? I bet you wouldn't have felt so passionate about them then.'

'Bet I would,' I huffed. I'd switched into my-dad's-bigger-than-your-dad mode, but I'd left out the 'so there'. It might have sounded childish.

And then I tried to make him understand. I pointed out that the Albion had come to mean more to me than just a football team; I reminded him about all the fantastic people I'd met, especially through the stadium campaign; how I felt as if my contribution, however tiny, may at least have counted for *something*; how I'd already bought my new season ticket because I knew I was in this for life now; how I'd come to feel part of a wonderful family; how I felt rejuvenated in the most forward-thinking sense. And then I decided to shut up. The second half was about to get underway, and I was starting to sound a bit wanky. 'Just watch the bloody game, OK?'

I wasn't so much annoyed by the point Andy was making, accurate or otherwise. I was annoyed that he felt he had to make it. What did it matter to him either way? I'd ended up happy. Couldn't he just humour me? He was meant to be my mate.

With the second half kicking off, each of us went off into his own frustrated sulk. Andy, I assumed, was frustrated because he'd only been able to deliver about a quarter of his I've-got-you-sussed-sunshine script. My own frustration stemmed from knowing that, somewhere among my muddle of thoughts, I'd had a valid point to put across. It was just that the right words, the clever-clogs turn of phrase, had eluded me, same as usual, just when it mattered.

For the next ten minutes, our stand-off was punctuated only by the occasional crack of a ring-pull.

And then something happened.

Out on the right, Freddie Ljungberg, the guy who'd scored Arsenal's glorious second goal against Chelsea in Saturday's FA Cup final, had broken free and started ploughing towards United's penalty box. And now he was unleashing a shot, low and hard. Barthez sprang to his right and got a palm to it, but all he could do was slap it away – straight into the path of Sylvain Wiltord. Surely Wiltord couldn't miss from there.

Actually, Wiltord could have done. But Wiltord didn't. And as the ball rolled into the back of the United net, I threw myself from the sofa, crumbled to my knees, and started thumping my fists on the floor, screaming like an animal. Just the way I'd done on 26 May, 1989, when Michael Thomas had hit Arsenal's title-winner at Anfield.

Andy stared at me. Nothing else. Just stared. I think he thought his stare said it all. I think he was probably right.

Thirty-five minutes later, the Double was Arsenal's. I didn't repeat the animal act because a final whistle never triggers quite the same response in me that a goal does. That, and I'd worried the dog. I just closed my eyes, threw my head back and raised my arms. I was soaking it up. For a moment, this was no longer 8 May 2002, but 8 May 1971, and I'd just turned 11, and Arsenal's Double-winning goal had been scored not by Sylvain Wiltord, what sort of a name is *that*, but by Charlie George. 'Char–leeee, Char–leeee, Char–leeee, Char–leee, born is the ki–ing of Hi–igh–bur–eeee!'

And then I opened them again.

'You despicable fucking glory-seeker!' shrieked Andy. 'What the hell do you think you're doing?'

'What do you *think* I'm doing?' I cried. 'I'm celebrating the fucking *Double.*'

Andy didn't seem wholly impressed. 'You can't fucking celebrate the fucking Double,' he cried. 'It's not yours to fucking celebrate. You abandoned this lot nine months ago, remember?' But he was laughing now, that was the thing. He'd obviously decided his razor-sharp logic was wasted on me.

'It doesn't mean I'm not allowed to be pleased,' I argued, taking a celebratory slurp.

'Pleased?!' he said. 'Look at you – you're virtually orgasmic!'

He had a point.

'Still,' he sighed. 'I suppose if it makes you happy . . .'

'Exactly,' I said. 'It does. You're looking at one very, very happy 42-year-old.'

Andy suddenly slapped his forehead in a way I'd only ever seen before on bad sitcoms. 'Forty-TWO?!' he exclaimed. 'Oh, shittitty shit – today's your bloody birthday, isn't it? Christ, I haven't even got you a prezzie.'

I couldn't help laughing myself now. 'Oh, shut your face and chuck us a beer,' I said.

'Failing that, just try and do the first bit.'

Epilogue

On Wednesday 12 June, 2002, Brighton and Hove City Council's planning committee met to discuss the Albion's application to build a stadium at Village Way North, Falmer. They voted in favour by 11 to one.

Three days later, the five members of Britain's Winter Olympic women's curling team were appointed MBEs.

On Monday, 15 July 2002, Martin Hinshelwood, previously Director of Youth, became Brighton and Hove Albion's new manager. 'I'm not a big name,' he admitted. 'Just a long one.'